f $r(T) = \sup\{|z| : z \in \sigma(T)\}$ is the spectral radius ?

Th 8.11 $r(T) = \lim_n \|T^n\|^{\frac{1}{n}}$

Proof $\sum a_n \lambda^n$ has rad of cvg
  + cvg $|\lambda| < R$
  $\therefore$ $\sum_1 \frac{T^n}{z^n}$ cgs $|z|^{-1} < (\lim$
    $\iff$ $|z| > \overline{\lim} \|T^n\|^n$
  dgs $|z| < \overline{\lim} \|T^n\|^{\frac{1}{n}}$ — but there

way poss be other versions of th inverse
  so $r(T) \leq \overline{\lim} \|T^n\|^{\frac{1}{n}}$

Lemma if $z_0 \in \rho(T)$ & $d(z_0; \sigma) = \inf_{z \in \sigma(T)} |z_0 - z|$
  then $\|R(z_0)\| \geq \dfrac{1}{d(z; \sigma(T))}$

if $|\mu| < \dfrac{1}{\|R(z_0)\|}$ then $z_0 + \mu \in \rho(T)$ by Th 8.5

Now $d(z_0; \sigma) = \inf_{z \in \sigma} |z_0 - z|$ now by contradiction
  $= \sup\{\lambda : |z_0 + z| = |z_0 + v| < $
  $\sup t \text{ such that } \{z : |x - z_0| < t\} \subseteq \rho$

$\therefore d(z_0; \sigma) \geq \dfrac{1}{\|R(z_0)\|}$.

Now by Lemma $\|R(z)\| \to \infty$ as $z \to \sigma(T)$, so (picture
$R(z; T)$ can't be analytic outside $\rho(T)$
                                 inside $\sigma(T)$

Now if $r(T) < \overline{\lim} \|T^n\|^{\frac{1}{n}}$ we get picture 2
which obv gives a contradiction $\therefore$ $R(z)$ is analytic
in th annulus
  $\therefore$ $r(T) = \overline{\lim} \|T^n\|^{\frac{1}{n}}$ we use $(T_1 T_2)^{-1} \in \mathcal{L}(X)$ T_j

Next   show $\overline{\lim} = \underline{\lim}$ $\Rightarrow T_1^{-1} \in \mathcal{L}(X)$
                                        $\therefore = T_2 (T_1 T_2)^{-1}$

First $\lambda \in \sigma(T) \Rightarrow \lambda^n \in \sigma(T^n)$
  if $\lambda^n \in \rho(T^n)$ $I = A(\lambda^n I - T^n) = A P_n(T)(\lambda I - T)$ = reversed
  $\Rightarrow \lambda \in \rho(T)$
  So $|\lambda|^n \leq \|T^n\|$ $\therefore$ $|\lambda| \leq \|T^n\|^{\frac{1}{n}}$
                So $r(T) \leq \underline{\lim} \|T^n\|^{\frac{1}{n}}$

from **Markings** by Seamus Heaney

We marked the pitch: four jackets for four goalposts,
That was all. The corners and the squares
Were there like longitude and latitude
Under the bumpy thistly ground, to be
Agreed about or disagreed about
When the time came. And then we picked the teams
And crossed the line our called names drew between us.

Youngsters shouting their heads off in a field
As the light died and they kept on playing
Because by then they were playing in their heads
And the actual kicked ball came to them
Like a dream heaviness, and their own hard
Breathing in the dark and skids on grass
Sounded like effort in another world …
It was quick and constant, a game that never need
Be played out. Some limit had been passed,
There was fleetness, furtherance, untiredness
In time that was extra, unforeseen and free.

Trevor West The Bold Collegian

Seamus Heaney

Mary Robinson

John West

Paul Colton

John McCarthy

Cyril Smyth

Mary Henry

Michael Halliday

Paul Coulson

Richard M. Timoney

Finbarr Holland

Charles Woodhouse

Gary Hufbauer and Carolyn Revelle

Michael Mortell

Andrew Bonar Law

Cathy Doyle

Roy Garland

Trevor West

The Bold Collegian

Hugo MacNeill

Tom Mitchell

John Tyrrell

Sean D. Barrett

Ulick O'Connor

Michael West

Iggy McGovern

THE LILLIPUT PRESS
DUBLIN

Charleston House,
Ballinacurra, Co. Cork.

Contents

Introduction Mary Robinson

Timothy Trevor West was a remarkable – and a remarkably engaging – man. In the year when I came up to Trinity College, 1963, he had just taken his degree in mathematics among a very small but distinguished group that included David Spearman and Nick's brother Michael Robinson. Trevor came back to Trinity a few years later to teach maths, armed with a doctorate from Cambridge. In 1968 I returned from Harvard to teach law and began thinking about how to become involved as a young independent voice in Irish politics. We met at various meetings of College societies, and I realized how committed to College Trevor was.

Passionate about College sports, from Gaelic games to cricket, Trevor had followed the fortunes of my rugby-playing brothers Oliver and Aubrey and cousins Frank Keane and Kevin Sheridan. His friendship with them and my other brothers Henry and Adrian meant that I got to know Trevor in his relaxed sporting mode as well. This emboldened me to ask him in the early summer of 1969 to become my election agent when I decided to run for one of three Dublin University seats in the Seanad. It was an inspired choice. Trevor's response was characteristically generous, energetic, and businesslike. Drawing on his popularity with Trinity graduates of every background, which stemmed in part from the practical, organizational support he was already giving – and would give throughout his life – to all the sports clubs within College, he went methodically through the electoral system to woo votes by postal ballot from all over Ireland and around the world. Against the odds, we won the seat!

Happily, having relished the task of helping me across the line, Trevor contested and won a by-election in the same constituency not long afterwards, following the untimely death of Owen Sheehy-Skeffington. He volunteered to join me and John Horgan (elected by NUI graduates) in co-sponsoring the Criminal Law (Amendment) Bill 1971 to remove the restrictions on access to contraception. He knew it would not be a very popular move – but it was the right thing to do. Perhaps uniquely in Irish parliamentary history, the Bill failed to be given even a

First Reading. Unperturbed, Trevor went on to make an important contribution to the Seanad detailed in the essay by Dr Mary Henry, herself a distinguished senator and university elder.

Other contributions spell out his role in academic life (starting with legendary escapades as an undergraduate!): his crucial involvement in the administration and development of sport in Irish universities; his researches on Horace Plunkett and the co-operative movement; his involvement in the Northern Ireland peace process and above all, the lasting contribution he made to the university he so loved.

It is fitting that Trevor's story would be known to, and inspire, future generations. Fortunately he has a champion in his widow Maura Lee, who understands the power of the personal story and the depth of the memories it evokes. Thanks to her commitment, this volume of essays will bring joy to many and hopefully inspiration to a new generation.

Mary Robinson, Chancellor,
Trinity College Dublin.

From back, left to right: John, Timothy Trevor, Brian and Neill West fishing in Waterville Co. Kerry.

Midleton College and garden, County Cork.

The Bold Collegian

Trevor's life is not easily summarized as he was involved in so many different areas. To begin with, the four of us siblings: Trevor, Neill, Brian and I, grew up in a warm, secure and happy environment in Midleton, in East Cork. Trevor was the eldest, I was a year behind. Then came Neill, who died when he was only fourteen years old. Brian, who has had a distinguished career as a pathologist in the United States, was the youngest in the family.

Trevor was at his happiest in the family home at Charleston. When our dad Timothy died, Trevor took it upon himself to look after our mother, Dorothy, in her later years. Most weekends Trevor would travel down to Cork from Dublin, often after watching a game in College Park. I know how much his love and attention were appreciated by Mum and he organized his timetable skilfully so that he had no lectures on Monday.

He also watched over our elderly cousin Margaret Moorhead who continued to live with us after Dorothy's death, and supported Tessie Finn, our faithful family cook, buying a house for her when she retired from Charleston.

Despite the variety of his interests and commitments he pursued most of them with extreme accomplishment. He seemed to be able to compartmentalize his time and attention, and switched seamlessly from one field to another, always giving his full concentration to the matter in hand. His early brilliance in mathematics led him to Trinity College Dublin and for four years he shared rooms in No. 2 Front Square with David Bird, a former classmate in Midleton College. It was at Front Square that I had my first introduction to the TCD sherry party, and have remained highly suspicious of Cyprus sherry ever since. David, with his wife Heather, have through the years been true friends to Trevor, particularly over the later difficult times.

As an undergraduate Trevor was involved in many student activities, some of them legal. I don't suppose that there are too many Senior Fellows who could claim that in the middle of the night they had painted the hands of the Regent House clock red. For this nocturnal adventure it was necessary to climb onto the roof and from there descend onto the ledge under the dial where he had to wait until approximately 5.30 am for the clock hands to come into range. The level of difficulty could be gauged by the fact that the hands remained red for three weeks. The Clerk of Works was not impressed. Trevor did not include this artistry on his CV.

His sympathy for those who were less skilful at evading capture by the authorities undoubtedly helped make his tenure as Junior Dean so successful. He was indulgent of transgression but didn't condone wilful violence or bad behaviour. Unnecessary confrontation could be avoided and problems solved over a pint in the Pavilion Bar. But he was also shrewd: hearing that one of the students had accepted a dare to streak naked around College Park during the Trinity Week Races, Trevor countered by inviting the lad's parents to sit out the afternoon with the good and the great. The lad spotted his mother and father. They saw a fully clothed son.

Trevor completed his doctorate in St John's College Cambridge and lived there for three years at 17 Barton Road, which became a safe and noisy house for the Trinity diaspora. He thoroughly enjoyed life at Cambridge, particularly the cricket in Fenners and around the colleges as both spectator and player, and he made lifelong friends at the university.

On his way back to Trinity he spent time in Glasgow University and at the University of California Los Angeles (UCLA). In both places, as well as his mathematical involvement, he immersed himself in the local soccer scene, ending up with a broken leg in Los Angeles. His soccer style was simple, direct and passionate, and he was deceptively slow.

Trevor's life was so full and busy, in sport, politics, culture and history, that if he had never been a mathematician most people wouldn't have noticed. But his original discipline underpinned everything. To it he dedicated his full commitment, and translated his early promise into scholarships and awards. Unlike many brilliant mathematicians he kept at it, publishing and researching until the end of his career, often (as he said himself) by cleverly encouraging the brighter students to co-write papers with him.

He wore his scholarship lightly and enjoyed meeting and sharing ideas with fellow mathematicians from other universities. By organizing symposia with Finbarr Holland of University College Cork, he helped advance the profile of mathematics in the Royal Irish Academy as well as nationally. The RIA's mathematicians have a custom that to mark the retirement of a member a day-long symposium is held, where they attack highly complex problems in challenging and difficult fields of abstract mathematics. They then adjourn for drinks and a meal, when, according to Trevor, they frequently need the help of the waitress and a calculator to sort out the bill when simple division proves far too complex for them.

Trevor was a dedicated teacher and a vibrant and enthusiastic lecturer. He particularly enjoyed teaching the engineers and thrived in this sometimes unruly and challenging atmosphere. He took a great interest in his students and was delighted with the election of the current provost: 'A good man,' he said. 'He will do well. One of my brighter students.'

With his enormous loyalty to Trinity, Trevor was proud that he could count ten TCD graduates in our immediate family, while he himself gave over fifty years of dedicated commitment to the university.

Of course DUCAC (Dublin University Central Athletic Club) was a major part of his life. Treasurer for nine years, Chairman for thirty-three, he gave enormous service to College and was fiercely proud of what was achieved under his stewardship. In this he was sustained, supported and encouraged by DUCAC staff, and in particular by Cathy, Geraldine and Drinda. As his legacy we have the Pavilion Bar, which he kick-started with Paul Coulson and Aidan Duggan, and the Sports Hall for which he fought both for the planning and the funding and which he happily saw to completion. An equally significant achievement was one that *didn't* happen during his watch. We have Trevor to thank for masterminding the routing of the barbarians who had the temerity to try to build on the pitch in our beloved College Park.

Intervarsity sports were very important to him. He was proud of the Irish Universities Rugby Union, of which he was Honorary Secretary for eleven years, during which he forged firm bonds with like-minded colleagues from the other universities. Coincidentally, his great friend Finbar Costello of UCD died within twenty-four hours of Trevor. They were the twin pillars of the IURU. Together they helped to organize highly successful tours to New Zealand, and later to Korea and Japan (both of which are still covered by the Official Secrets Act). Trevor also followed the IURU side on subsequent tours to South Africa and Australia.

But of course it was not just rugby he supported. He loved the camaraderie and socializing with the Knights of the Campanile. He was an avid soccer supporter and enjoyed TCD's Collingwood Cup triumphs. He was highly protective of the cricket wicket in College Park, and with Murray Power he formed the Irish Universities Cricket Association, sharing the delight in winning the British Universities Championship in 1986 and 1988 – great wins for Ireland. He was patron of Irish University Athletics and founder of CUSI, an organization set up to encourage the sports administrators of all the universities to socialize and share their problems. He was their first honorary secretary and set up their office in the DUCAC rooms at TCD. Recently he was elected posthumously as an honorary patron of that organization, now rebranded and renamed Student Sport Ireland.

Trevor supported all Trinity games – Gaelic football and hurling, hockey, squash, even rowing. He told me he had found the perfect way to enjoy the rowing regattas: 'With a pint in my hand and my back to the river.'

He was in his element at Sporting Commons, jumping onto the table to announce Trinity triumphs in a wide field of sporting achievements. Here his wit and vivacity really shone through. These evenings were huge fun and tremendous for the undergraduate *esprit de corps*. They were thoroughly enjoyed by all and led to the inevitable post-mortem and celebration in the Pav.

Trevor's first engagement with the Senate was when he acted as agent for Mary Robinson on her successful first election. Later, having resigned from his student affiliation to Fianna Fáil, he was elected himself as an independent member for the Senate. One of the defeated candidates referred tartly to the victory as being one for the Fianna Fáil machine but as Trevor's political career went on to show the remark was self-evidently untrue. Shortly afterwards Jack Lynch met Dad at a rugby match in Cork. 'Tim,' he said, 'if you're finished with our machine, could we please have it back?'

Trevor was proud to be independent and part of the small liberal wing of a very conservative Oireachtas, but strove to maintain relationships with politicians of every hue. Early differences of opinion with Kader Asmal of TCD's law department and Secretary of the Irish Anti-Apartheid Movement transformed into a firm, long-lasting friendship. Trevor was open-minded and not afraid to allow his own political positions to evolve.

He always took a keen interest in Northern Ireland and was President of the Irish Association for Cultural, Economic and Social Relations in 1980. He saw it as an urgent necessity to get both sides of the divide talking to each other. He visited Gusty Spence, the UVF commander, in Long Kesh prison, and later helped persuade the Home Secretary that Spence could be a force for good as a paramilitary leader who had renounced violence. This was by no means an obvious proposition at the time and Trevor was in a unique position as a Protestant politician from the Republic to make it.

He was particularly proud of organizing the first Oireachtas Soccer XI to play the British House of Commons in 1969. In the context of the time, this innocent-sounding activity was an amazing political breakthrough. There is a splendid team photo of the Irish side, resplendent in IURU jerseys, including Liam Lawlor, Enda, Bertie and Trevor (as captain) all looking like choirboys, still mounted in the Members' Bar of Dáil Éireann.

Simultaneously with all these interests, Trevor still found time to be Chairman of the Board of Midleton College for twenty-four years and helped in continuing to build its reputation as a top-class school. He researched and wrote several books, most notably a biography of Horace Plunkett, which is considered the definitive work on that fascinating contributor to Irish politics and agriculture (*Horace Plunkett: Co-Operation and Politics* (1986)). He also wrote the brilliant *Malting the Barley* (2006), a history of the family malting business in Ballinacurra and a subject very close to his heart.

Crest of the Philosophical Society.

A current leader of the Church of Ireland surprised me recently by saying that he was involved in one of Trevor's missions. I had become accustomed to hearing of yet another of Trevor's hitherto unknown and unheralded vocations but I was taken aback by this one, until he explained that the mission was to educate Northeners how to drink socially. The returns are not fully in, but it appears it met with some success.

One of Trevor's great strengths was getting people to socialize together easily. Yet anyone who knew him knew also that he didn't do transitions. He would appear and disappear with sometimes startling abruptness. He did not discuss his responsibilities, he just carried them out. He never talked about the many students he helped with advice and frequently with financial aid. He never had conversations about how proud and fond he was of his nieces and nephews, though he followed their careers with great interest and enormous generosity; and with considerable heckling.

Trevor's life, and indeed his style of fashion, changed dramatically when during the celebration for Trinity's quarter-centenary he met the television producer Maura Lee. He fell fully and deeply in love with her. They celebrated their marriage in the college chapel and spent twenty years together, travelling extensively here and abroad. They made an enor-

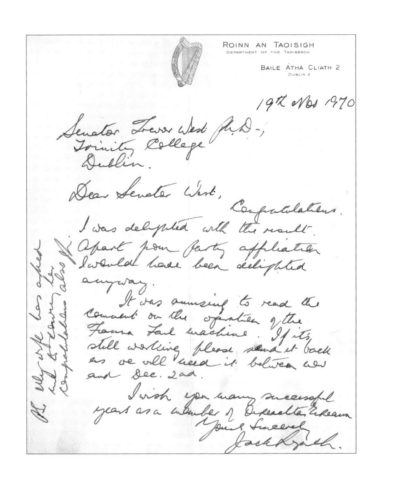

ROINN AN TAOISIGH
DEPARTMENT OF THE TAOISEACH

BAILE ÁTHA CLIATH 2
DUBLIN 2

19th Nov 1970

Senator Trevor West Ph.D.,
Trinity College
Dublin.

Dear Senator West,
Congratulations.
I was delighted with the result.
Apart from Party affiliation
I would have been delighted
anyway.
It was amusing to read the
comment on the operation of the
Fianna Fáil machine. If it's
still working please send it back
as we will need it between now
and Dec. 2nd.
I wish you many successful
years as a member of Seanad Éireann
Yours sincerely
Jack Lynch.

*It why wife has often
had to serve her
congratulations also*

Letter of congratulation from the then
Taoiseach, Jack Lynch, on Trevor's election
to Seanad Éireann, November 1970.

mously lively, generous and hospitable partnership and Maura Lee quickly became Trevor's most determined champion and his staunch supporter in all his many causes.

As his memory diminished, he became more and more reliant on her. 'Where's Maura Lee?' I can hear him say. 'Where's Maura Lee?' It was extraordinarily demanding on her, but she was brilliant at looking after him with patience and great love. Thanks to her he was at his most relaxed at his beloved Charleston and she made him very happy.

Towards the end, when his mind was slipping, he still had lucid moments. He said to me: 'John, you, Brian and I should write a joint book together about the family. Brian could cover the zoology department, ringing cormorants in Inniskea, founding the salmon farm in Donegal and working in clinical pathology in the USA. My section would include Trinity, DUCAC, the maths department, the Senate, Midleton College and the Irish Universities. You could write a bit about the rugby.' He paused, thought for a moment and added, 'But yours would need a good deal of editing.'

In all these achievements he touched few areas that he did not improve with a combination of diligence, exuberance, loyalty and humour. In such a full life, and one lived much of the time in the public sphere, possibly his most lasting legacy is the way he unselfishly helped so many, many people in a quiet, unobtrusive manner.

I am enormously proud of him.

Trevor West at his Commencements at TCD, 1960.

A Good Church and College Life

A portrait of George Chinnery, Bishop of Cloyne, hangs on a wall of the first-floor landing of the Bishop's Palace in Cork. The small portrait of the bewigged figure who was Bishop of Cloyne for less than one year (1780) is the sole episcopal portrait on that landing. It stands out. It also exemplifies the links for over three centuries between the Church of Ireland and Midleton College. Trevor West personified those links. Membership of the Church of Ireland on the one hand, and his nurture and commitment to Midleton College on the other, were two formative and enduring threads in Trevor's life.

The Reverend George Chinnery Junior served as Rector of Killeagh, Prebendary of Caherulton, Rector of Castleblayney, and Dean of Cork before being consecrated Bishop of Killaloe and Kilfenora in 1779. He didn't stay there long. He moved to Cloyne on 15 February 1780 and died six months later on 13 August 1870. Chinnery Junior may only have been Bishop of Cloyne for six months, but he had been Headmaster of Midleton College for twenty-five years from 1750 to 1775. He succeeded his father, the Reverend George Chinnery, first Headmaster of the College who served from the year it opened to students in 1717 until 1750 when his son succeeded him. The Chinnerys set one trend: of the seventeen headmasters to date, nine have been priests of the Church of Ireland.

All of this is set out comprehensively and accessibly in Trevor's very readable history of Midleton College, written to mark the 300th anniversary in 1996 of the Countess of Orkney's indenture of 23 October 1696, granting the land for the school. The Bishop of Cork was to be an *ex-officio* governor from the outset, further cementing the link between Church and school. On 1 July 1747 there was a further episcopal addition to the board of governors: the philosopher Bishop, George Berkeley, of Cloyne.

I knew of Trevor West. He had a public profile in the county and diocese in which I grew up. When it became time to leave primary school, friends of my time in Cork went our separate ways, some to schools in Dublin, most of us to Cork Grammar School or Rochelle School (soon jointly to become Ashton School), and then there were those who went

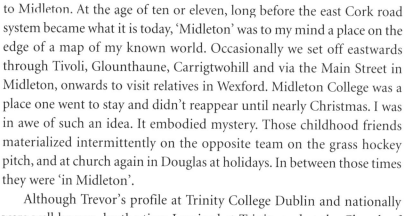

Trevor as a schoolboy with his aunt Miss Sidney West, Matron at Midleton College. Trevor wears his red Munster cricket cap.

to Midleton. At the age of ten or eleven, long before the east Cork road system became what it is today, 'Midleton' was to my mind a place on the edge of a map of my known world. Occasionally we set off eastwards through Tivoli, Glounthaune, Carrigtwohill and via the Main Street in Midleton, onwards to visit relatives in Wexford. Midleton College was a place one went to stay and didn't reappear until nearly Christmas. I was in awe of such an idea. It embodied mystery. Those childhood friends materialized intermittently on the opposite team on the grass hockey pitch, and at church again in Douglas at holidays. In between those times they were 'in Midleton'.

Although Trevor's profile at Trinity College Dublin and nationally were well known, by the time I arrived at Trinity and at the Church of Ireland Theological College he was in his final term as a member of Seanad Éireann. We would cross paths occasionally at College chapel. It was on Mothering Sunday, 21 March 1993, when I was rector of Castleknock, that I first met him properly. We were doing a radio broadcast for RTÉ Radio One. The producer was Maura Lee, who I knew from my own work in RTÉ as coordinator of religious programmes involving the Protestant churches. The epiphany to me on that occasion was that she was accompanied by her future husband Professor, Trevor West, who came along 'to carry things' and assist with the taxi.

In 1999 I returned to my home diocese as Bishop of Cork, Cloyne and Ross. Trevor, ever the gentleman, always gave the bishop of the day due deference. However, from the mid 1960s he was somewhat wary of bishops. The debates about the Irish education system in the 1960s brought the entire established framework of second-level schools under scrutiny. The then Bishop of Cork, Gordon Perdue, was very involved in that debate and felt convinced that he should bring to bear what was being envisioned nationally on the schools of Cork, Cloyne and Ross. The closure of Midleton College was proposed, and it was suggested that, with the amalgamation of Cork Grammar School and Rochelle School, all of the focus of Protestant second-level education for East Cork and Cork City might be concentrated in one new comprehensive school: Ashton School, with the former Rochelle School building as a boarding residence for students, mainly from around the diocese.

This proposal, made in 1965, did not find favour in Midleton. Trevor described it as 'a bombshell'. It was further complicated locally in that the bishop was chairman of both the national committee making the rec-

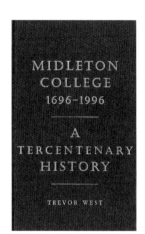

Cover of *Midleton College, a Tercentenary History.*

MIDLETON
COLLEGE
1696–1996

A
TERCENTENARY
HISTORY

TREVOR WEST

ommendations (advocating that Midleton be closed) and also of the Midleton College Board of Governors. The report had the backing of the Department of Education. A flurry of meetings followed between interested parties in the diocese but by 1968 the Department was pushing for just one Protestant school in each of Limerick, Waterford and Cork, with, perhaps, some leeway for a second in Cork. At an open meeting of the Board of Midleton College (also attended by staff) in 1968, the bishop indicated that he could not support a resolution maintaining the college. At a crunch meeting at Midleton on 6 May 1971 the bishop was told that he was in a position 'of divided loyalty' and that there was 'disquiet amongst the Board'. The bishop's riposte was that he had made his position clear three years before in 1968. Nonetheless, Perdue held on to his position as Chairman of the Midleton Board until he announced his retirement on 16 February 1978 when H.E. Kenworthy succeeded him. The new Ashton Comprehensive School in Cork had been up and running since 1973.

This episode loomed ever large in Trevor's mind. As recently as 1999 at a function (one of my first at Midleton) in the Jameson Institute for the Natural Sciences at the college he welcomed me as bishop, but referred again to that earlier era of uncertainty in the college's life when its existence had been threatened, as he saw it, by local episcopal leadership. It has to be noted that the Ashton School component of Bishop Perdue's vision, seen through to completion in spite of much local opposition, was vindicated. Today there is a large Church of Ireland school at Ashton in Cork City with new school buildings recently opened. The boarding school element of that plan (at the old Rochelle School) only survived, however, until 1999. Today Bandon Grammar School and Midleton College continue to grow and to serve the needs of the diocese as well as others who seek an education according to a Church of Ireland ethos for their children. Both sides of the argument have won the day.

When it came to bishops, therefore, Trevor, like an able batsman defending a wicket, sizing up a menacing bowler, certainly kept his eye on the bishop of the day, but yet, at the same time, was genuine in his respect for and appreciation of continuing episcopal involvement at Midleton College. When I first joined the Board in 1999, this (and the former chairmanship of the Bishop of the Board) was symbolized by the fact that at the table in the boardroom Trevor, as chairman, sat at one end presiding, but the corresponding seat at the opposite end was reserved for the

19

The Bold Collegian

bishop. The result was an interesting equilibrium and partnership in the work of Midleton College. Latterly, following his own retirement as chairman, and following the short chairmanship (2007–8) of Ken Brookes, a past pupil, Trevor seconded the proposal on 22 September 2008 that I be elected as chairman. He expressed himself to be delighted at my election. We got on extremely well: a shared interest in TCD, concern for the well-being of both the Church of Ireland and also Midleton College, as well as an interest in sport, and periodic collusion on charitable enterprises, strengthened our friendship.

Interestingly, when it came to bishops, Trevor had a near miss at the very outset of his life. He was born on 8 May 1938. His father had already been headmaster of Midleton College for ten years and was a member of the Diocesan Synod and of the General Synod of the Church of Ireland. The family were living in the main school building in the town of Midleton before they later moved across the road to the Estate House. The baptismal register of the local parish church records Trevor's baptism on 27 July 1938 by none other than the Archdeacon, Robert Thomas Hearn. Hearn had been Incumbent of St Anne, Shandon, since 1904 and was appointed Archdeacon in 1934. Within three months (on 19 October 1938) Hearn would be elected bishop of the diocese. The consecration was in St Patrick's Cathedral, Dublin on 13 November 1938. Trevor narrowly missed being baptized by a bishop! Hearn's wife, Dr Mary T. Hearn, Sir John Cameron and Miss S.E. West are recorded in the register's margin as the sponsors, and the Reverend H.D. Townsend, Rector of Midleton, officiated.

That local parish church, St John the Baptist, erected in 1823, is described by Samuel Lewis as 'a handsome structure, in the later English style, with an embattled tower crowned with pinnacles, and surmounted by a light and elegant spire'. The parish church and Midleton College (in spite of intervening buildings within the town) are aligned with each other, much as the axis of two key reference points in Trevor's life. The spire is clearly visible from the main steps of the college and from many aspects throughout the college grounds. Seasonal college services are still held in the parish church, including at Christmas and Easter, and the weekend boarders attend Sunday worship there. The Rector of the Parish, the Dean of Cloyne, Alan Marley, works closely with the college in pastoral care and in overseeing the college chaplaincy.

The Diocesan Confirmation register, now computerized, records that Timothy Trevor West was confirmed on Sunday, 24 May 1953 in the

Church of St John the Baptist. The name of the bishop is not given, although George Simms, one-time Dean of Residence of Trinity College, later to be Archbishop of Dublin and subsequently Archbishop of Armagh, was Bishop of Cork, Cloyne and Ross at that time.

At the annual Governors' Ball at Midleton College for the departing sixth form, Trevor, like his friend Brian Cairns, exhorted all students each year 'to have a good Church life'. Trevor's friend and contemporary, also a past pupil of Midleton, David Bird, recollects that Trevor was a 'loyal church attender who was also very caring of his mother and his cousin'. This constancy in Sunday worship and church attendance, whether in Trinity College Chapel, at home in Midleton, in St Colman's Cathedral Cloyne, and later in life at St Fin Barre's Cathedral, Cork, was a hallmark of Trevor's life. He was a man of faith and tradition. As at high table at Commons in Trinity, grace was said before and after a meal, no matter where one was. I recall being asked to say grace, before and after eating, when dining at Ballymaloe at a large gathering hosted by Trevor and Maura. Like so much in Trevor's life, his approach to religion and religious practice was unashamed, straightforward, routine and matter-of-fact. He told me once that his favourite television programme was the BBC's *Songs of Praise*.

Officers of the Trinity College Dublin Philosophical Society, 1959–60:
Back, left to right: A.M. Gann, G.B. McAvoy, L. Roche, M.J. Riggs, T.H. Daniels, J.A. Lutton, J.F.R. Gillam.
Front, left to right: T.C.D. Mulraine (Hon. Librarian), R.H. Johnston (Sch. Hon. Secretary), J.A.D. Bird (President), T.T. West (Sch. Hon Treasurer), J.R. West (Hon. Registrar).

21

The Bold Collegian

The Archbishop of Armagh, Richard Clarke, who was Dean of Residence at Trinity from 1979 until 1984, remembers Trevor as 'a member of staff who gave real support to the chaplaincy and real loyalty to the life of the Chapel'. Similarly, Bishop Michael Burrows, also a former Dean of Residence, describes his 'numerous warm encounters' with Trevor on the stone stairs of House 27:

> The offices of DUCAC, the University Central Athletic club over which Trevor presided and which coordinated the organization and funding of sports clubs in the college were on the third floor. We often met and talked on the dim stone stairs. I had to ascend forty-eight of them. He had to do seventy-two. He affirmed and valued chaplaincy and chapel as, like sport, a key part of the gel of a large collegiate community. He expected worship and liturgy to be ordered and seemly, with reasonably intelligent preaching, a good peppering of wit, and awareness of the political reality of the outside world and indeed of the college. He valued good college tradition, and while he did not bestow many compliments concerning sermons, one felt one really deserved the occasional ones received, often offered with a kind of distinctive backhand gruffness. Maura Lee and he had shared views about worship. It had to be very well prepared, executed in a tidy, seemly, efficient and thoughtful way, and all humbug was to be abominated. Preparing for it was indeed like the Pauline athlete making ready for the contest.

That was indeed the case. Senator Seán Barrett, Trevor's colleague at Trinity, bears this out: 'Trevor was loyal, hard-working and committed to the Church in which he grew up. He inclined to the traditional church.' Tracey Cairns Brown, a past pupil of Midleton College, was well placed also to get to know Trevor, as her father, Brian D. Cairns, was headmaster from 1981 until 2003. She remembers Trevor as

> a frequent visitor to the College and a well-known face. He sat behind us in church in St John the Baptist when he was in Midleton at the weekends (prior to marriage) and was always a line ahead of the congregation during the prayers. He was a traditionalist as far as church services were concerned.

Trevor and Bishop Peter F. Barrett (who was Dean of Residence from 1994 to 1998) got on particularly well because of their shared interest in sport, as well as in the chaplaincy. Barrett describes him as 'truly collegiate in the fullest possible way' and as a faithful member of the chapel congregation. Trevor looked forward to receiving the Term Card listing services and special events and, when present, which was more often than not, sat in his fellow's stall. Together they collaborated on initiating the annual Sportspersons' Service in the chapel and together they prepared the liturgy for his marriage to Maura Lee, presided over by Trevor's close friend, Archbishop Donald Caird. This was a truly happy and memorable College celebration.

Derek Johnston, a Diocesan Reader and former deputy principal at Midleton College, knew Trevor in both the Midleton College setting and in a Church of Ireland context, particularly when ministering as a lay reader in Cloyne Union of parishes:

> One of the hazards of ministering where a number of one's bois-
> terous colleagues may be present is that, as they leave church, they
> tend to fire figures at one, e.g. 'nine minutes, Johnston'. The ser-
> mon has been timed. I once saw two watch wrists rise simulta-
> neously to eye level as I entered the pulpit. On a different
> occasion I was startled to be greeted at the end by a grinning
> Trevor: 'Thirty-five minutes!' However, there had been no
> organist in Cloyne Cathedral and consequently no hymns that
> morning; it was, to my surprise, the length of the entire service!

Trevor's involvement in the Church of Ireland was not only local. According to the journals of the General Synod of the Church of Ireland, his father was elected first to represent the Diocese of Cloyne in 1934. Women were not elected to the General Synod until 1952 when Mrs G. Ruth from the Diocese of Ardfert was elected. Trevor's mother, Dorothy, was first elected six years later in 1958 and served alongside her husband. The attendance of both on all three days of the 1972 session is recorded. However, Trevor's father's died in 1973 and Mrs West did not attend at all that year. She continued as a member of the General Synod with full at-tendances each year from 1974 until 1981. The journals record that her son, Senator Trevor West, joined her there in 1976. Undoubtedly his busy work at Trinity and in Seanad Éireann precluded full, weekday involvement in the sessions of the General Synod. Weekday sessions do not suit most members of the Church. Membership of the General Synod of itself, how-ever, opened doors to more practical engagement with Church affairs.

In 1970 the Standing Committee of the General Synod reported that, at the request of the primate, it had appointed, in 1969, a working group 'to study the positive role of the Church in all aspects of political, social and economic life in Ireland'. From the outset it was interested in the sit-

uation in Northern Ireland, in north-south relations, violence, intern-
ment, 'mixed marriages' and family planning, for example. Its brief fell
well within the range of Trevor's political interests and activity. In his first
year on the General Synod he was elected to the role of the Church Committee. Over the years the committee deliberated on the following topics:
the Northern Ireland situation, the American factor in politics and public
life in Ireland, 'Cooperation North', family planning in the Republic of
Ireland, ethics and medicine, adoption, integrated education, peace-
building efforts, homosexuality, the status of women, Church-State relationships, human rights in Northern Ireland, unemployment, the
challenge of change, inter-church relations, pluralism in Ireland, and the
economy.

Trevor's citizenship and his religious affiliation within the Church of
Ireland were important to him. In December 1970 in his second speech
as a senator, he addressed the subject of relationships between the two
parts of this island; the rights of Protestant minorities in the twenty-six

Midleton College, Co. Cork, south-west facade.

counties; the perception of Protestants in the twenty-six counties among their co-religionists in the six; and the friction caused by the *Ne Temere* decree as a 'real barrier to harmony'. He referred to his family holidays and very strong contacts in the North of Ireland and said, in the midst of the speech: 'As a Protestant member of the Seanad, I should be able to make a special contribution in helping relations between these two parts of the country.' He did so with political subtlety and personal bravery.

The role of the Church Committee was indeed an appropriate forum for his talents, energy and insights. In 1981 the following topics were addressed: the attitude of Christians to violence; security in border areas; crime and punishment in Ireland; the death penalty; the relationship between the Republic of Ireland and the United Kingdom; the political situation in Northern Ireland; unemployment; industrial relations and industrial action; nuclear disarmament; inter-church marriages; a recommendation that the prohibition on divorce in the Irish Constitution be removed; and family planning. Eight years previously, along with Senator John Horgan, Trevor had given his support in November 1973 to the Family Planning Bill proposed by Senator Mary Robinson. Trevor served on the Role of the Church Committee from 1976 until 1982. David Bird (Trevor's contemporary at Midleton), also a member of the Committee, says that Trevor's time on the Committee 'was at a time of particular tension south and north, and he brought a balanced and far-seeing approach to its deliberations.'

Trevor also represented the Diocese of Cork, Cloyne and Ross on the Board of Education of the General Synod of the Church of Ireland from 1976 to 1984. In 1990 he again became involved in the education work of the Church. He was elected by the General Synod as one of the Church of Ireland representatives on the Secondary Education Committee. That Committee was established in 1965 by resolution of the sponsoring churches (the Church of Ireland, the Methodist Church, the Presbyterian Church) and the Religious Society of Friends. Its role was, and is, to distribute the block grant provided by the Department of Education and Skills to eligible families who need assistance to send their children to Protestant secondary schools. It also seeks to represent the interests of the member churches in the post-primary education system. Trevor resigned from the committee in December 1999, not in anticipation of my becoming its chairman in January 2000 (I hope); I recollect it was because the Committee met on a Monday, and Mondays were Trevor's day for Midleton College before taking the train back to Dublin.

My predecessor, Bishop Roy Warke, sums up Trevor's commitment to Midleton College when he says that Trevor was 'totally committed to enhancing the reputation of Midleton College in all aspects of his life'. Moreover, he believes that Trevor's high academic standing enhanced Midleton College's reputation as a place of learning. Timothy West, Trevor's father, was headmaster of Midleton College from 1928 to 1960. Trevor's aunt, Miss Sydney West, was Matron. He attended there from the preparatory school to the college itself until the Intermediate Certificate in 1953. In that year's examination he was one of two students in Ireland to achieve 100 per cent in mathematics (the other being C.E. Fleury). The High School in Dublin, a day school, was his next stop, and Trevor lived out in Rathmines for the two years of senior cycle before going to Trinity in 1956 to read mathematics. In 1960, the year his father retired as Headmaster, Trevor graduated with a bachelor in arts with first class honours in mathematics.

Paula Stead, Midleton College Librarian and Archivist, discovered an array of references to Trevor's time in the school in the *Midleton College Magazine*, which was revived in 1933 after a twelve-year lapse. The first mention of the young Trevor was in 1945–46 when he received Second Prize in the Lower Preparatory Class. By 1946–47 he was in Form II and was again in receipt of a Second Prize. Still in Form II the following year (1947–48) he had established his place with a First Prize at the top of the class. In 1949–50 he was again top of the class and was awarded a Science Notebook Prize, a First Prize for Religious Knowledge and a First Prize awarded by the General Synod of the Church of Ireland. In that year also, father and son appear in photographs of the fathers and sons cricket match at the college. In 1951–52 he was first in Lower Fourth Form, and again there was a Science Notebook Prize. Trevor also features in team photographs of the winners in the Munster Schools' Cricket Cup, the Munster Schools' Junior Hockey League and a junior cricket team that played against Presentation Brothers College Cork.

Dean Herbie O'Driscoll, Corkman, past pupil of Midleton, and a former Dean of Vancouver Cathedral in British Columbia, remembers Trevor as 'the quiet one', 'thoughtful', and 'very capable in school debates, no histrionics, incisive and insightful'.

Trevor's Intermediate Certificate results are listed in the 1952–53 magazine and again in that of 1954–55: honours in English, Latin, science, drawing, history and geography and, of course, mathematics. That same year he was awarded the Earl of Midleton Scholarship, the J.H. Bennett

Memorial Prize for Intermediate Science and a scripture prize presented by the Very Reverend J.A. Warner, Dean of Cloyne. Photographs from that year show Trevor on the winning side of the Munster Senior Schools' Cricket Cup, and as Captain of the Junior Cup team.

In 1954–55 the college had five first places in Ireland in the religious knowledge examination: Trevor was one of them, and received the Morgan Jellett Memorial Exhibition. Along with his (by then customary) science prize he received a prize for first place in languages. In 1954, only one year after sitting the Intermediate Certificate, Trevor sat three subjects in the Leaving Certificate and attained honours in English, Latin and French. He also received an exemption from the entrance examination for Trinity College, and was awarded the Moore Memorial Scholarship.

In the 1955–56 issue the magazine reports that Trevor is a past pupil who 'hopes to enter Trinity College in October and has been appointed Head Prefect in High School, Dublin'. Over the subsequent years Trevor's achievements from 'Scholar of the House' (the only one in 1958 in mathematics) to his array of scholarships, including his research scholarship to St John's College Cambridge, as well as his active membership and proficiency in the Philosophical Society are all recorded. The sporting theme continues in the photographs, in one of which Trevor is face to face with Professor J.V. Luce in the Fellows *versus* Scholars cricket match.

The award of the 1851 Exhibition to Trevor is reported in 1961 and, in 1962, it is announced that Trevor had given a lecture at the Advanced Institute of Studies in Dublin and would be giving one later that year at the International Congress of Mathematicians in Oslo. His appointment to a research lectureship in mathematics at Glasgow University featured in the 1963 edition. An account and photograph of the award of his doctorate from Cambridge University on 29 May 1965 are published, together with the news of his departure for Los Angeles to take up the post of visiting professor at California University. On 7 July 1970 the Board of Governors recorded 'with great pleasure that an Old Boy, Dr T.T. West, had been elected a Fellow of Trinity College Dublin'. Trevor became a governor of Midleton College on 12 September 1974, the year after his father died. On 24 June 1985 he was elected as Chairman of the Board of Governors. He served as a governor for thirty-six years, twenty-two of those as chairman. Successive headmasters were indebted to him. Simon Thompson (Principal from 2003 to 2014) was the last to serve under Trevor's chairmanship. He describes Trevor as

> a crucial support to Headmasters … He and his wife Maura were

exceedingly generous in giving their time to the College. Indeed they went further, making their home, Charleston, available for receptions and functions. I am personally indebted to him for his confidence, his encouragement and his loyalty.

Patrick Hitchmough, a governor of Midleton College during Trevor's time as chairman, recalls how Trevor had the capacity 'to get to the point quickly and to back it up with facts'. What stood out for Hitchmough was Trevor's 'understanding of the history of the College … At all times, in making key decisions, he wanted to achieve the highest standards for the pupils.'

The minute books from Trevor's era attest to the usual round of business: enrolment, improvements and repairs of buildings, insurance, negotiations with public authorities and the Department of Education, finance, outstanding fees, recruitment of headmasters, staffing, the library, security (a torch was stolen one evening from the headmaster's study), arrangements for prize days, policies, discipline, church services, sporting fixtures and other college events.

Not everything was routine. Trevor's nationwide connections resulted in a glittering array of distinguished speakers at prize day while Green and White papers in education, resulting ultimately in the Education Act 1998, dominated the 1990s. From 1991 onwards energies were directed towards the Tercentennial Appeal. On 16 November 1992 the governors decided to build a natural science teaching block. The first day of teaching in this new building – the Jameson Institute – was on 7 January 1998 and the official opening on 29 May 1998. The Millennium Project, chaired by past pupil Ken Brookes, followed. In January 1999 it was decided to replace the all-weather hockey pitch laid in 1978 (and which had drainage problems) with a synthetic turf pitch, now known as the Cairns Field. In 2004 (on 11 October) another sub-committee was established to coordinate the future development of the college. A new kindergarten – Singing in the Rain – was built and opened on college grounds. All of these things happened on Trevor's watch. He decided to step down as chairman on 16 May 2007, just as the development plan was being finalized. The minutes record that thanks to Trevor were expressed by the bishop and the headmaster – the Church of Ireland and Midleton College strands once again – and 'the expressions of gratitude were greeted with acclamation'.

Trevor's interest in Midleton College did not begin and end at the boardroom table. Former Deputy Principal, John Levis, recalls the attention that Trevor himself gave to the cricket wicket at the college during

FINALISTS MUNSTER SCHOOLS' JUNIOR CUP

J. R. West, J. R. D. Ford, A. T. Jeffers, G. S. Tomkins, C. E. Fleury, G. A. Boyle,
I. H. E. Johnston, J. E. Hornibrook, T. T. West, (Capt.), J. A. Hill, G. R. J. Caldwell.

29

Junior Cricket at Midleton, 1951–52.

summer term. He adds that 'Trevor's support for Midleton College students attending Trinity College Dublin was legendary. He enjoyed their success, academic and non-academic.' Former Deputy Principal, Derek Johnston, who taught in Midleton College for thirty-six years, chiefly encountered Trevor when, as chairman, he wished to communicate with the staff:

> He often did this through me as deputy principal. He was punctilious in writing to the staff to congratulate them on hard work, particularly at exam results time. I always found him friendly, open and gregarious; he loved to stop and chat. Sport, politics, Trinity and Midleton College were among his chief interests ... He had a deep interest and knowledge of the people who made up the college community. What particularly struck me was his knowledge of, and interest in, the Midleton people who had long associations with the college: grounds staff, household staff, people involved in the trades and professions, which supplied the college. There were often family connections, frequently going back over a number of generations and Trevor knew them all and the family histories they bore.

JUNIOR XV. 1953

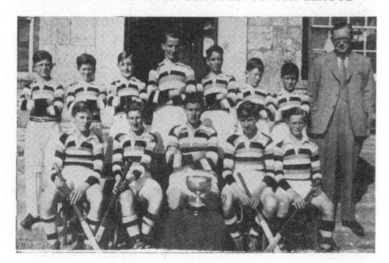

Back: M. J. Nichols, G. R. J. Caldwell, P. R. O'Driscoll, J. R. McCluskey, G. R. Northridge, G. A. Boyle, J. E. Hornibrook.
Front: T. T. West, A. T. Jeffers, B. T. Moore, G. S. Tomkins, J. R. D. Ford, E. K. Wilson, J. C. Moore.

WINNERS OF MUNSTER SCHOOLS' JUNIOR LEAGUE

Back: G. R. J. Caldwell, G. A. Boyle, J. R. D. Ford, S. G. Tomkins, R. K. O'Connell, T. T. West, J. E. Hornibrook, Mr. T. West.
Front: W. T. Perrott, C. E. Fleury, R. E. Mollard, (Capt.), D. T. Hosford, G. H. Redden.

Junior Rugby XV at Midleton, 1953.
Munster Schools' Junior League hockey winners.

The last word from Midleton College comes from our newest principal, Dr Edward Gash. He and Trevor would have got on famously as he too is a mathematician and a cricketer, having played for Ireland at under-21 level. Even though he is new in the post, Gash says that 'already I have observed the legacy of Trevor West. His enduring place in the ongoing life and affections of Midleton College is clear for all to see.'

In preparing this perspective on the Midleton College and Church of Ireland strands in Trevor's life, I contacted many who knew Trevor within either of those settings. The range of words used is both broad and consistent: humorous, sporting, concerned, committed, courteous, fun, irreverent (in the best sense of the word), entertaining, irrepressible, hospitable, genial, political, rugged, determined, steely, convivial, amusing, clever, generous, loyal, highly intelligent, eccentric, polymath, supportive, friendly, witty, dedicated, passionate, thoughtful, straight-talking, extremely welcoming to college events, and understated about his remarkable range of achievements. The last of these is undoubtedly true, and no doubt Trevor himself would have guffawed if he were to read the list himself.

Trevor died on 30 October 2012. His funeral service was held in St Fin Barre's Cathedral, Cork, which was full to capacity. In paying tribute to Trevor I referred to the gallery of yachting photographs at Charleston in my sermon:

> There is a gallery of yachts at Charleston. One of those boats pictured in the glorious photographs of yesteryear was named *Verve*. It was the 52-foot cutter – a racing yacht modelled on the King's *Britannia* and bought in 1913 by Trevor's grandfather. *Verve* is photographed speeding, ploughing and dancing on the energetic and lumpy seas, a parable of life itself, perhaps. Enthralled by the photographs, it struck me that *Verve* might be a paradigm for Trevor's own life, for what else is *Verve* but vivacity, energy, vitality, animation, liveliness, enthusiasm, spirit and vigour?

Following the funeral at the Diocesan Cathedral of the Church of Ireland we drove back to Midleton – home – where Trevor was buried not far from the west door of the parish church, its spire visible from Midleton College. Staff and students of Midleton College provided a guard of honour at the cathedral. Midleton College and the Church of Ireland stood by him, as he did them, to the end.

UNIVERSITY OF DUBLIN
SCHOOL OF ENGLISH

Telephone: 772941
Extension: 1111/1839

ARTS BUILDING
TRINITY COLLEGE
DUBLIN 2

30/7/93

Dear Young Mc Carthy,

The Ballinacurra greyhound is long-necked and lusty at the moment, the nose is up, smelling the Dublin air. He's wearing the ould grey trousers and the ould brown coat, and the stride has noticeably lengthened, and also he glances left and right with an air of primitive speculation. He scratches the what's left of the hair with sudden ferocity, then subsides with equal suddenness. He gives tips about stocks and shares. He vanishes for days on end. And, guess what, after all that, he's still doing the sums!

love,
Young Kennelly.

Letter from Brendan Kennelly to John McCarthy, July 1993.

The Greyhound of Ballinacurra

I first met Trevor when I went to Trinity in 1957. He was at that time an outstanding student and talented mathematician, but his interest went far beyond his chosen subject. Though possessing a brilliant mind and destined to become a top academic there was no pretension in the student Trevor, a characteristic he carried with him throughout his life. He had, though, a rather wicked and boyish sense of humour and I can count myself among the many victims of Trevor's practical jokes. Early one morning my skip awoke me to tell me that while very few students had milk delivered that day, over thirty pints of that precious liquid were found in my rooms. I knew immediately who the practical joker was and had to concede that Trevor had done a fine breaking-and-entering job. I was duly interviewed by the celebrated Junior Dean R.B. McDowell. Having pleaded not guilty to the charge, McDowell opined that he could not understand the whole affair. It was, he further stated, far too stupid to be a student prank. Now I often think to myself that it was rather ironic that one day in the future Trevor would become Trinity's Junior Dean.

The late sixties and early seventies were difficult though interesting days for a South of Ireland cleric in the Loyalist town of Portadown. Paramilitaries were making their presence felt in the area and many of my young parishioners were being recruited as junior members into organizations. To keep in touch with the boys I formed a parish soccer group and tried to get as many of them as possible onto our team. In those days one of our popular guests was none other than T T West, who always seemed available for a game of football wherever the match was played. A fit, fast and solid man in defence, the 'Ballinacurra Greyhound', as Brendan Kennelly called him, became a firm favourite with the young Loyalists of Portadown. It was during this time that Trevor was first elected to Seanad Éireann for the constituency of Dublin University. He still found time to play on our team and while Irish politicians were not the rage of the day in Portadown, Trevor, so the team considered, was of a different kind. His election, if anything, rather enhanced his reputation among the players and years later when meeting any of this group they invariably enquired about him and also referred to him as The Senator long after the constituents of Dublin University decided, inexplicably, not to return him to the Senate.

In common with all the other contributors to this publication I feel honoured that my friendship with Trevor, forged in our shining college days, would continue, and I was happy that he visited me regularly in all the parishes in which I served. My last appointment in the Church of Ireland was as Rector of St Macartin's Cathedral in Enniskillen. My ministry in Enniskillen commenced in the autumn of 1986 and though the Troubles in Northern Ireland were raging at that time, Enniskillen was comparatively quiet and peaceful. All this was shortly to change. On 8 November 1987 a bomb planted by the Provisional IRA exploded at the Remembrance Day parade, killing eleven people and injuring sixty-four. The Remembrance Service in the cathedral had to be cancelled and a renewed Act of Remembrance was organized for 22 November.

The presentation of an award to Rev. John McCarthy in 1977 marking his twenty years playing senior hockey in Ireland. *Left to right*: Trevor West, Aubrey McCallister, David McCrory, John McCarthy, Kevin Heffernan, Eric Walker and Brendan Kennelly.

Trevor and Brendan Kennelly at Trevor's seventieth birthday party.

John and Isobel McCarthy.

Typically for Trevor he was one of the first people to contact me. He was, of course, loyal to all his friends but above all he was devastated that this would be a huge blow to the cause of peace in Northern Ireland to which cause he had given so much time and effort. However, the bombing in Enniskillen did help the cause of peace and good citizenship because there emerged from the stony grief of that day the compelling and forgiving voice of Gordon Wilson.

Gordon's daughter Marie died beside her father in the deep rubble of an exploding building and as Gordon recalled to a BBC interviewer her last words were, 'Daddy I love you.' Gordon also added, 'I bear no ill will. I bear no grudge.' His words had a powerful and emotional impact and resounded throughout the land.

In 1993 Taoiseach Albert Reynolds invited Gordon to take a seat in Seanad Éireann. It was a big appointment for the man from Enniskillen and he called and asked me if I could suggest a person to guide him in this undertaking. I immediately contacted Trevor, who came to Enniskillen and arranged to introduce Gordon to the appropriate people in Seanad Éireann. As I expected, Trevor and Gordon became firm friends. Here were two outstanding men who in their lives displayed the common values of compassion and deep concern for all with whom they came in contact. Trevor was a man of many talents and he found success as an academic, author and politician, but I like to think that his greatness lay elsewhere. Despite all his achievements there was not a trace of arrogance in this good man, but rather he was clothed with a penetrating and child-like humility. T.S. Eliot wrote: 'The only wisdom we can hope to acquire is the wisdom of humility: humility is endless.' Trevor had this wisdom to the full and in that lay his beauty, his goodness and his greatness.

Imitate him if you dare.

35

The Bold Collegian

J.V. Luce, FTCD, Captain of the Fellows and Trevor West, Captain of the Scholars, at the Fellows *vs* Scholars cricket match at TCD, 1960. (*The Irish Times*)

Invitation to the 1851 Exhibition Scholars Alumni Reception at Buckingham Palace, 2006.

Jamie Heaslip celebrates with Trinity Lions:
Back row, left to right: Jamie Heaslip, Kingsley Aikins, Gerry Kelly, Mike Roberts, Sheamus Considine, Des FitzGerald, Brendan Mullin, Mick FitzPatrick, Philip Orr, John Dillon.
Front row: Kay Bowen (former President D.U.F.C.), Trevor West, Drinda Jones, Roly Meates.

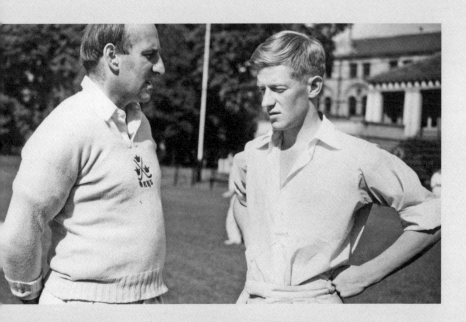

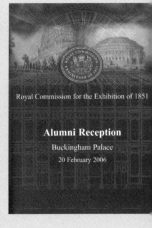

In Memoriam: Timothy Trevor West

When Timothy Trevor West was born in Midleton, Co. Cork, Trinity College, sport and sports administration were already in his genes. His father, Timothy West, was a graduate of Dublin University (BA 1924, MA 1929) and after graduation taught at Mountjoy School where he coached the Senior Rugby XV. He played rugby with Wanderers RFC and became Captain from 1925 to 1926, gaining three caps for Leinster in the back row. He was also Hon. Secretary of the Leinster Schools' Rugby Football Committee before taking up his appointment as Headmaster of Midleton College in 1928, a post he held until 1960.

Midleton College prospered under the leadership of Timothy West. High sporting and academic standards were pursued and achieved. He continued his rugby career with Cork Constitution RFC and then applied his rugby experience and expertise to refereeing. He attained inter-provincial referee status when he refereed the Connacht v Leinster match in 1939. Elected Hon. President of Cork Constitution RFC 1939–1940, he was a founding member of the Munster Schools' Rugby Football Committee and was to remain its Hon. Secretary for forty years. He became Hon. President of the Munster Branch IRFU 1962–1963, the season in which Munster won its fourth outright inter-provincial championship.

Timothy's son, Timothy Trevor West, was educated at Midleton College to Intermediate Certificate level and completed his secondary education at The High School in Dublin. He entered Trinity College Dublin in 1956 and was elected to Scholarship in Pure Mathematics in 1958. The golden jubilee of his election was celebrated at the New Scholars' and Fellows' Dinner in 2008. He graduated BA with First Class Honours in Mathematics in 1960.

Trevor West was awarded a prestigious Overseas Scholarship by the Commissioners for the Exhibition of 1851 to study for his Ph.D. at St John's College Cambridge. The Great Exhibition of 1851 was held in The Crystal Palace, London, and was a popular and financial success, making a surplus of £186,000 (approximately £21 million in 2012). From this, a trust fund, established and administered by the 1851 Royal Commissioners, provides scholarships, fellowships and grants for research in science and engineering. Trevor's research supervisor was Dr Frank Smithies FRSE, a distinguished mathematician who has been described as 'the father of functional analysis in Great Britain'. Smithies had a reputation for pointing his students to areas of mathematical research where he had a shrewd inkling that interesting problems existed. He guided T.T. West into the field of operators, i.e., symbols or functions representing mathematical operations (the actions or procedures that produce new values from one or more input values).

After graduating from Cambridge, Trevor's first academic appointment was to the Department of Mathematics in the University of Glasgow. He then taught at the University of California Los Angeles, before joining the staff of the Department of Pure Mathematics in Trinity College as a lecturer in October 1966. In this role he succeeded in teaching mathematics with panache, enthusiasm and repartee to large classes of engineers. He was elected a Fellow of Trinity College Dublin in 1970 and to membership of the Royal Irish Academy in 1972. Promoted to Associate Professor of Mathematics in 1977, he became a Senior Fellow of Trinity College Dublin in 2000 and formally retired from the Department of Mathematics in September 2004. His thirty-eight years on the staff of the department were celebrated with a *Westfest* symposium on 19–20 December 2005.

Trevor's principal research field was operator theory. One of his seminal papers in 1966, published in *Proceedings of the Edinburgh Mathematical Society*, was entitled 'Operators with a single spectrum'. In life, however, Trevor was an operator with a kaleidoscopic spectrum of talents, which he brought to bear on the multitude of functions he undertook both in Trinity College and in wider Irish community. He served as an Assistant Junior Dean from 1968–1970 and then as Junior Dean and Registrar of Chambers from 1974–1978. In addition, he was a Reserve Assistant Junior Dean from 1983–1986 and from 1997–2004. He was by all accounts a JD very much in the tradition and mould of R.B. McDowell and Brendan Kennelly.

His active engagement in sport in College gave him great insight into the antics of students, while his strong understanding of and relationship with them earned him their esteem and respect. Trevor served on the board of the College as a representative of the Junior Fellows from 1984–88, 1992–94 and 1999–2000 and as an elected member for the Fellows' and Fellow Professors' constituency from 2000–4. He was a member of the Central Fellowship Committee from 1987–90, of the Foundation

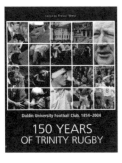

Irish Universities Tour of New Zealand, 1978.
Back row, left to right: Dr Malcolm Little, Hugh McGuire, J.A.D. Langbroek, Moss Finn, John Cambell, Donal Spring, Paul Joyce, Noel Ardiss, Jerry Holland, Tom Kavanagh, Mike Gibson, Pat Shaffrey, Roly Meates.
Middle row, left to right: Ronan Kearney, Stephen Wall, Anthony O'Leary, John Robbie (Captain), Brendan Mayes, Chris Cantillon, Alan Irwin, Peter Rolls.
Front row: *left to right*: Willie Ryan, John Barry, Ray Finn, Chris Gardner, Ricky Stewart, Darragh Coakley.

Cover of *150 years of Trinity Rugby* by Trevor West.

Wanderers RFC 1925–26 including Timothy West (Captain), fourth left in front row.

Scholarship/Central Scholarship Committee from 1988–96 and of the Chapel Committee from 1991–96. He was Chairman of the Fellows from 1990–93. He was also a member of the Executive Committee of the TCD Trust from 1975–87 and, following the amalgamation of the TCD Trust and the TCD Association into the TCD Association and Trust in 1987, a member of its Standing Committee through to his retirement in 2004.

With a brief break, Trevor West was one of Dublin University's three senators for twelve years. He was elected as an Independent Senator to the 12th Seanad Éireann (1969–73) on 19 November 1970 at a by-election for the University of Dublin constituency occasioned by the death of Dr Owen Sheehy-Skeffington, Department of French (a member of the 8th, 9th, 11th and 12th Seanad Éireann). He was re-elected to the 13th Seanad in 1973 and to the 14th Seanad in 1977. Losing his seat in the 1981 election, he was re-elected to the 16th Seanad (1982–83). He lost his seat again at the 1983 election. Along with his fellow Trinity Senator Mary Robinson he championed many social issues including the liberalization of the avail-ability of contraception. During this time he was placed under consider-able pressure to choose between his academic career in Trinity and a career in politics. However, Provost F.S.L. Lyons supported the principle of people in Trevor's position being able to contribute to Irish governance without resigning their main occupations.

From 1980–82 Senator West was President of the Irish Association for Cultural, Economic and Social Relations, a body dedicated to the promo-tion of communication, understanding and co-operation between all people of Ireland, north and south. Trevor earnestly believed that sport was a major vehicle for breaking down sectarian passion and prejudice. He also engaged actively in the peace process, with possible risk to himself, to get the paramilitary organizations within the Unionist community, the UDA and UDF, to the talks table to break the cycle of violence, intimida-tion and revenge killings.

Trevor's own sporting forte was cricket. He played for Cork County, Phoenix and Munster. He was a useful, lower-order to middle-order bats-man and a leg spinner bowler. In 1961, while he was at Cambridge, he toured Ireland with Peterhouse College. On 21 June against the Dublin University XI, he took 4/40 in College Park, including the wicket of his brother John, leg before for a single run, and held two catches. Having dismissed Dublin University Cricket Club for 144 runs, Peterhouse went on to win by a wicket in an exciting and tense finish with the last Cam-bridge pair on the pitch. For the record Trevor scored seven runs in Pe-terhouse's 145 total.

Trevor West's contributions to College sport and to Irish university sport have been considerable. From 1966 he served for forty-three years on the Dublin University Central Athletic Club Executive Committee. To this role he brought passion, drive, vitality, vibrancy, sparkle, energy and total commitment, attributes that would remain with him throughout his years of service to sport in College. He succeeded Simon Newman as Hon. Treasurer of DUCAC in 1967, a post he would occupy for nine years. He ably helped to fend off College's plans to build residences on the rugby pitch in 1970–71. He saw the need for a permanent secretary in the DUCAC office and was instrumental in the appointment of Joan Taylor to that post in 1970. In 1961 the Pavilion Bar had opened with very limited opening hours and trading conditions by edict of the board and in 1971, Trevor, with Aidan Duggan and Paul Coulson, examined the feasibility of setting up the Pavilion Bar with regular trading hours and adequate facilities. This was brought to fruition in 1972 with the appointment of a permanent steward. In 1975 when the Students' Union tried to seize control of the disbursement of the Capitation Fund through a student referendum, Trevor mobilized support from the College's sporting community to defeat the referendum.

When John V. Luce retired as Chairman of DUCAC, Trevor was the obvious choice as his successor, becoming only the fourth chairman after William E. Thrift (1919–37), Harry Thrift (1937–56) and John V. Luce (1956–76). Trevor stepped down as Chairman of DUCAC in 2009 after thirty-three years in the post, the longest-serving incumbent. As chairman he oversaw the development of the Luce Hall Sports Centre project to its completion and served as Hon. President of Dublin University Association Football Club from 1968 to 1971.

He was Hon. President of Dublin University Cricket Club from 1974–1980 and again from 1983 1904, during which periods he worked hard to strengthen the club's profile in College. He was instrumental in an Irish Universities XI first competing against the Leprechauns in College Park in July 1972 and also umpired the Universities v Leprechauns matches for several years. The Irish Universities Cricket Association was founded two years later. Trevor was a driving force in the development of the Irish Universities Cricket tournament. This led to an Irish Universities team, drawn from all Irish universities, being allowed to compete in the British Universities Championship, replacing a team drawn solely from Queen's University of Belfast and the University of Ulster. Trevor West, Murray

Irish Universities *vs* Leprechauns, July 1973 at College Park.
Back row, left to right: John Hall (C.U.), John Frankland (C.U.), Johnny Shaw (C.U.), Stephen Molins (Leps), Dessie Kane (C.U.), Chris Harte (Leps), Bertie McGill (C.U.), Douggie Goodwin (Leps).
Middle row, left to right:: Tony Leon (Leps), Gerry Duffy (Leps), David Hayes (C.U.), Jack Short (C.U.), Ian Lewis (Leps), Michael Halliday (Leps), Corrie Halliday (C.U.), Alan McCully (C.U.), Ken Hope (Leps), Murray Power (C.U.).
Front row, left to right: Paddy Tynan, (Leps), Alfie Linehan (Leps), Pat Dineen (Captain, Leps), Des Cashell (Leps), Trevor West (C.U.), Graham Crothers (Captain, C.U.), Alec O'Riordan (Leps), Philip Marshall (C.U.).

Power (QUB) and Alan Sharp (UU) argued that such an Irish Universities team would be fitter for the stiff opposition in the British Universities Championship than a team drawn from only the two Northern university clubs. The fruits of these endeavours led to the Irish Universities XI winning the British Championship in 1986 and 1988 and to the successful hosting of the British Championships in Dublin in 1985.

Upon completion of the Luce Hall, Trevor West pushed for the appointment of a physical recreation officer and in January 1981 Terence McAuley took up this post. He was promoted to Facilities Officer in 1985, including responsibility for sports facilities. Trevor had taught Terry mathematics during his undergraduate years and the pair developed a very close working synergy over their twenty-eight years together in sport in Trinity. The need for a larger and better-equipped sport centre in College became critical in the 1990s with the considerable expansion in student numbers. To raise funds towards the project a referendum for a sports levy, to be paid by all students over five years, had to be passed.

Trevor again engaged persuasively with the College's sporting community to ensure approval of the levy referendum by the student body. As a result, a substantial private donation to the College for a building that would benefit students in a non-academic sphere was earmarked for the project. The development of an all-weather hockey pitch at Santry was incorporated into the project. Terry and Trevor worked tirelessly together on the Sports Complex Planning Committee from 1998 through 2003 and subsequently on the North-East Corner Planning Committee once the decision for the joint construction of the Centre for Research on Adaptive Nanostructures and Nanodevices (CRANN) and the sports centre complex was taken. He proudly saw the completion of the College's new sports centre in 2007 and its official opening by the Minister for Arts, Sport & Tourism, Séamus Brennan, in April 2008. From Terry McAuley's appointment as Director of Sport and Recreation in May 1999, Trevor West guided and facilitated the smooth transition of DUCAC's role in College sport and the transfer of many of DUCAC's erstwhile responsibilities to the Department of Sport.

Trevor West's influence on university sport was not restricted to Trinity College. He foresaw the need in the early 1980s for better coordination and organization of university sport in Ireland, north and south. Together with fellow university sports administrators, he helped to found the Council for University Sports Administrators in Ireland (CUSAI), becoming its first Hon. Secretary. Through Trevor, the nascent organization was provided with office space in House 27 alongside DUCAC.

From 1977–88 Trevor was Hon. Secretary of the Irish Universities Rugby Union, the representative body for university rugby union in Ireland. In 1978 he organized and accompanied the 25-strong Irish Universities team to New Zealand on its first-ever tour, which cost £23,000. The Dublin University members of the team were John Robbie (Captain), John Langbroek, Donal Spring and Michael Gibson, and the coach and assistant manager was Roland Meates. The team won six of their nine matches, some of which attracted crowds of up to 40,000 spectators. At Wellington they lost their first match 15–10 against New Zealand Universities, the only non-test side to have beaten the Lions the previous year. In the closing minutes the Irish were awarded a try by the referee but he then changed his mind, a decision the Irish players accepted in the best sporting manner. The Irish Universities XV turned the tables in the second Universities test at Dunedin 18–4. The final match of the tour was against the New Zealand Colts, the New Zealand National U21 team, at

43

The Bold Collegian

Eden Park, Auckland, in a quagmire of mud, the Irish Universities XV winning 9–6.

Trevor also organized and managed the Irish Universities rugby tour to Korea and Japan in 1987. He was proud of the fact that of the team of twenty-six players, nine were from Dublin University: Fergus Dunlea, John Sexton, Paul Bell, John Feehan, Patrick Kenny, John Collins, Mark Egan, Richard Murray and Donal Sheehan, with former DU player Roly Meates again as assistant manager and coach. The first match was against a South Korean Army XV in Seoul and was won 15–12, followed by five games in Japan (one loss against Waseda University 16–15), culminating in a test against the full national Japan XV in Tokyo, which the Irish Universities XV won 24–12. Trevor toured subsequently with the Irish Universities teams to South Africa in 1994 and Australia in 1997. He was succeeded in the role of Hon. Secretary of the Irish University Rugby Union by his brother, John West, also a graduate of Trinity College, DUFC President 1999–2000, and an international rugby union referee.

Trevor was a fervent supporter of the Boat Club and a loyal attendee at the Trinity Regatta, albeit that he found the perfect way to enjoy it was 'with a pint in my hand and my back to the river'. However he never lost an opportunity to press the flesh to the advantage of sport in College and social occasions such as the Trinity Regatta were the ideal vehicle for a pre-planned offensive. He employed his extraordinary skills to maximize any possibility of funding from the good and great and used his magnetic charm with purposeful engagement and witty repartee. I had the honour to serve as Hon. Treasurer of DUCAC for ten years (1991–2001) under Trevor's 'fiscal guidance'. Supposedly I controlled the purse strings with Scottish frugality (and was known as DUCAC's Scrooge), but that was far from the truth: the strings were parted by Trevor to support the Boat Club more times than I would care to admit. If I was invited over to the Pavilion for a pint, I could sense that it was to persuade me of the virtues of extra funds that just had to be made available. He usually got his way!

The Club VAT Act 1994 was the godsend required by DUCAC, according to T.T. West. DUCAC could now solve the backlog of capital requests in one fell swoop, including a new eight and oars for the Boat Club, and claim the VAT back. Unfortunately I did not read the small print. Money spent, the Revenue Commissioners informed DUCAC that it was ineligible as a 'Club' under the terms of the Act. To Trevor it was not the end of the world, but I had my head on the block at the following AGM waiting for the guillotine to fall as I endeavoured to explain away this mix-up over VAT to the attendance. Trevor had the solution: he encouraged clubs to drink earlier and often in the Pav to make up the difference. Both of us survived the questioning to continue in post!

Trevor retained a deep affinity with his *alma mater*, Midleton College. He became a governor of Midleton College in 1974 in succession to his father, Timothy Sr, a role he would fulfil for thirty-six years. For twenty-four of those years he was Chairman of the Board of Governors. With the establishment of Midleton College Limited in October 2008, and with responsibility for all financial matters relating to the college, he also served as a director until November 2011. From November 1996 until June 2002 Trevor was a director of the Sick and Indigent Roomkeepers' Society (Incorporated), a charitable society for all religious persuasions founded in 1790 to relieve poverty in the City of Dublin, and he served on the Council of the Royal Irish Academy from 1990 to 1994.

Aside from his mathematical research papers, Trevor West wrote several books. In 1986 he produced a biography of Horace Plunkett, the founder of the Irish Co-operative movement (*Horace Plunkett: Co-operation and Politics*). His history of Trinity's sporting community (*The Bold Collegian: The Development of Sport in Trinity College, Dublin*) appeared in 1991, tracing the development of the university's clubs and the contributions of Trinity's sportsmen and sportswomen to the codification of sports and to the participation of women in sport. He marked the tercentenary of his old school in 1996 with a short history, *Midleton College: A Tercentennary History*. In 2003 Trevor edited a history of Dublin University Football Club to celebrate its sesquicentenary as the world's oldest senior rugby club in continuous existence (*Dublin University Football Club, 1854–2004: 150 years of Trinity Rugby*). In 2006 Trevor related the 200-year history in malting barley, primarily for Guinness, of the firm of John H. Bennett at Ballinacurra in Co. Cork (*Malting the Barley: John H. Bennett, The Man and His Firm*). John H. Bennett was Trevor's step-grandfather. The book brought Trevor back to his family roots and was very much a labour of love.

Aside from *The Bold Collegians*, Trevor West contributed immensely to the rich sporting heritage of Trinity College, a legacy of which he can be justifiably proud. The anecdotal evidence of his sporting *joie de vivre* has become the subject of legend, whether true or not. Throughout his service to DUCAC Trevor was generous in time and deed to sport and to sportsmen and sportswomen in college. He took a personal interest in Dublin University sports clubs and encouraged athletes in all sports.

Trevor used his good offices to assist sporting students from disadvantaged backgrounds or students who were experiencing financial difficulties. He offered advice, used his network of contacts to assist, and smoothed out ruffled feathers over a pint of Guinness in the Pavilion Bar. He gave financial aid to students anonymously, using trusted third parties. Over his forty-three years he was the guiding hand of DUCAC, always steady on the tiller in stormy weather. He developed many lifelong friendships with sporting alumni of the College, all of whom share DUCAC's profound sense of loss. Trevor was keen that the end of each sporting year in College should be celebrated with an ecumenical 'Service for the Gift of Sport'. His favourite hymn to be sung by the College choir on these occasions was '*Non Nobis Domine*' ('Not unto us the Praise'), which was the Olympic hymn for the opening ceremony of the XIV Summer Olympiad in London in 1948.

Trevor West was not to be granted the long healthy years of retirement he richly deserved. He died peacefully on 30 October 2012. He will be sorely missed, not only within DUCAC and Trinity College but also in wider Irish sporting circles, for his character, wisdom, spirit, humour, counsel, kindness and craic. He greatly enjoyed the social aspects of sport, especially those hosted in College. His catchphrase was 'DUCAC always throws the best parties' on these occasions. In the many facets of Trevor's life of service to the College and to the community at large he epitomized the oft-cited passage in John F. Kennedy's inauguration address as President of the United States of America: 'Ask not what your country can do for you – ask what you can do for your country.' The flame of his torch has now been passed to a new generation of Irish men and women, of Trinity graduates and of sportsmen and sportswomen throughout Ireland.

In his *Epitaph on William Muir* Robert Burns remembered his very good friend in lines that are appropriate to Timothy Trevor West:

'An honest man here lies at rest.'

In the Senate

A warm welcome awaited Trevor West when he was first elected to the Seanad in a by-election in November 1970 caused by the untimely death of Senator Owen Sheehy-Skeffington.

Mary Robinson, then Mary Bourke, had been elected to the Seanad in 1969 (Trevor was her election agent) together with Professor W.J.E. Jessop and Dr Sheehy-Skeffington. In her election address she had promised to bring forward legislation to decriminalize the importation and use of contraceptives and to make information on family planning freely available. A bill was prepared by her (which eventually became The Family Planning Bill 1971) with John Horgan, a senator elected from the National University of Ireland panel, and Dr Sheehy-Skeffington as supporting signatories. On Dr Sheehy-Skeffington's death another signatory was needed but none of those who were already members of the Seanad were enthusiastic about supporting the bill.

The by-election count took place in the Public Theatre (Examination Hall) in Trinity College. The candidates were Dr David Cabot, Mrs Catherine McGuinness, Mr W.G. Kirkpatrick, Mr A.E. Ashmore, Mrs C.M. Doolan and Trevor. All but David Cabot, Catherine McGuinness and Trevor were eliminated on the first count and Trevor was elected on the third count, beating David Cabot by 2214 votes to 1694. Catherine McGuinness was eliminated on the second count when she had 1025 votes. Trevor was not at the count when the result was announced; he had gone to conduct a rugby training session for College freshmen. His parents were there, however, and his mother thanked all concerned in the election and said she 'hoped her son would represent all that was best in Trinity in radically changing times'.

Radically changing times they may have been but change was not too fast in the Seanad. When Mary Robinson tried to introduce her original Family Planning Bill in 1971 the First Reading of the bill, which allows for its publication, was opposed by some Seanad members (the First Reading of a bill simply allows for it to be printed so that the public could know what was in it). This opposition meant the bill could not be printed. Indeed, such was the antipathy to the bill in the Seanad that the Leader of

Govt. Family Planning Bill in a fortnight

THE GOVERNMENT would have its own Family Planning Bill ready within a fortnight, as it was presently being drafted, the Minister for Justice, Mr. Cooney, announced in the Senate last night.

The Minister, who was speaking during the resumed debate on the Second Stage of Senator Mrs. Mary Robinson's Family Planning Bill, said he didn't propose to give details of the Government's Bill to the House not that he wanted to keep it secret, but to uphold the proprieties that exist between both houses of the Oireachtas.

He said with reference to the Magee case, the Government made known its intention to introduce its own Bill. This was the dominant feature in the whole debate, but he was dis appointed at the few muted references made to it in the Senate. He wished to clarify the position following the findings of the Supreme Court. Under section 17 sub-section 3 of the Criminal Amendment Act 1935, the prohibition on the importation of contraceptives was deemed unconstitutional. The judgment of the court was that married couples have the right by law to have contraceptives legally available to them in this country. He said the legal position up to now had been turned completely upside down. There was nothing the Oireachtas could do to change that position which was decided by the Supreme Court as a constitutional right.

Act, 1929 which prohibited the sale or distribution of literature on "unnatural" methods of contraception. It was not open to them to dictate in laws what were natural and what were "unnatural" methods of contraception, and in doing so adopt the viewpoint of one denominational church. The interference in what would be that we did not respect the viewpoint of other churches or of other individuals, she said.

Mrs. Robinson said the viewpoint of the whole population had evolved since 1929 and all the churches now approved of family planning. Yet, there was a total prohibition of advertisements on any method of family planning "natural or unnatural"

One of the real dangers was that people would do themselves harm because of the lack of information available about family planning. "How can people address themselves with

Mr. Cooney.

believed in the Catholic Church. Some people might not like them,

within the criminal law code.

It was invidious to ignore appeals from conscientious minorities. Was it not unfair to ask those who felt that the law should be changed if they were prepared to have similar legal protection afforded to people who claimed the right to take life, have abortions, mercy killings on the grounds of personal civil rights? What was the difference in principle if both claims were advanced on constitutional grounds?

Neither majorities nor minorities possed the "right", in inverted comas, to flout the natural law. But minorities would have to subordinate themselves to the common good.

Misleading people

Dr. Noel Browne - he Catholic church accepts a just war. The contraceptive argument

Robinson's was regarded as too conservative because it did not allow slot machines.

Pope's plea

He said it was right to put on record the appeal by the Pope to legislators. He quoted from Humanae Vitae a section where the pope urged legislators not to allow the morals of their people to be undermined and not to tolerate any legislation which would allow into the family practices which were contrary to the natural law. There were other ways in which governments could solve the world population problem.

Mr. O'Higgins said if he supported Mrs. Robinson's Bill he would receive bouquets of praise from the media, the drug companies and those who are trying to knock the teaching of the Catholic Church.

"But by doing so we might bt

---

the House, Senator Tomás Ó Maoláin, refused to hold the Order Paper for the day in his hand.

Trevor had long had an interest in Irish politics both as an undergraduate and as a staff member in the Department of Mathematics. While an undergraduate he was a member of the National Progressive Democrats, a liberal socialist party of which his good friend Larry Roche was a founder member. Another Trinity member, David Thornley, was involved, as was Noel Browne, who was a TCD medical graduate.

The party had a short but dynamic career and was disbanded in 1963. Some time after its demise Trevor joined the Trinity Fianna Fáil Cumann and was chairman of it when he decided to become a by-election candidate. However, he resigned from this position before his election, feeling that his independence as a senator should never be in doubt.

He had been involved in various political campaigns, such as that for the retention of proportional representation when it was proposed to change our voting system to 'first past the post'. The referendum was held

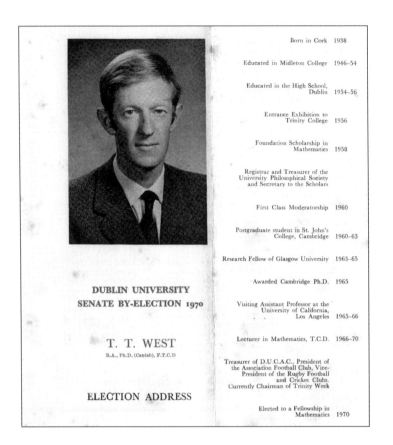

Report in *The Cork Examiner* on the Senate debate on the Family Planning Bill, February 1974.

Trevor West's Seanad Éireann election address, 1970.

DUBLIN UNIVERSITY
SENATE BY-ELECTION 1970

T. T. WEST
B.A., Ph.D. (Cantab), F.T.C.D

ELECTION ADDRESS

Born in Cork	1938
Educated in Midleton College	1946–54
Educated in the High School, Dublin	1954–56
Entrance Exhibition to Trinity College	1956
Foundation Scholarship in Mathematics	1958
Registrar and Treasurer of the University Philosophical Society and Secretary to the Scholars	
First Class Moderatorship	1960
Postgraduate student in St. John's College, Cambridge	1960–63
Research Fellow of Glasgow University	1963–65
Awarded Cambridge Ph.D.	1965
Visiting Assistant Professor at the University of California, Los Angeles	1965–66
Lecturer in Mathematics, T.C.D.	1966–70
Treasurer of D.U.C.A.C., President of the Association Football Club, Vice-President of the Rugby Football and Cricket Clubs. Currently Chairman of Trinity Week	
Elected to a Fellowship in Mathematics	1970

49

The Bold Collegian

on Wednesday, 17 June 1959 on the same day as a presidential election. Éamon de Valera was elected President of Ireland but the referendum was rejected. This referendum had been put forward by the Fianna Fáil party at a time when Trevor was probably still involved in the National Progressive Democrats.

Trevor was re-elected to the Seanad in the 1973 General Election from a very strong field, which included Noel Browne, a former Minister of Health, and Mary Robinson, both of whom were elected with Trevor. This time, following a debate on 17 December 1974, the Family Planning Bill 1974, proposed by Robinson, John Horgan and West did pass the First Stage in the Seanad but not without a vote, which they won by 23 votes to 16.

There is no need to continue with the history of the snail's-pace progress of legislation on family planning in this country but Trevor, a bachelor in his thirties, was instrumental in getting it started. During his contribution to the Seanad debate he said he hoped that the legislation

Senate row over hospital posts

THE idea that there could be two kinds of medicine practice in this State — Catholic medicine and Protestant medicine should be nailed, Senator T. West told the Senate yesterday.

He said they must get to the stage where the best man was appointed and was seen to be so appointed.

Senator West who was speaking on the Health Hospital Boards Regulations 1972 which had been laid before the House, said it seemed that they would perpetuate a system which had existed in the voluntary hospitals.

This was a system under which it seemed that two types of medicine existed — and that Protestant doctors were not going to be appointed to Catholic hospitals and vice versa.

IT was tremendously important that this idea should be nailed.

Mr. Childers, Minister for Health, said that the Senator was undertaking propaganda of a most scandalous kind.

Was the Senator suggesting that in 1972 Comhairle na n-Oispideal would say "We are appointing a surgeon from Ardkeen Hospital he must be a Catholic."

Senator West said that he wanted to nail the idea that the voluntary hospitals would be prohibiting appointments because of any religious qualifications or lack of them. He was not trying to put out any insidious propaganda.

RELIGIOUS GROUNDS

What he was worried about was that the voluntary hospitals, whether Protestant or Catholic controlled might stop the appointment of the best candidate on religious grounds.

Mr. Childers said that Comhairle na n-Oispideal had not got the power to make that kind of selection.

Senator T. O Maolain said the Senator should name names.

Senator West said that there were hospitals in Dublin which were basically controlled by religious orders. He would be the last person to denigrate the work of the religious orders in hospitals and schools but they should be clear that in the case of these hospitals the best person was appointed irrespective of his religion.

Senator Mullen — Is the

Senator West should be prepared to name names.

Senator West — There are hospitals on both sides of the religious divide.

Senator Mullen — Of course there are.

SNOB PROBLEM.

Senator Mrs. Mary Robinson said that consultants in voluntary hospitals were regarded by people as being better than those in health authority hospitals. Apart from the religious problems there was also a snob

Senator T. West

problem. She was disappointed that they had not introduced a system of a common pool of consultants.

Earlier Senator Prof. J. E. Jessop who said he was involved with eight of the 16 voluntary hospitals in Dublin, stated that it was the policy of each of these to advertise vacancies and to assess and appoint the best candidates as far as was humanly possible.

These hospitals had no objection to the regulations before the House.

Senator G. E. Russell said the feeling still persisted to some degree that it was a pity to break up the Limerick Joint Health Authority which had been operating successfully for years and replace it with a Regional Health Board. But there was a desire to give the new boards a chance to see if they would function effectively in the interests of the patient.

He hoped that this "period of organisation" would settle down

injection of three regional hospital boards into the system of health and hospital administration. But if they were going to have these he thought there was a strong case for having a fourth board based on the Limerick region, which was the only area in the country with two regional hospitals.

EXPANSION.

Mr. Childers interjected, as the Senator was proceeding, to say that there was no intention to downgrade the Limerick Regional Hospital. In fact, there were plans for a great expansion of the facilities there.

Senator Russell appealed to the Minister to withdraw his plans to introduce these three hospital boards which he felt would lead to overlapping and to a costlier service.

Senator W. O'Brien said that there was no great demand in the health boards for the expansion of the hospital boards and he thought the Minister should be slow to move in this regard. He feared that the additional boards would increase taxation.

Mr. Childers replying to the debate, said that he knew of no single case where vested interests in the Health Boards were ganging up together to secure something for a selfish interest.

He said that they had now reached the stage where they must see how they could get the voluntary hospitals and the health board hospitals to co-operate and co-ordinate. Some success had been achieved so far in this regard.

Mr. Childers pledged that in the creation of the new boards and their administrations there would be no "gobbledegook Parkinsonian empire building". He would not tolerate it.

The motion to approve the regulations was agreed to by 20, votes to 13.

SENATOR URGES PROTESTANTS TO SPEAK THEIR MINDS

Irish Times Reporter

"THE REMARKS of Dr. McQuaid, Archbishop of Dublin, sometimes send shivers down Protestant spines," Senator Trevor West told parents at a Charter Day ceremony yesterday in The King's Hospital, Palmerstown, Co. Dublin.

Senator West said he would like to see The King's Hospital taking in Roman Catholic pupils. The sooner we faced up to inter-denominational education the better, he said.

It was about time Protestants stopped bending over backwards and said exactly what they thought about such matters as the Ne Temere decree, interdenominational education and community schools. "We will not gain respect, nor will we deserve respect, if we do not stand up and state our objections."

Senator West said there now appeared to be a new possibility of Protestant schools working together with Catholic schools. "I think the gap in the barrier has already appeared."

Education could overcome old animosities. Protestant schools had something to be proud of in their liberal approach. Religion was often used as an offensive instrument. "We should be looking at education tradition from a constant point of view and we should want to share this tradition with other people no mater what their background may be."

The headmaster, the Rev. G. S. Magahy, said that Protestant parents must make their minds known as to what types of schools they wished to have. The whole patern of our educational system

was changing rapidly, but no clear pattern had yet emerged for the Protestant population.

"Few Protestants can have read the recent statements of Dr. McQuaid with an easy mind. There are places, in country areas especially, where the joining of schools into a community school must mean the inclusion of a Protestant school, and if these are to be directly under the control of the Roman Catholic Hierarchy it will mean the eventual disappearance of schools under Protestant management."

He said he was not discussing the pros and cons of segregated education but only trying to state that he considered that Protestant parents of this generation have an obligation to ensure that schools under Protestant management would continue, so that parents who wished to send their children to them might be able to do so.

One of the best solutions put forward so far was that schools should be fostered and boarding facilities provided in areas where there was already a school with a large day pupil population.

"Protestants have been too willing in the past to sit back and let things happen and then make the best of them. How much better they would be if they got inside and helped to formulate decisions. They must encourage their children to do this," he said.

Reports in *The Cork Examiner* and *The Irish Times* on the Senate debate about the Family Planning Bill, February 1974.

would not be diluted, as some speakers had suggested, by limiting the use of contraceptives to married people only and foreseeing Charlie Haughey's eventual legislation in 1979 when he was Minister for Health – an Irish solution to an Irish problem. Trevor also spoke on the need for adequate sex education in schools at various levels and for appropriate literature to be available in relation to family planning. 'We should not make the changes down here mainly because of the people of Northern Ireland,' he said, 'but we should make them for our own purposes.' A lot had been said about the possibility of a downgrading of the quality of life as a result of the use of contraception, but he had found 'no sign of the lowering of the quality of life in Northern Ireland'.

A member of the Church of Ireland, and for many years a lay member representing the diocese of Cork, Cloyne and Ross at the General Synod of the church, Trevor's religion was very important to him. He felt a particular responsibility to speak on behalf of members of the minority churches in the Republic. The ban imposed by Archbishop John Charles McQuaid on Roman Catholics attending Trinity College had recently been rescinded by the bishops' meeting at Maynooth in 1970 towards the end of McQuaid's episcopacy, but had been in place when Trevor was an undergraduate and a junior staff member. Archbishop McQuaid was a very powerful influence on life in Ireland at that time.

Trevor was particularly concerned about the small Dublin hospitals, which were described as having a 'Protestant ethos' (although 'liberal' might have been a better description) – and with reason. Some time after Trevor's election to the Seanad in December 1969 the new St Vincent's Hospital opened at Elm Park in Dublin. At the opening ceremony in 1970 Archbishop McQuaid spoke. The general tone of his speech was so sectarian that it led Dr Noel Browne (Trevor's erstwhile colleague in the National Progressive Democratic Party), who was then in the Dáil, to put a question to the Minister for Health, Erskine Childers. Browne asked, if, in view of the fact that public money was spent on the building of this institution

> [the Minister] would care to comment, and to condemn or to criticize, the very bigoted and sectarian speech made by the chairman of the board, Dr John Charles McQuaid, Archbishop of Dublin, at the opening of the institution in which, by implication, he excluded members of the religious minority of the nursing and medical profession from employment there and also those of the minority who fall sick in this State and who have as much

51

The Bold Collegian

right to access to this hospital as anybody else and to treatment
in accordance with their religious beliefs?

The Ceann Comhairle told Deputy Browne the question did not arise but
Browne continued to ask Minister Childers why he, as a member of the
Church of Ireland, did not condemn sectarianism and defend the reli-
gious minority.

Trevor drew attention to McQuaid's speeches when speaking at the
Charter Day at The King's Hospital School in October 1971 saying that
'the remarks of Dr McQuaid, Archbishop of Dublin, sometimes send
shivers down Protestant spines'. He also crossed swords with Minister
Childers on the hospital issue at the end of June 1972 during the debate
in the Seanad on the Health (Hospital Bodies) Regulations 1972. As reported in the *Cork Examiner* on Friday, 30 June 1972, Trevor said 'the idea
that there could be two kinds of medicine practised in this State –
Catholic medicine and Protestant medicine – should be nailed'. He said
that they must get to the stage where the best man for the job was appointed and was seen to be appointed. (There wasn't much question of
women being appointed then due to the ban on married women working
in the public services. This was removed in 1973.) Trevor felt the regulations before the House perpetuated the system that existed in the voluntary hospitals – that Protestant doctors were not going to be appointed
to Catholic hospitals and vice versa.

Mr Childers responded that Trevor was undertaking propaganda of
the most scandalous kind by suggesting that in 1972 Comhairle na
nOspidéal (the State body that appointed medical consultants) would say
when they were appointing a surgeon that he must be a Catholic. But
Trevor persisted and said that there were hospitals in Dublin that were
basically controlled by religious orders. He was, he said, the last person
to denigrate the work of religious orders in hospitals and schools but they
should be clear that in the case of these hospitals the best person was appointed irrespective of religion, and that there was a problem on both
sides of the religious divide.

As someone who always urged Protestants to speak their minds
Trevor may have been disappointed that in the debate Professor W.J.E.
Jessop, also a member of a religious minority, stated that he was involved
in eight of the sixteen voluntary hospitals in Dublin and that these hospitals had no objections to the regulations. But Professor Jessop may have
seen no problems because, he said 'it was the policy of each of these hos-

pitals to advertise vacancies and to assess and appoint the best candidates as far as is humanly possible'.

In that Charter Day speech at The King's Hospital in Dublin Trevor had urged Protestants to 'stop bending over backwards and say exactly what they thought'. He spoke several times about the effect of the *Ne Temere* decree on the Protestant population in the Republic, which insisted that the children of marriages between a Protestant and a Roman Catholic had to be brought up as Roman Catholics, and the interdenominational disharmony this caused in communities. His interest in education at all levels was not confined to areas where minority groups were affected but he paid particular attention to their situation, and he welcomed Roman Catholic children to schools such as The King's Hospital.

Because he was a member of the Church of Ireland – an all-Ireland church – he availed of his position as a co-religionist to involve himself in affairs in Northern Ireland. Many Northerners came to Trinity when Trevor was an undergraduate; as indeed did his maternal grandfather John Hill Trevor McNeill from Belfast. Recognizing in his first election address that 'tension springs from prejudice which is deeply held' he felt it could only be removed if Protestants and Catholics meet each other in schools and to that end promised to promote non-denominational education.

While always ready to defend members of the minority in the Republic he was quick to explain the true situation here if he felt it was being misrepresented. He wrote a great response to two depressing articles by 'Cromlyn', the pseudonym of a writer who was almost certainly a Northerner, in the *Church of Ireland Gazette* of 17 December 1976 and 14 January 1977, on the situation of Protestants in the Republic. Trevor's reply was published in the *Gazette* on 28 January 1977. He recognized that Protestants had problems here but he pointed to the changes as well – the deletion of Article 44 of the Constitution, which had removed the special position of the Catholic Church, and he believed that 'increasingly numbers of southern Roman Catholics are coming to value open-mindedness and liberal standards, which are an essential part of Protestantism'.

He wrote that the change in Southern society is 'in part due to social and economic improvements, to greatly increased educational opportunities, and as a reaction against the authoritarianism of the Irish Roman Catholic Church'. While he agreed with 'Cromlyn' about the entanglement of Church and State in the South and the lack of enthusiasm by the two main political parties to address this issue, he finished by writing that the Southern Protestant never feels part of a beleaguered community:

> Unlike his predecessors in 1921 who for very obvious reasons had problems of dual allegiance he has no such problem. His allegiance is to the State in which he pays his taxes (in amounts which are somewhat too large most Southern Protestants would agree). His relations with his fellow Roman Catholics on an individual level are extremely good. As a member of a community he feels himself (as do members of all minorities) at certain disadvantages. He will strive to rectify these disadvantages and he believes that he has a role to play in the future, acting as a catalyst to improve inter-community relations in the whole island– and this Trevor certainly did.

Less well known is Trevor's considerable contribution to the Peace Process, especially during some of the most violent years, particularly his influence on the Unionist communities and on paramilitaries in the UDA and the UVF. In his address at Trevor's funeral, Bishop Paul Colton, Church of Ireland Bishop of Cork Cloyne and Ross, quoted from Ulick O'Connor's obituary of Gusty Spence: 'Trevor', O'Connor wrote, 'had a huge effect in bringing opposing sides together in Northern Ireland.' It was Spence who announced the Loyalist ceasefire in 1994. Trevor had a close association with Spence and had visited him in Long Kesh in the mid 1970s. Bishop Colton continued: 'Trevor's service to us all on this island, in the Peace Process, by helping to bring those Loyalist paramilitaries to the table of discussion should not be forgotten.'

Amazingly, he also had an influence on IRA prisoners. An article in *The Irish Times* on 17 February 1975 describes Trevor and Senator Michael Mullen, then General Secretary of the ITGWU, as the 'middle men' in achieving the ending of a very serious hunger strike by some members of the Provisional IRA in Portlaoise Gaol. One man had been without food for forty-four days.

Little of this was publicly known and certainly not trumpeted by Trevor. As early as August 1971 he and fellow University senators Bryan Alton, John Horgan, William Jessop, Patrick Quinlan and Mary Robinson wrote to the parliaments of Westminster and Stormont urging 'a political solution to the problems of Northern Ireland' and pointing out that 'responsibility for bringing this about lies on each member of the parliaments involved'.

Described often as a 'Renaissance Man' Trevor was an enthusiastic debater in the Seanad chamber. The debates on our entry to the European

Economic Community (as the European Union then was) were under way when he entered the Seanad. He publicly urged people to vote yes in the subsequent referendum on entry. Long a supporter of the decimalization of our currency, he was a most useful contributor to the debate on the Decimal Currency Bill 1970, urging that 'errors in conversion would be rounded down rather than up, as this would be good psychologically for acceptance of decimalization'. A practical man as ever! He also asked the government to be vigilant in guarding against excessive rises in prices, suggesting that 'our archaic system of weights and measures would also be rationalized as soon as possible'. Again, about twenty years before his time.

As one would hope a mathematician would do, he kept a close eye on monetary issues. As reported in the *Cork Examiner* on 7 May 1975, Trevor was one of the nine senators who in April had put their names to a motion urging the establishment of a Select Committee of the Senate to examine the implications of breaking the link with sterling. Trevor is quoted as saying that the best information available indicated that a devaluation of sterling was 'just around the corner', and that an 'abnormal' effort should be made to have the issue debated. 'Otherwise,' he said 'we could be faced with a sterling devaluation,' and the only people having a chance to think about it would be the civil servants in the Central Bank. The next day Trevor was on his feet again on the Order of Business asking the Minister for Finance to address the issue. In April 1976, exactly a year after he and the other eight senators had put forward the motion for a debate, Trevor expressed his regret in the House that the Select Committee had not been set up as the value of sterling was plummeting!

Trevor frequently looked to the future in Seanad debates: for example on the Nuclear Energy Bill 1971 he pointed out that this country had no control over institutions using radioactive isotopes, while in the United Kingdom there were two separate acts to ensure safety. He pointed to incompatibilities in the bill and said it was vital safety standards were set by an entirely independent body instead of the Nuclear Energy Board, so that these standards could be used as a stick to beat the constructors of the station. At Committee stage the Minister, Mr Brian Lenihan (Senior), assured Trevor that the Board would look after the safety arrangements of the nuclear station until a separate body was set up to cater for that. The Minister continued that he envisaged the bill being amended within a relatively short time to incorporate this. 'To set up such a body at this time would be putting the cart before the horse.' In this case Trevor was forty-odd years before his time, as we still do not have a nuclear power station in Ireland!

Minister Lenihan and Trevor were involved in some jousting again over the Transport (Miscellaneous Provisions) Bill in 1971 with Trevor urging the subsidisation of loss-making parts of CIE by profitable ones – and while CIE is now divided up it is still a case of *plus ça change, plus c'est la même chose.*

As the only scientist among the university senators for much of his time in the Seanad, Trevor's contributions to the debates on science were very significant. In the debate on the science budget in February 1981 he spoke about the small number of students taking the Honours Mathematics papers in the Leaving Certificate (still a problem today) and suggested ways in which this could be rectified. Students might not have known that he said the papers were too hard. He gave a lovely practical example of this. He had been asked to check some papers and started to do so one day on the train to Cork. The journey to Cork took three hours and three hours was allotted for each paper: 'So I thought I would finish the couple of papers I had to check. I am supposed to be good at it. I was halfway through the first paper when we got to Mallow.'

Trevor gave great praise to the excellence of the Young Scientist Competition run by Aer Lingus at the Royal Dublin Society each year, which has stimulated great interest in project-type work in schools. He frequently stressed the importance of making science exciting and praised the Irish Mathematical Society for organizing mathematical Olympiads, explaining the Russian tradition where young mathematicians competed with each other on a local basis and on a national level.

Trevor had a practical interest in encouraging scientific development in agriculture and industry as his family's malting business had been involved in experiments with the Department of Agriculture and Messrs Guinness to develop the best type of malting barley for the Irish climate. He spoke in this debate in 1981 of Sir Horace Plunkett's emphasis on the importance of education in agriculture. On that occasion in 1981 he promoted the importance of an interplay between private industry and education (Trinity had just started a foundation aimed at this project):

> What one has to do is to persuade industrialists and others that it is of direct benefit to them that levels of research funding are raised and that there is a limit to what the Government can spend. I am not proposing to set any limit nor am I trying to ab-

solve the Government from responsibilities, but the universities should also look to the private sector and to the other third level institutions.

During Trevor's years in the Seanad he was from time to time placed under considerable pressure to choose between his academic career in Trinity and his career in politics. This seems unfair, seeing that his commitment to College life was incredible and not just in the sporting area. From 1968 to 1970 he was Assistant Junior Dean and then from 1974 to 1978 he was Junior Dean and Registrar of Chambers, at the same time being a very active member of the Seanad. However, Provost F.S.L. Lyons supported the principle of people in Trevor's position being able to contribute to Irish governance without resigning their main occupation. He had a good relationship with students and a strong understanding of them and of their problems. In the debate on the Misuse of Drugs Bill 1973 introduced by Brendan Corish, Minister for Health, he said that as officer in charge of student discipline in Trinity the drugs problem had impinged on him when, six or seven years before, there had been a severe increase in drug-taking but it had fortunately decreased.

Trevor West umpires a cricket match in College Park during the Senate election count, August 1977. (*The Irish Times*)

The election to the twenty-first Dáil and Seanad took place in the summer of 1977. Once again there was an ex-minister in the Dublin University Seanad race: Connor Cruise O'Brien was well known not only as a politician but as a writer, journalist and former diplomat. High-profile candidates are always likely to do well in the Trinity elections where so many of the voters live overseas and name recognition is important. The other candidates beside outgoing senators Mary Robinson and Trevor were Trinity 'insiders' such as Vincent McBrierty from the Department of Physics and David Norris from the Department of English. Some of the 'outsiders' were well known also as they included Catherine McGuinness and David Cabot, who were running again, and Shane Ross, son of the former Senator John Ross. Those with the highest number of votes on the first count eventually won: Robinson with 1562, West 1407 and Cruise O'Brien 1378 with McGuinness in fourth position with 868 votes.

We entered a turbulent time in Irish politics during the twenty-first Dáil and for some years after. A backbench revolt against the then Taoiseach Jack Lynch led to the election of Charles J. Haughey as leader of Fianna Fáil and hence Taoiseach in December 1979. There were four changes of Taoiseach, six changes of minister for finance and three changes of government between December 1979 and December 1982 and

57

The Bold Collegian

the country was already in an economic crisis. There was great instability in the Dáil and Haughey called an election in June 1981. Fianna Fáil narrowly lost the election and a Fine Gael-Labour coalition led by Garret FitzGerald came to power.

No matter who is in power, as night follows day a Seanad election must follow a Dáil election. The Seanad election following the election of the twenty-second Dáil took place in the summer of 1982. Outgoing senators Robinson and West ran, but O'Brien had resigned from the Seanad in 1969 and gone to London to edit *The Observer* newspaper. In the by-election held in 1979 due to O'Brien's resignation Catherine McGuinness had been elected so when an election was called for the Seanad following the twenty-second Dáil election in 1981 she, Mary Robinson and Trevor were the outgoing senators. Despite getting good transfers on every count Trevor was not able to catch up with the front runners Robinson, Ross and McGuinness, and lost his seat.

The Fine Gael-Labour coalition did not last long, falling on a budget vote. By February 1982 Fianna Fáil was back in power. Trevor ran again in the subsequent Seanad election: as he regained a huge number of first-preference votes he had lost in the previous election he returned to the Seanad with Mary Robinson and Shane Ross, Catherine McGuinness losing out on this occasion.

However, there were not to be tranquil years ahead in the Seanad. Times were terrible for Charlie Haughey: there were allegations of impersonation and of illegal phone-tapping, and earlier in 1982 he had a major revolt by Dessie O'Malley on his hands. In the summer his Attorney General Patrick Connolly had to resign after a man found by the gardaí in his apartment was charged with two murders. There were other problems too. Haughey, after the Attorney General's resignation, described the events as 'grotesque, unprecedented, bizarre and unbelievable', allowing Cruise O'Brien to coin the word GUBU, which is in our vocabulary to this day.

It all led to yet another general election in November 1982, the count for the Seanad election following the twenty-fourth Dáil election being in January 1983. This time, while Trevor's first preference vote held up well, he was not so lucky in transfers. There were several of the usual suspects from previous elections and the outgoing senators McGuinness, Robinson and Ross ran. After Robinson and Ross were elected McGuinness passed Trevor on the sixth and final count with 1631 to his 1565 – very close in a tough race.

The Chinese curse of 'may you live in interesting times' comes to mind: had Trevor been senator when politics in Ireland were less chaotic he would probably have been able to continue to contribute to the governance of Ireland in the measured way he did for so many years. How useful he would have been, in particular on Northern Ireland. Not that he did not continue his contacts with Gusty Spence – he saw him often – and his attendance at church in Enniskillen on the Sunday after the Remembrance Day bombing in 1987 made a huge impression.

In the course of research for this chapter I came across some undated notes Trevor had made in preparation for a speech, in this case on 'The Role of the Minority in Ireland'. The material emphasized his contributions to the Seanad, especially as a member of the Church of Ireland. It is worth quoting, and although we are still challenged by some of these issues today, the material is further evidence of Trevor's great foresight in his political career in Seanad Éireann:

> In a country in which the majority makes up 95 per cent of the population the role of the minority is to be independent in a firm and constructive way. Ireland faces great changes, not just because of the situation in the North, but on account of the increased awareness, especially among younger people, resulting from the broadening of our educational horizons.
>
> We have not, as yet, taken political account of this increased awareness. Younger people find our present political system unattractive, the parties are controlled by an older group, their approach has been to maintain the status quo unless forced to do otherwise. Consequently many have turned to Sinn Féin or Marxist politics [This surely showed amazing foresight in view of what we are seeing in politics today.] We are making a serious mistake if we ignore the ideas put forward by these groups: their plans for putting such ideas into practice by violent or disruptive means must be totally rejected. An urgent first priority is to lower the voting age to eighteen to enable youthful views to be expressed through the ballot box.
>
> As a young person in an independent position in politics, I would criticize the government, and the system as a whole, on its caution and timidity, its lack of daring and initiative in facing our major problems. These problems can no longer be side-stepped, they must be dealt with. Some of these problems are ones on which Protestant and Roman Catholic views differ. These include

59

Taoiseach Charles J. Haughey presents a mascot to the Irish Parliamentary Soccer Team prior to their match against Westminster Wanderers, June 1978.

Introducing seven-year old Elizabeth O'Connell of Templeogue to President Éamon de Valera at College Races, 1972. (*The Irish Press*) problems in the Constitution, problems of divorce, family planning, adoption. It is a sad reflexion that during fifty years of independence we talked so much of Irish unity and yet made few constructive moves to attract Northern Protestants. Now, with political changes imminent we find that our legislation dealing with matters of private morality is one-sided and desperately needs to be altered.

I would like also to deal with the need to change our view of ownership of money, property, land, talents and resources. For too long in Ireland we have taken a purely individual point of view. Everything owned by an individual or group of people should be regarded as being held in trust for the nation. Money should not be invested just so as to give the maximum return without consideration of national needs and priorities. Land should not be farmed or developed regardless of consequences to the surrounding areas and population. Industrial organizations must not be allowed to exploit our natural resources in a thoughtless fashion. These questions arise in the areas of planning and the preservation of the environment. Legislation with teeth is urgently needed for preservation of existing amenities. But more urgently we need to change our whole attitude to ownership and possession. The warning signals are all about us and we need to recognize them before it is too late.

As a university representative I know that independents play an important role in our political life. It is just as important that religious minorities take a full, active and vigorous part in the running of the country. We are challenged by our many problems, that of Irish unity, accession to the EEC, environmental preservation, economic growth. All our citizens must work together as Irishmen if these problems are to be solved.

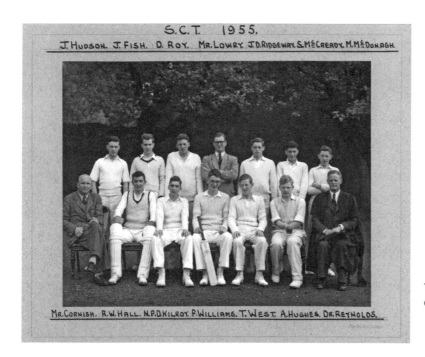

S.C.T. 1955.

J. HUDSON. J. FISH. D. ROY. MR. LOWRY. J.D. RIDGEWAY. S. McCREADY. M. McDONAGH.

MR. CORNISH. R.W. HALL. N.P.O. KILROY. P. WILLIAMS. T. WEST. A. HUGHES. DR. REYNOLDS.

The High School Senior Cricket Cup team, 1955.

Charity GAA match featuring Connaught/Munster *vs* Leinster/Ulster:
Back row, left to right: Paddy Cooney T.D., Paudge Brennan T.D., Hugh Byrne T.D., Patrick Lawlor T.D., Jim Gibbons T.D., Brendan Corish T.D., Jim Tunney T.D., Larry McMahon T.D., Sean Moore T.D., Paddy Harte, T.D., John Boland T.D. (unidentified).

This Sporting Life

Trevor West was competitive. He competed as a schoolboy to win scholarships in maths, as a young university lecturer to win a seat in the Senate and as a sportsman to win every time he took to the pitch in whatever game he was playing. When he reached an age that precluded him from being an active sportsman he continued his competitive sporting life by making every possible effort to see sportspeople from Trinity or Irish universities teams perform to the best of their abilities. In fact he became a champion for sport when he started his teaching career in Trinity in 1966, long before his playing days could be deemed over. However, in sport he never departed from what is best described as the Corinthian ideal. As a willing volunteer, enthusiast and chairman of Dublin University Central Athletic Committee (DUCAC) he had the task of trying not to relegate this ideal to the recycling bin while university sport pressed ahead towards the twenty-first century.

It was at Midleton College in the late 1940s that Trevor's sporting life began, and undoubtedly it was hugely influenced by his sports-mad father, Timothy West, who was the headmaster. West Senior was a hard taskmaster and strict disciplinarian who had been in charge since 1928, when the school was threatened with closure and had only seven pupils. The new head resurrected Midleton in those difficult times, which of course included the Second World War. When Trevor was a pupil the numbers were hovering between seventy and eighty and it became possible for the school to compete successfully in Munster Schools' competitions in hockey and cricket.

Rugby was much more difficult given the strength and numbers in the traditional rugby schools such as Presentation and Christian Brothers Cork. Tim had been captain of Wanderers in Dublin during 1925–6, had three Leinster caps and on moving to Midleton played for Cork Constitution. He introduced the club colours of Wanderers and of Cork Con, which happened to be the same (blue, black and white) for Midleton College. Trevor played rugby as a wing forward, as had his father, but did not have the physical presence to make sufficient impression when becoming an undergraduate. Partly for this reason he turned to soccer and had a long career playing for various 'social' teams, nearly always organized by himself.

He was most successful as a cricketer and continued to wear an old faded red Munster Schools' cap whenever donning whites. In Trevor's time as a pupil in Midleton there existed probably the most bizarre cricket field ever seen. Jack White, past pupil, poet, journalist and RTÉ Assistant Controller of Programmes, but not a cricket fan, described the setting: 'It is one of the few fields in the world where cricket is exciting, because one boundary is ten yards from the wicket and another two hundred, and the furthest fielders are completely hidden from sight in the deep gully of a dry stream.' Jack White is allowed some poetic licence but past pupils have been heard to say that when the ball was hit to the long boundary it was necessary to shout to tell the fielder that the ball was on its way.

Due to his prowess in maths Trevor was sent to finish his education at The High School in Dublin, where a renowned mathematician, Pip Graham, who also taught in Trinity, specialized in preparing students for Trinity Entrance Scholarships and Exhibitions. The Trinity that Trevor attended in 1956 was a peculiar mixture of Northern Ireland Protestants, English ex-public school pupils, middle-class southerners and the odd slightly exotic African, Asian or American. It was an ideal environment in which to develop an understanding of how it was possible for many diverse sorts to unite for the common good. Captain of the Cricket Club in 1955 was 'Kiki Coker' from Sierra Leone, and he was in charge of a team that included Rhodesians, Irishmen and Englishmen. Background was irrelevant when it came to building a team to compete on a field of sport. The lessons were obvious to the young maths student.

On the second floor lobby of the new Department of Sport in Trinity are photographs of the College's Olympians. These are all people of whom Trevor was very proud, but was his Corinthian ideal fundamentally at odds with that other Olympian principle, 'Faster, Higher, Stronger', where the limits required for achievement were being pushed ever higher? Professionalism in sport is increasingly unavoidable. Trevor however, did embrace change, despite remaining a Victorian at heart. His ideal assumed that sport could teach virtues complementary to those acquired in classrooms, lecture halls, libraries and around the family dinner table: team spirit, fair play, courage, swiftness of judgment, deference to arbitration, attention to detail, mastery of rules. He also had a vision of sport as a means of bringing people together, especially political opposites in Ireland, and helped by his own sporting connections, worked to assist in reconciliation, North and South. He would have seen his efforts in this area as a competition with himself: what can I achieve?

Throughout his life Trevor compiled a huge dossier of contacts and this started when he was an undergraduate. Wherever he travelled in later years he always knew who to look up in the area being visited. Many were from his sporting connections, others were ex-students and colleagues and some were contacts from his political life. He did not think that his extensive address book would one day be used in his successful campaign for the Senate in 1970, but it certainly was a major factor.

Trevor bowled off-breaks and batted. He practised religiously, often with his schoolmate Norman Kilroy, on their own, in Leinster Cricket Club. High School then played in Belgrave Square, another quirky cricket ground, just big enough to fit a rugby pitch in the winter season. The ball was pretty regularly dispatched into the surrounding roads and gardens. Trevor flirted a bit with leg-breaks as he felt he had 'mastered' the off-break but in his later playing career he didn't bowl at all and was just seen as a batsman. In Trinity from 1956 to 1960 he did not make it on to the Colours team. In fact all the sport that Trevor played began to take on a slightly casual nature, as his wide range of interests gradually precluded him from being available on a consistent basis. Perhaps his most memorable moment in College Park came in 1961 when guesting for Peterhouse College in Cambridge while he was working for his Ph.D. in St John's College. Not only did Trevor take four wickets to assist the visitors to a narrow victory but one of his dismissals was his brother John, LBW for one. It certainly is one of the most memorable moments of John's career as a cricketer. When Trevor returned to Dublin in 1966 he was inveigled up to Phoenix Cricket Club by John, who was captain in 1967 and 1969. He played intermittently for Phoenix in those years and also in Cork for Cork County, C of I, and occasionally for Munster.

Trevor was always keen to travel when required, usually in Northern Ireland, when Munster found it difficult to field their strongest team. It would not have bothered him that he was obviously seen as a useful extra in the general scheme of Munster cricket. He was never available to play in Cork, on the beautiful Mardyke ground, until all his Trinity responsibilities were finished in June, leaving him available for the second half of the season only. Apart from his successful outing for Peterhouse, his most memorable game was probably a two-day match for Munster in Armagh against the Northern Cricket Union. Representing Munster was Tom Kiernan, the Lions captain and a close friend of Trevor's, and on the Ulster team was Raymond Hunter, a Lions and Ireland teammate. After the first day's play there was a magnificent dinner after which Tom and Raymond combined, with great enthusiasm, in a rendition of 'The Sash'. The probability that sport could overcome any political or religious differences was obvious to onlookers, even if inebriation played a role.

His willingness to travel for any particular event, sporting or non-sporting, brought him finally to play for DUCC in Belfast, against Queen's, in 1972. This was an annual two-day fixture and held in similar circumstances to those that saw him playing away matches for Munster, the Trinity XI needing a willing substitute. Rather more than a mature student at this stage, he opened the batting with the Trinity captain, Johnny Silverstone. The pair put on 144 for the first wicket with Trevor scoring 69, and DUCC proceeded to win the match. Making connections was always on the agenda in these games and Trevor was a senator at this stage and keen to expand his sporting contacts.

Following this match the first ever Irish Universities match took place in College Park on 13–14 July 1972. This was played against the Irish touring club, the Leprechauns, and was organized by Trevor with Des Cashell and Tony Leon of the Leps. The significance of this fixture was that it was the beginning of the general organization of Irish University sport for which Trevor's vision was largely responsible. There were Irish Universities rugby teams, which were occasionally selected to play against southern hemisphere tourists, GAA teams who played some games despite there being no international opposition, and an All-Ireland Association Football team had been selected in the past despite the North/South division in the respective football associations.

However, nobody took responsibility for the organization of university sport on an all-Ireland basis in the early 1970s. Two years later, on 22 March 1974, the Irish Universities Cricket Association was formed and Trevor was unanimously elected President, a position he held for thirty-five years. He would seldom miss a tournament or AGM. Enthusiastic support for this initiative came from Murray Power (Queen's) and Alan Sharp (University of Ulster). Significantly, the first team manager was Philip Carson (UU), who later became Head of Sport in the University of Ulster. The Irish Universities XI played every year in the British Uni-

Michael Halliday, off spinner and former captain of Dublin University Cricket Club who was capped ninety-three times for Ireland. (Photograph Billy Strickland)

versities tournament and managed to win it in 1986 and 1988. Trevor usually turned up at the tournament wherever it was held, combining it with a visit to an old academic or sporting friend who lived nearby. College Park successfully staged the tournament in 1985 and also in 2000 when the side defeated the English, Welsh and Scottish sides to take the title again. Dominick Joyce of DUCC was the dominant batsman who engineered this victory. It is possible that this brought more pleasure to Trevor than dismissing his brother for one run back in 1961, but that is doubtful.

Apart from his role as Treasurer of DUCAC up to 1976 and then as Chairman until 2009, Trevor had direct involvement in the Association Football, Rugby and Cricket Clubs. He was President of DUAFC from 1968–71 and DUCC from 1974–80 and again in 1983–84. He organized his own social soccer team, which frequently included a vocal left winger in Ulick O'Connor. This team played a wide range of opponents, ranging from schools, literary selections, prisons and teams selected from deprived areas of Dublin such as the Hardwicke Street Flats. However, the most notable team that he captained was an Oireachtas XI, which played against a parliamentary selection from Westminster on 10 June 1978. In the photographs it is possible to see such aspiring athletes and politicians as Enda Kenny, Bertie Ahern and Liam Lawlor. Another picture displays a Munster/Leinster team of politicians at Croke Park about to play a Connacht/Ulster selection in a fundraising Gaelic football encounter.

As President of DUAFC Trevor was very keen that the Collingwood Cup (the inter-varsity championship) should be won and later in 1979/80 DUCAC and the soccer club employed the renowned Liam Tuohy to coach the side. They duly won the final for the second time with two goals from rugby international Hugo MacNeill greatly helping the cause, along with one or two earnest students of Biblical studies controlling midfield. Captain in 1972 and 1973 was solicitor Pat Finucane, who became a good friend of Trevor's. Pat was a fine winger whom Trevor entertained at home in Midleton with his family. His murder by the UDA in 1989 was a shock to all who knew him and a setback to hopes for an end to civil strife in the North. However connections on both side of the divide enabled Trevor to play a largely undocumented role in helping the peace process over a long period.

Trevor was secretary of the Irish Universities Rugby Association from 1977 to 1988 and organized and led two major tours. In 1978 the side, captained by John Robbie and coached by Roly Meates, travelled to New

Zealand, winning six of their nine matches. Two Tests were played against New Zealand Universities, resulting in one win and one loss and the New Zealand Under-21 side was defeated in the last match. A second tour was undertaken in 1987, this time to Korea and Japan with Roly Meates again coaching. Trevor was delighted to have nine DUFC players in the squad of twenty-six. The full national Japanese side was beaten 24–12 in the final game in Tokyo. When he was succeeded as secretary by brother John, Trevor subsequently went on tours to the new South Africa in 1994 and Australia in 1997.

DUCAC was set up to revive sport after the First World War. It was essentially a federation of the college sports clubs with four representatives from the rugby, cricket, hockey and boat clubs, and two from the rest. The board had three sitting members and a chairman. Remarkably there have only been five chairmen to date and all played a major role, despite their other responsibilities. Two brothers, W.E. (later Provost) and Harry Thrift took the first two shifts, followed by J.V. Luce from 1956 to 1976. In Luce's period of chairmanship the capitation fee was introduced, which gave DUCAC a stable financial base. DUCAC was given No. 27 as offices, rooms that were shared with the Knights of the Campanile, the sporting society based on the equivalent clubs in Oxford and Cambridge, Vincents and Hawks. One of Trevor's favourite stories surrounds the search for funding for the resurfacing and renovation of the tennis courts in Botany Bay in the late 1960s. All graduate members of the Knights were asked for monetary support for which they would be sent a Knights tie. Sam Beckett replied from Paris, enclosing £20 and the following inscription: 'Delighted to help the tennis court appeal. Don't bother to send a tie. I don't wear one.' Much to Trevor's annoyance the note was lost or stolen from the Library Manuscripts Room.

Trevor became Treasurer in 1967 and succeeded John Luce as Chairman in 1976. The disbursement of funds thus became his main job. In 1970 Trevor successfully argued that DUCAC employ secretarial staff and appointed Joan Taylor. The secretarial and administrative staff of DUCAC from now on effectively acted as personal assistants to Trevor and strong working relationships were set up with Joan Taylor and others in following years including Cathy Doyle, Geraldine McAuley and Drinda Jones. This was pretty important as the chairman resisted the personal use of technology. All these administrators speak fondly of their boss and he certainly had a knack of running a smooth ship with little in the way of dissension. It probably helped that he appears to have headhunted almost all who worked with him.

The Pavilion Bar was a potential source of funding for DUCAC and up to 1971 it only opened after matches in College Park. It was run on a very amateur basis by the Rugby and Cricket Clubs, who each appointed a member to take responsibility for ordering, accounting and serving (only beer and soft drinks). DUCAC minutes indicate that there were frequent problems, usually involving the disappearance of barrels. The author of this particular chapter can vouch for the accuracy of the minutes and the amateurish nature of the arrangement: at one stage he received permission to order beer for the 'Pav' on his own account so as to have an operating bar at all! A member of staff had nominally been a monitor but no money was made and the situation required a complete refit of the pavilion with a permanent staff that would open at regular hours. Trevor had little difficulty in inveigling hockey-playing entrepreneur Paul Coulson to get involved and he started his role while an undergraduate and continued on the bar committee for over ten years. Aidan Duggan was chairman and continued in that role even after taking a new job in the Royal Irish Academy.

The minutes describe the annual efforts to rebuild the bar area and make it into a profitable enterprise. This eventually paid dividends although the costs of renovating and extending spiralled throughout the seventies. It was not until 1990 that a complete refurbishment was completed at a cost of over £250,000, of which the College contributed a fifth. Sport benefited hugely as DUCAC now had a major extra source of funding along with the student capitation. The Pav is, in a way, one of the visible results of Trevor's period in charge, perched above his beloved College Park, a social centre for all College sports people and undergraduates in general while helping to fund sport. The Lincoln Inn and Kennedy's outside back gate had provided the location for a couple of generations of Trinity sports people but this gradually changed in the period from about 1980 onwards.

Another of Trevor's responsibilities was Trinity Week, of which he was chairman well into the seventies (Paul Coulson was also involved, and under his charge Trinity Week finally began making money). Invitation cricket and football matches were held, either organized by or supported by Trevor, along with seven-a-side rugby and the traditional College Races. Also in the DUCAC minutes at the end of the sixties is the first mention of a proposed 'new gymnasium' plus swimming pool and squash courts. An estimate of £350,000, which would need government support, indicates that this idea was an ambitious challenge. Unfortunately a development on this scale remained aspirational and the subsequent building of the Luce Hall, which was dedicated in 1982, did not include the space or facilities envisaged in the earlier plan. This project was government-funded and the compromise was that the ground floor would be used as a science library.

Trevor also had experience, in other universities such as Cambridge, UCLA and Queen's Belfast, of seeing professional physical education teachers operating programmes and managing facilities, but it was not until 1981 that Terry McAuley was appointed as the first Physical Recreation Officer. Terry was a soccer-playing Trinity graduate with experience in Queen's and Loughborough and both he and his wife Geraldine (later administrative assistant of DUCAC) were to have a long association with Trevor and sport in College. Queen's opened a state-of-the-art sports centre in 1972–3 and many of Trevor's and Terry's ideas came from Alastair McDonald who was Director of Sport in Queen's from 1948 to 1978.

It became increasingly obvious that the building of the Luce Hall, with its limitations for a rapidly expanding student population in the eighties and nineties, was inadequate, and a new sports centre facility was required. The need for a major development became increasingly apparent, as did the creation of a dedicated department of sport. Trevor realized that the facilities, development and administration of sport in College, mainly organized by DUCAC to date, were no longer fit for purpose and required a professional approach. In the mid nineties he approached Ken Ryan of KPMG with the idea of a feasibility study, which became a report named *Sport in Trinity: a Strategic Plan for the Next Decade*. Ken Ryan was well known to Trevor as father of two rugby colours, one for DUFC and one for UCD, for his Trinity involvement in graduate recruitment and as a lecturer in economics in the College. Trevor lobbied hard for the plan and was supported by the new Provost, Tom Mitchell. This ensured that sporting issues came regularly to the attention of the board. There were meetings with staff, students, alumni and local residents. Students voted in a referendum to accept a new sports capital investment levy, the carrot being a discount for graduate membership and immediate facilities for fitness and the hockey club. This raised about £3 million from students; £9 million came from Chuck Feeney's Atlantic Philanthropies organization. Tom Mitchell was on the board of Atlantic Philanthropies and was a friend of the entrepreneur who supported a number of Irish ventures over the years. Despite the cash being available there was a delay of five years before building started due to various planning and design issues.

As with many aspects of his life as a sports advocate, Trevor let the professionals or players and participants get on with it. This was even more apparent with the new Department of Sport in 2000. The DUCAC role as safeguard of the clubs would continue alongside the department's role in overseeing the development of the new sports and leisure facilities. Terry McAuley, who had been promoted to Facilities Officer in 1985, was encouraged by Trevor to apply for the role of Director of Sport. Trevor's mate Tony O'Neill of UCD, in his capacity as external advisor to the College for the appointment, fully supported the appointment of Terry and also explained the UCD structure. Michelle Tanner had become Physical Recreation Officer in 1997 and there were now two sports and leisure professionals driving the plans first enumerated in the Ryan report.

With the experience of involvement with Irish University matches, tournaments and tours, sports administration in DUCAC and frequent visits to the Pavilion Bar in the aftermath of matches in College Park, the seeds of a committee to oversee the development and progress of university sport were sown. The Council of University Sports Administrators (CUSAI) was founded in 1986 with Professor John Meenan of UCD as Chairman. At a meeting in the Gresham Hotel, Kieran Dowd of UCC, T.T. West, John Kerrane of DCU and Kevin Barnes of UCD agreed on a formula for this new body 'to promote the development of university sport particularly at inter-varsity and international student level'. It was said, by one of those mentioned, to have been 'organized over a pint'. All of the existing universities, North and South, the NIHE sports clubs and Thomond College Sports and Recreation Committee joined what became CUSAI. Trevor built up a close relationship with Tony O'Neill, the Director of Sport in UCD, based on their friendly rivalry surrounding Trinity and UCD sport in particular and their co-operation in CUSAI. They were described by others involved in sports administration as 'being like two schoolboys'.

There is no doubt that Trevor West, through his enthusiasm, energy and position, made a major contribution to sport in Trinity and his vision, along with sports administrators in the other universities, was responsible for a much-needed organizational revolution in inter-varsity and international student sport. In all the discussion of his work and organization there is no evidence provided as to what sort of 'guy' he was.

Many people, students and friends alike, will say that he was eccentric, and it is worth remembering that he was very much an institutionalized university don, living in the Rubrics in the centre of the College alongside a group of eccentric and distinguished lecturers and professors. These included the legendary R.B. McDowell (History), David Webb (Botany), John Gaskin (Philosophy), George Dawson (Genetics) and Brendan Kennelly (English Literature).

As an assistant Junior Dean, Trevor found himself a bit like a poacher turned gamekeeper. As he was constantly involved with students engaged in the many sports clubs there were times when he had to deal with high-spirited nocturnal activity. This was not an easy task and the problem is one well known to teachers in many institutions. One of his worst experiences was dealing with a group of the rugby club members at a party in No. 38 who had decided to launch a piano down the stairwell. He also had to handle a major bout of destructiveness when the Boat House in Islandbridge was wrecked during a Sigerson Cup function (the Gaelic Football intervarsity competition) in 1990. Cyril Smyth writes in his obituary of Trevor, 'His active engagement in sport in College gave him great insight into the antics of students.' True, but this one-liner does not quite get to grips with the problems he faced from time to time.

The trio of McDowell in his pork-pie hat, overcoats and long scarves, Webb in his dirty jeans and West in his ill-fitting fawn duffle coat certainly made recognition easy. However, a dramatic change came about for Trevor in the nineties with his relationship and subsequent marriage to Maura Lee. Duffle coats were out, Magee suits and jackets were in and Louis Copeland became a close buddy. Friends have been heard talking about Trevor in terms of pm or am (pre Maura or after Maura). This of course was said as a compliment to Maura who enthusiastically embraced all aspects of Trevor's life with its many different and compartmentalized interests and engagements: maths, politics, sport, history, literature, Trinity staff issues and his chairmanship of the board of Midleton College for twenty-four years. Sometimes they overlapped, notably when the board dreamed up the idea of building residences on the rugby pitch in 1970. In fact one of his most valuable assets was that he was in a position to point out to the more ivory-tower, book-bound members of the board or fellows (he was also a chairman of the Fellows Committee) the value of green grass in the centre, not only of Trinity, but also of Dublin.

Because he had so many things going on at any one time he often disappeared from company, usually unexplained. Seen imbibing in the Pav, usually exhibiting the normal raucous laughter, he would leave as suddenly as he had arrived. 'Where has T.T. gone?' It may have been just to Commons but could well have been to attend to any number of other current responsibilities, or simply to meet Maura at the National Concert Hall. History and sport also overlapped and to those who knew nothing about maths he came across as a historian.

The sporting archives in the manuscript room of the library would have little on Trinity sport over the last forty years were it not for Trevor's interest and of course his history of sport in the College, *The Bold Collegians* (1991), which brought together all that was available on the subject in one book. He also edited *150 Years of Trinity Rugby* (2003), the book produced to mark the 150th anniversary of the Rugby Club. An interest in farming and agriculture led to him writing a book on Horace Plunkett, the founder of the Irish Agricultural Organization Society: *Horace Plunkett: Co-operation and Politics* (1986). Because of these many interests he did not have a hands-on involvement in the running of the many clubs overseen by DUCAC. His approach was to make sure a club was operating properly and received its available share of funding and then let its student members get on with the business of running it. DUCAC only intervened if there were queries, usually about how money was being spent.

One of the benefits of playing for a college team is the experience to be gained, at a young age, of running a club, captaincy, taking responsibility, learning how to get on with people and appreciating the importance of team spirit. Trevor did not see it as his role to be involved, unless asked for help, and at least 90 per cent of the time the help requested would be financial. In his book *The Bold Collegians* Trevor delves into Plato and Huizinga's philosophy for their thoughts on the physical, on sport and relaxation. Plato argued for an educational balance between the physical and the philosophical, offering appropriate challenges to both body and mind. Huizinga, a Dutch historian and philosopher who died in 1945 as a prisoner of the Nazis, clearly had an influence on the sports-mad maths lecturer. In 1938 Huizinga published *Homo Ludens (The Sportsman)* in which he discussed the possibility that play is the primary formative element in human culture. Possessed of aesthetic qualities as well as tension and humour, sport offers relaxation, rhythm, challenge. It is an embodiment of youth, of strength, of life; above all else, playing must be fun: 'Man only plays when in the full meaning of the word he is a man, and he is only completely a man when he plays.'

The Beginning of a Business Career

Trevor West was the first member of the Trinity establishment I met when I arrived in 1969. Our meeting led to a lifelong friendship and was a life-changing experience for me.

Trevor was an extraordinary genius – a brilliant academic yet at the same time a practical and shrewd administrator who had a wonderful way with people. His energy and enthusiasm for all aspects of Trinity life was supercharged. On campus he was everywhere: teaching, organizing, playing and watching all forms of sport. He was also an active member of Seanad Éireann and a shrewd College politician, as some of his adversaries in provost electoral campaigns were to discover to their cost.

Early on in my college life Trevor persuaded me to become involved in Trinity Week and DUCAC. This started with the Trinity Ball, which in the late sixties was far too expensive and way beyond the means of most students. It was also a loss-making event. Together we decided that the whole occasion had to be completely revamped, made affordable to the average student and returned to profitability. We slashed the price of the tickets to a quarter of their previous level and the ball quickly became a sell-out and a significant contributor to DUCAC and to the cost of the Trinity Week celebrations. This formula was sustainable and repeated each year. For Trevor nothing was impossible and he never gave up no matter what the problem or opposition.

He and I spent many hours together protecting existing sports facilities such as the rugby pitch and negotiating with College administrators regarding the provision of facilities appropriate to a university of Trinity's standing. Our meetings with Colonel Walsh, the agent in Trinity, were fascinating, as John Walsh was a great administrator and negotiator. To be sitting in the middle of Trevor and John trying to outwit each other was far more educational than attending lectures in the Business Studies department. Because Trevor was very trusting and gave me tremendous freedom to get on with things, he provided me with my first business career within the walls of Trinity.

Once the Trinity Ball had been successfully restructured, Trevor pushed me to become active in DUCAC. He recognized that the financing

The Campanile
in TCD's Front Square.

of College sport was precarious and subject to threat from undergraduates such as Michael Colgan and members of the various arts societies. Trevor was adamant that DUCAC had to develop new sources of funding if sport in Trinity was to thrive. We decided with the help and encouragement of Aidan Duggan, a prominent College administrator, to turn the upstairs of the pavilion in College Park into a bar. We were convinced that students would support a well-run, properly priced facilty. So we did, and the Pavilion Bar with Peadar Byrne at the helm became an overnight success, providing significant new funding for College sport from the outset. Many in the College establishment opposed the project but Trevor was not prepared to take no for an answer and his determination and political skills carried the day.

When it came to Seanad elections Trevor had no peers. He was incredible in his approach and energy. Again, I learned a lot from acting as his agent in one of his successful Seanad campaigns. He took enormous personal risks in his role as a senator and his contacts with all sides in the Northern Irish conflict proved very important, a fact which has only been recognized in more recent times.

Trevor West was a wonderful friend to my family. He became close to my parents with whom he spent endless Saturday afternoons in College

Park and Santry watching my sister Jane playing hockey for Trinity. When Jane was capped for Ireland, Trevor was even more excited about it than anyone in our family. I am sure that without his constant encouragement and support, Jane would have found it much harder to become the player she did.

He had a wonderful, sometimes mischievous, sense of humour and wherever he was there was fun and energy. He truly loved all aspects of Trinity and its people. His range of interests both inside and outside the university was extraordinary and his lifelong contribution to Trinity was immense.

Later on he developed the most important relationship of his life, with Maura Lee. It was fascinating to watch the transformation of Trevor as the nylon mustard-coloured shirts were gradually replaced by a new, dapper wardrobe! Together Maura Lee and Trevor travelled the world and their closeness was there for all his friends to see.

It is hard to imagine how one man could contribute to an institution such as Trinity and touch as many people's lives as Trevor did. A great, great friend who is so much missed.

77

College Park and the Pavilion as they are today.

Officers of TCD's Mathematical Society 1957–58: *Back row*: A.J. Solomons, T.T. West, R.E. Harte, A.L.R. Beck. *Front row*: T.D. Spearman, T.S. Broderick, J.A. Lutton.

The Mathematician

We can start our story of Trevor as mathematician from his admission to Trinity College Dublin as an undergraduate in 1956, although we should first mention that he finished his schooling at The High School in Dublin, where Victor Graham was surely an influence on him. Victor was in the somewhat unusual position of holding two posts, one as mathematics teacher at The High School and the other as a lecturer in Trinity. While Victor always kept a fatherly eye on the progress of his High School pupils, he had more opportunity to do that on students who entered Trinity to study engineering, where Victor lectured the majority of the mathematicians while Trevor was a mathematics student.

One imagines that Trevor met his classmate Robin Harte as soon as they entered Trinity, and the pair of them maintained a lifelong amicable rivalry of sorts thereafter. When both went to Cambridge together as Ph.D. students they had different supervisors but their topics were so close that they could well have written joint papers, although that never did happen. Trevor was good at engaging with colleagues from far and near to work on problems that did lead to joint papers, but presumably the rivalry between him and Robin was one factor that prevented that happening.

Robin has written in a memorial issue of the *Mathematical Proceedings of the Royal Irish Academy* (2013 no. 2,) of their interactions. He recounts that he outsmarted Trevor by getting a Foundation Scholarship in his Junior Freshman year, whereas Trevor got his in the more standard Senior Freshman year. It seems though that Trevor became the ringleader of the Robin & Trevor gang by the time they both went to Cambridge, with Robin claiming that he obeyed strict instructions from Trevor not to reveal the extent of their mathematical ignorance in Cambridge. Moreover, Trevor outclassed Robin in the Senior Freshman examinations, due partly to the fact that Robin was slacking while Trevor put in the efforts for his scholarship. I think it is true to say that Trevor was competitive, though perhaps always in a good-natured way as befits a sportsman. He seems to have been influenced by other successful Trinity students who were near-contemporaries, such as John Miller and David Spearman, as

TCD mathematics lecturer and High School teacher Victor Graham with Trevor West.

well as Robin. I recall him comparing himself to them in typical Trevor-speak, so that one was never quite sure where the borderline was between truth and the colourful details added to make the message more entertaining.

In the period when Trevor was a student at Trinity, the College was not in a very healthy state. David Simms (who was a TCD graduate from 1954 and on the staff in Mathematics at TCD since 1964) recalled at the Scholars' Dinner 2012 (on the sixtieth anniversary of his scholarship) some of the near-Dickensian conditions that prevailed while he was a student – and there were not many improvements before Trevor entered in 1956. While the applied mathematician A.J. McConnell became Provost in 1952 in a sort of revolution by the Junior Fellows, and perhaps set the College on an improving path, this would not necessarily have been a great benefit for mathematics students. They lost one of their professors – at least partly because McConnell retained his chair as well as the provostship until 1957. That chair (the applied one) is listed as vacant from 1957–62, covering most of Trevor's time as an undergraduate. T.S. Broderick, who held the (pure) Erasmus Smith's Chair of Mathematics from 1944 to 1962, had published some papers prior to becoming professor, most recently a note with Erwin Schrödinger in the *Proceedings of the Royal Irish Academy* (Section A, 1940), but that was his last publication.

David Simms recalls that amongst the lecturers in pure mathematics the only one who had any real contact with current research was Arthur Allen. Allen obtained his Ph.D. from Princeton in 1952 and had made a preliminary report on his work (presumably his thesis work) on harmonic analysis to a meeting of the American Mathematical Society held in Columbia University in April 1952. However, Allen never published any paper in a journal. Born in 1928, Allen, who died in 2010, had been an undergraduate at Cambridge before Princeton and David Simms credits him with arranging for Simms to study at Cambridge, rather than Princeton. This was the place where some Trinity students had gone earlier as research students (such as Brian Murdoch, 1955 Ph.D. Princeton on probability supervised by Feller, Erasmus Smith's professor of mathematics at TCD from 1966 to 1989). Simms says that Allen arranged that he would study with W.V.D. Hodge, a major figure who was then still supervising Michael Atiyah, later to become a mathematical superstar. Robin Harte also credits Allen with organizing for Trevor and himself to go to Cambridge, both working in related areas but under different supervisors, Frank Smithies and John Williamson.

Smithies is not as well known as David Simms's supervisor Hodge (who has his name attached to Hodge theory), but Smithies supervised many doctoral students and he surely was a good supervisor to have. Smithies had built up a large group in the UK working on functional analysis, or at the very least was instrumental in building the group. Perhaps Frank Bonsall (who held the mathematics chair at Newcastle 1959–63 and later at Edinburgh) also deserves a considerable share of the credit for the health of functional analysis in the UK at that time; indeed, some of Trevor's research later on was motivated by questions posed by Bonsall. Smithies was also fortunate in that some of his students became very prominent and built up considerable reputations. While Trevor also gained a considerable reputation, he retained close links throughout his career with his leading contemporaries and their collaborators and students. In this way he was close to the cutting edge of the topics that interested him and that in turn allowed him to publish on questions that were of widespread interest.

A few years before Trevor, a Nigerian-born student at Trinity called P.A. Olagunju had gone to Cambridge to study with Smithies (also influenced to do so by Arthur Allen). While Olagunju prospered as a research student and had submitted a nice paper for publication, he was killed in a motor accident in Nigeria in 1960, before he could complete the final stages of his paper. It seems then that Smithies asked Trevor to look at the points raised in the referee's report on Olagunju's paper. Not only did Trevor do that, he also extended some of the work and published a joint paper with the late Olagunju.

Trevor's own doctoral thesis contained the result that become known as the 'West Decomposition' and continues to make him famous. The thesis was certainly influenced by the work of Olagunju in that Trevor cites him in several places, but the work was also well placed at the time because of the strong group working in functional analysis – not only UK-based people but also groups in the US in particular. While there is an eternal truth to mathematics, there are also fashions or themes so that questions studied intensively in one century or decade may be of minority interest in the next period. Functional analysis was doing very well when Trevor was a student, undergoing a period of rapid and strong development, and Trevor's work was close to the mainstream. This is possibly a significant part of the job of a doctoral supervisor; to suggest a topic on which progress is possible but that can also lead on to further interesting questions.

Even before his thesis was fully completed Trevor was appointed to a position in Glasgow in 1963. After two years there he got the opportunity to spend a year at the University of California Los Angeles. While the initial idea was to work with Angus Taylor, this did not happen because Taylor was appointed to higher office in the University of California and moved to Berkeley. However, despite this, Trevor really flourished at UCLA. During that year he considerably extended his network of mathematical contacts, adding to his already impressive network in the UK.

While in Glasgow he had started to collaborate with Alastair Gillespie, a student of Bonsall who spent most of his career at the University of Edinburgh. Gillespie and West continued to publish together off and on for over a decade. In UCLA he met a Dutch mathematician, Rien Kaashoek, and they worked intensively together for some years, leading to a research monograph in 1974, the first of Trevor's books.

Paul Halmos (1916–2006) was an international figure in operator theory, at close to the height of his powers in the mid 1960s. Trevor had met Halmos in Scotland, but Halmos invited Trevor to Indiana from California to give a talk and that cemented a relationship between Trevor and a number of significant figures in Indiana.

Appointed to a lectureship in Trinity in 1966, Trevor brought a huge amount of energy with him back to Ireland. He quickly set about building relationships with others such as Finbarr Holland in Cork, Maurice Kennedy and later Tom Laffey at UCD and David Simms at TCD, and managed to kick-start several important initiatives designed to inspire mathematical research in Ireland. A proposal to set up a completely new mathematical organization or society was diverted by Father J.R. McConnell (an influential mathematical physicist) and taken under the auspices of the Royal Irish Academy. The RIA set up a 'symposium sub-committee' of the National Committee for Mathematics, in such a way that Trevor was in effective control as secretary of the sub-committee. This was probably the beginning of Trevor's involvement with the RIA, of which he was elected a member in 1972. He maintained an active involvement with the RIA even after the sub-committee ceased its work, in particular with the academy's publication in mathematics, which under Trevor's influence was eventually reformed into a journal framework and renamed the *Mathematical Proceedings of the RIA*. The formation of the

Irish Mathematical Society in 1976 was another outcome of Trevor's influence, more or less a revival of his plans in the late 1960s.

Although the first symposium organized by the RIA sub-committee
in summer 1969 was on group representations and quantum mechanics
(not really Trevor's interest), it did nevertheless have lecturers who were
closely associated with him among those with a more obvious connection
to quantum theory. Later there were symposia directly related to Trevor
in 1974 and 1975. Looking at the lists of speakers, and the related papers
that appeared in the RIA journal, it is clear that Trevor's networks of
mathematical collaborators and acquaintances were well represented. The
events leading to the symposium sub-committee are described in rather
more detail by Finbarr Holland in that memorial volume of the *RIA
Mathematical Proceedings* mentioned earlier, and Trevor himself wrote
an account of the start of the Irish Mathematical Society in the *Bulletin
of the Society* (no. 51, 2003, available online).

While these organizational initiatives were progressing, Trevor was
active on many other fronts, including his research and lecturing commitments. His lecturing style was unique I would say, perhaps influenced
to some extent by the Victor Graham approach, but also featuring a type
of interaction that might be more common between a sports coach and
his team. I think it worked well for Trevor and enabled him to build up a
very good rapport with his students, some of whom also interacted with
him in other aspects of his college life, such as through sports clubs or in
his time as Junior Dean by taking a short cut across the cricket pitch or
by organizing an impromptu soccer match without authorization. Trevor
lectured many students over the years and I'm sure most recall him
fondly, despite his no-nonsense class discipline coupled with an informal
interactive style.

Some of his students were deserving of particular interest ever after.
One of those was Gerard Murphy (1948–2006), who had a close relationship with Trevor although he was not a Ph.D. student of his. Gerard came
from a working-class background in Dublin and missed out on a normal
secondary education, but came to the notice of the School of Mathematics
in Trinity. Trevor took a special interest in Gerard, and was delighted that
he turned out to be an outstanding mathematics undergraduate. Gerard
did his doctorate at Cambridge – not with Trevor's supervisor Smithies
but with one of Smithies' mathematical descendants – finishing in 1977.
Then he got a postdoctoral fellowship back at Trinity, where he worked
closely with Trevor. Following three years at TCD Gerard held some po-

sitions in North America before being appointed in Cork, where he was again within close reach of Trevor from the West family home in Midleton. Trevor encouraged Gerard to organize international research meetings in Cork, of which there were quite a few, and Trevor was always in the thick of them.

Among the many joint Murphy and West papers, Finbarr Holland picks out a spectral radius formula for special mention in an obituary of Gerard that appeared in the *Bulletin of the Irish Mathematical Society* (no. 59, 2007). It is a particularly elegant formula for the spectral radius of an element in a C*-algebra that was published in a paper in the *Proceedings of the Edinburgh Mathematical Society* in 1979.

One should also mention that Gerard was elected to membership of the RIA and became editor of the *Mathematical Proceedings*, surely aided by Trevor in both cases. As with many things, Trevor would not miss opportunities to plug his favourites and the considerable merits of Gerard were easy to extol, but of course Gerard's terminal illness was a blow. Maybe the most notable joint effort between them was Trevor's second mathematical monograph, often referred to as 'the little red book', which was in fact a joint effort between four authors: Bruce Barnes of Oregon, Gerard Murphy, Roger Smyth (a former doctoral student) and Trevor. The book appeared in 1982 and has a lasting and noteworthy value. It is not so much that the overall thrust of the book is still current, but rather that it contains definitions and lemmas that remain useful and are not available elsewhere.

Roger Smyth was the first of Trevor's two Ph.D. students and Trevor always spoke enthusiastically about their work together, which spanned many years. Roger was employed as a civil servant in the Northern Ireland Department of Health and Social Services, and so did his mathematics outside of his working hours. Apart from the fact that Trevor got on very well with Roger, it suited Trevor to have Roger among his Northern Ireland friends and informants on political matters. In a different way, Alastair Gillespie was well placed in Edinburgh where there were rugby matches to attend every now and again, while the Cork connection with Gerard was a different kind of overlap of interests. By the way, the collaboration with Rien Kaashoek did not seem to have any similar coincidence but they did travel often between Dublin and Amsterdam. Rainer Nagel of Tübingen was also a close contact of Trevor's but not a co-author.

MATHEMATICAL PROCEEDINGS

of the

ROYAL IRISH ACADEMY

DECEMBER 2013 · VOLUME 113A · NUMBER 2

Edited by Martin Mathieu

RIA

Cover of the programme for the *Mathematical Proceedings of the Royal Irish Academy*, 2013.

With regard to the red book (actually entitled *Riesz and Fredholm Theory in Banach Algebras* and published by Pitman in 1982), Roger Smyth credits Trevor with being the mastermind and driving force behind the book. For instance, Trevor would have been the host for Bruce Barnes during his sabbatical year in Trinity (1979–80) and Roger also recalls Trevor deciding rather late on that a significant section of the book was not written in the 'right way' and coming up with a new and clearer approach during the final stages of preparation. It seems Trevor also did the management work such as dealing with the publisher and managing the production of the camera-ready copy (in those days using a typist with a golf-ball typewriter). Roger's influence on the book is quite clearly related to his doctoral and subsequent work with Trevor. Bruce Barnes' research at the time was also close to the topics discussed and perhaps Gerard was more interested in the parts where C^*-algebras enter. It is appropriate to quote the last paragraph from the *Mathematical Review* write-up of the book:

> The aim of the authors is to highlight the interplay between algebra and spectral theory which emerges in any penetrating analysis of compact, Riesz and Fredholm operators on Banach spaces'. Their little book proves, among other things, that they have fully (and beautifully) achieved this aim.

> Possibly an important contribution from Gerard Murphy to the book, or maybe something he picked up while engaged in it, was a facility for explaining things particularly well. Later, in 1990, Gerard published a book called *C*-algebras and operator theory* (Academic Press), which has remained a standard reference. It covers the basics of the theory but also dips into the more advanced and modern aspects in such a way that many new students of C^*-algebras continue to find it a valuable introduction, preferable for the beginner to many fatter and more encyclopedic volumes.

One of the themes of Trevor's work in more recent years was the Perron Frobenius theorem (asserting that for a square matrix with nonnegative entries, the largest absolute value of any eigenvalue is actually a positive eigenvalue) and he had many discussions with Roger Smyth on this theme. They published a joint paper on it in 1998, Roger published on it in 2002 and Trevor's last mathematical publication in 2003 was related to that and also to the work of Bonsall some decades before. So it seems that Trevor had that topic on his mind for a long time, along with his other research. I have discussed Trevor's mathematical works in more technical terms in an obituary published by the *Bulletin of the London Mathematical Society* in 2013 (vol. 45, no. 6).)

To try to convey the topics of Trevor's mathematical works in greater detail, let us start with what functional analysis is about. In undergraduate courses, many students learn linear algebra after calculus. Linear algebra includes matrices and these have been found to be useful in many ways. But linear algebra is also so very satisfactory because most things are rather well understood – not only is it known that many calculations can be carried out, in many cases there are super-efficient ways of doing the calculations and these ways are used often for many practical purposes. More or less, we can say that linear algebra is about solving linear equations, that is systems of linear algebraic equations. The theoretical basis for the subject, including matrices, vector spaces and linear transformations, is what allows the complicated problems to be understood and solved. There are at least two sources of problems that seem as if they could be understood in a way that would be just a souped-up version of the linear algebra theory. Differential equations are a bit more complicated than algebraic ones and for linear differential equations (which cover quite a range of problems), mathematicians hope to solve almost all problems. Quantum theory, as developed in physics some decades before Trevor started his mathematical career, was another incentive to understand operators that can be thought of as infinite matrices.

At the time Trevor went to Cambridge, and more or less to the present day, these and other motivations caused us to look at operators on infinite dimensional spaces with a view to understanding both the spaces and the operators as far as one can along the lines that work so well for finite dimensional vector spaces and matrices. For instance in differential equations the unknowns are functions, which then have infinitely many values rather than the finitely many variables that are to be found when solving systems of linear equations in linear algebra. Because of this the unknown function in a differential equation should be sought among all possible functions, and these functions will form an infinite dimensional space. Actually, we need to be able to differentiate a function for it to be able to be a solution of a differential equation and the domain of the function will be dictated by the situation we are considering. Because of this we end up considering not just one space of functions, but many different ones. These are the substitutes for the finite dimensional vector spaces of linear algebra and one aspect of functional analysis is to get an understanding of the spaces that arise.

In linear algebra, the next step after considering the space where we seek the solutions (the space) is to consider the problem as an operator on the space of unknowns. In finite dimensions, these are the linear transformations and we typically represent them by matrices. In the infinite dimensional world of functional analysis, we typically need to assume that our operator is well-behaved, or in more technical terms a continuous operator or a bounded operator. At least some of the time we can represent such an operator as an infinite matrix.

One of the more satisfying parts of the theory of finite matrices deals with eigenvectors and eigenvalues. If A is a matrix, an eigenvector is a nonzero vector v such that Av is a multiple v of v, and the multiple is called the eigenvalue. At least when we deal with complex numbers, all finite (square) matrices have eigenvalues and eigenvectors and one understands lots about how a matrix A works by looking at the eigenvectors and eigenvalues. Because of this, one of the first things to do with an infinite dimensional operator T is to find eigenvalues. But there may not be any! So we need to think about what we need about T to have any eigenvalues (and preferably plenty of them). There had already been some good progress on this before Trevor started his Ph.D. in Cambridge. In particular when T is an operator on a Banach space, it was known that if T is assumed to be a compact operator, then the situation was very satisfactory, a theory developed in particular by Riesz.

In 1954 Ruston had considered a wider class of operators that he called Riesz operators, where the same statements about eigenvalues and eigenvectors (and also generalized eigenvectors) hold for T, even though T need not be compact. The West decomposition is a result about Riesz operators and is an important step in understanding the class and the limits of this avenue of the study of operators. A Riesz operator has eigenvalues forming a sequence that converges to the origin in the complex plane and $=0$ may or may not be an actual eigen value. The whole space can be made up from (generalized) eigenvectors for the nonzero eigenvalues plus vectors that are related to $=0$. Amongst the Ricsz operators there are those with no nonzero eigenvalues called quasinilpotent. They can be a bit tricky to deal with, but still they are rather obvious examples of Riesz operators. A question that arose was whether every Riesz operator T had to be of the form $T = Q + C$ with Q quasinilpotent and C compact and Q commuting with C (that is with $QC = CQ$). Trevor proved that it was possible for Riesz operators T acting on a Hilbert space to write $T = Q + C$

with Q quasinilpotent and C compact. That was the famous West decomposition. He did not have Q commuting with C in his result and part of the breakthrough was to consider omitting this condition. Not long afterwards, Trevor collaborated with Alastair Gillespie (in 1968) to produce examples of Riesz operators, which could *not* be decomposed as $T = Q + C$ with Q and C also commuting.

The question of whether the West decomposition must hold for Riesz operators on Banach spaces (rather than the important but more restrictive case of Hilbert spaces) remains open. Trevor did deal fully with the case where T has only finitely many non-zero eigenvalues in his paper and there were various papers over the years on this question. Perhaps the most complete results were by Davidson & Herrero in 1986, who established a West decomposition result for certain kinds of Banach spaces.

This work belongs to the theory of single operators, where we start with a single operator T and try to understand it. However, another strong theme in modern functional analysis involves considering not just one operator T but several at a time. For example, the powers of T form what is called a semigroup (where you can multiply but probably not divide) and Trevor's extensive collaboration with Kaashoek relates to this. If you also allow sums, scalar multiples and products of operators, you are dealing with an algebra of operators and this is the basis for much of Trevor's later work. For instance 'the red book' with Barnes, Murphy and Smyth fits into this theme.

Within the class of algebras, there are those called C*-algebras, which have been the focus of much study. They are algebras of operators on a Hilbert space that allow adjoints T^* to be still in the algebra. (For matrices, the star operation is the complex conjugate of the transpose.) C*-algebras attracted a lot of attention because of their strong connections to quantum theory and Trevor delved into aspects of C*-theory that were close enough to his other works that he could make a significant contribution. In particular, Gerard Murphy spent most of his career on problems related to C*-algebra theory and several of their joint papers reflect this aspect of Trevor's work. For instance we have already noted the elegant work they did on a spectral radius formula of an element in a C*-algebra in 1979.

As mentioned, Trevor more or less delegated organizing mathematical research meetings to Gerard Murphy in Cork, but an exception was the first joint meeting of the London and Irish Mathematical Societies held in Dublin in 1986. Trevor arranged four top-notch speakers from France, the UK and the US and his social skills were to the fore during and outside the lecture sessions.

Following Trevor's retirement from lecturing, our Trinity mathematics colleague Donal O'Donovan organized the 'WestFest' in TCD in December 2005, a short conference where many of Trevor's collaborators were able to attend and speak, together with eminent speakers who were not collaborators (such as Rob Archbold of Aberdeen, Seán Dineen of UCD, Tony Carbery of Edinburgh, John Erdos of London, Tony O'Farrell of Maynooth, Rainer Nagel of Tübingen, Philip Spain and Simon Wassermann of Glasgow, Tony Wickstead of Belfast, Geoff Wood of Swansea, Jaroslav Zemánek of Warsaw) and past students such as David Malone and Ollie Mason. Alastair Gillespie, Rien Kaashoek, Tom Laffey, Roger Smyth and I were also speakers, as was Harry Dowson of Glasgow. Harry was a research student at the same time as Trevor and one of those people with whom he maintained close connections. Unfortunately, Harry, who had taken early retirement from Glasgow in 1990, died suddenly in 2008.

Another attendee and speaker at the meeting was Lothrop Mittenthal, unknown to many of us, but a research student of sorts of Trevor's and Rien Kaashoek's during their UCLA year. Mittenthal was officially a student of the absent Angus Taylor but Trevor and Rien took on the job of supervising him on a regular basis. In fact Mittenthal was older than either of them, being an officer in the US army, and he was known to Trevor's older friends as the 'Colonel'. Trevor's second official doctoral student, Ed Bach, was also present, and we've already mentioned Roger Smyth. (Bach completed his Ph.D. in 1988, Smyth in 1972.) A photograph (taken by John Erdos) of Trevor speaking at the meeting was used in the obituary I wrote for the Bulletin of the *LMS*.

The last event to mention was a meeting held in December 2013 at the Royal Irish Academy and co-sponsored by the School of Mathematics at Trinity on the occasion of the launch of the memorial volume of the *Mathematical Proceedings* mentioned earlier. The editor who succeeded Gerard Murphy is Martin Mathieu of Belfast, once a student of Rainer Nagel's in Tübingen. This time there were three speakers: Rainer Nagel, Rien Kaashoek and Wilhelm Winter of Münster. Winter did not have direct contact with Trevor but he is a current leading light in C*-algebras and fills the role of the leading speakers Trevor organized at the symposia he managed in the 1970s or at the joint meeting with the London Mathematical Society in 1986.

Quite a few of those who had been at the 'WestFest' attended, including Alastair Gillespie from Edinburgh and Lothrop Mittenthal from California. Robin Harte was there also, of course, as was Micheal O Searcoid of UCD, who got his Ph.D. in Cork with Harte and who was always regarded by Trevor as a player on the same team. Indeed O Searcoid co-authored a paper with Trevor in 1989. Many younger mathematicians attended the meeting as well as some more senior ones who had known Trevor for most of his career, including Finbarr Holland, Seán Dineen and Stephen Gardiner of UCD, as well as colleagues from TCD – a strong turnout from the island of Ireland. There were also some of a number of Trevor's friends from outside mathematics, for example from DUCAC. A mathematical meeting with a social dimension – a fitting posthumous tribute!

Charleston Visitors' Book, 1987.

Participants at the Westfest in 2005 included John Erdos, Sean Dineen, Simon Wasserman, Trevor West, Mícheál Ó Searcóid, Maurice O'Reilly, David Malone, Philip Spain, Dan Moynihan, Geoff Wood, Alastair Gillespie, Donal O'Donovan, Robin Harte, Derek Kitson, Rainer Nagel, Jaroslav Zemánek, Lothrop Mittenthal, Richard Timoney, David Simms, Finbarr Holland, Thomas Laffey, Anthony O'Farrell and Roger Smyth.

Robin E. Harte speaks at the Westfest dinner at the Arts Club in Dublin, 2005.

The Mathematical Community

I spent much of my early and teenage years on my aunt's farm in Trabolgan, Co. Cork. Long before making Trevor's acquaintance I knew about the West family of Midleton, and was particularly knowledgeable about the part his mother played in managing the mill at Ballinacurra, and how much she was admired for her business acumen by the farming community in East Cork.

Trevor's mother Dorothy West, testing barley in east Cork, 1953.

However, I believe I first encountered Trevor himself at the 1961 Christmast two-day mathematical symposium organized by J.L. Synge at the Dublin Institute for Advanced Studies (DIAS), then based on Merrion Square. On that occasion, accompanied by Robin Harte, he would have been on his way home for the Christmas holidays from Cambridge University, where both he and Robin were doing their Ph.Ds. As a fellow participant at the symposium, I had come up from Cork where I was studying for my master's degree at UCC. Along with others who attended the symposium, we would have availed of the generous travel and accommodation expenses offered by the DIAS, which were very welcome, especially to impecunious students! (In those days, in order to boost attendance at the symposium, travel and accommodation expenses for one night were paid to attendees who were not in receipt of travel grants from their home institutions; and speakers also received an honorarium.)

On the second occasion he surprised me when he arrived unexpectedly at my office in UCC shortly after his return in 1966 from UCLA. I had taken up a position in UCC the previous year, having returned from the California Institute of Technology where I had held a one-year research fellowship. Though coming from different sporting and cultural backgrounds we quickly established common ground, and, from that moment on, our friendship grew and solidified over the following decades, during which we collaborated on several ventures to improve the standing of mathematics in Ireland, though we never did any joint research work.

What follows is an attempt to summarize the work Trevor did for the Irish mathematical community. To put things in perspective, it pays to recall how the world changed at the end of the 1950s when the first Sputnik encircled the globe, and the space race began: it made a huge impact

93

on curious scientifically minded teenagers, and led many of them to surge into our universities to fulfill their wildest dreams. Trevor and I were among them, both of us wanting to become mathematicians, whatever that meant.

Seemingly unrelated to the space race but yet largely driven by it, university science programmes were being revamped, and research efforts were beginning to be funded by national agencies, which in turn made it possible for professors to support many more students who were given a licence to engage in fundamental as well as applied research. For instance, fellowship opportunities abounded, especially in American universities, which were keen to recruit bright students from all over the world, and offered them attractive study packages in many scientific areas to whet their appetite.

Inevitably, these changes impacted on mathematics as well, and brought about major changes in curricula at every level, leading, for instance, to the 'New Math for Secondary Schools' under the banner 'Down with Euclid'. This was promulgated by many eminent European mathematicians who were concerned by the lack of preparedness of students taking their courses. At a result, in programmes for university degrees in mathematics, more emphasis was placed on understanding concepts rather than developing mathematical techniques and computational ability, and more attention was devoted to an axiomatic development of every aspect of the subject, which served to emphasize the distinction between pure and applied mathematics. In this way, new branches of the subject, or abstract versions of old ones, were opened up, analysed, developed and applied within and without the parent branch. In particular, it became fashionable to study the properties of families of similar functions rather then the behaviour of any single one, resulting, for example, in the emergence of a new branch of mathematics called functional analysis. All told, it was a very fertile period for open-minded young Ph.D. students pursuing the subject, many of whom were likely to know more about their chosen topic than their supervisor, especially if he or she was more than forty years old.

It was into this milieu that Trevor ventured when he went to Cambridge University to study for his Ph.D. in pure mathematics, supported by an 1851 Exhibition Scholarship. There his interest in operator theory took hold and never waned. He wrote his 1964 Ph.D. thesis, entitled *Riesz operators in Banach spaces*, under the nominal supervision of Professor Frank Smithies. Thereafter he made other important contributions in this field, and throughout his career he inspired others to do likewise. He published about twenty-eight mathematical articles in prestigious peer-reviewed journals, many of which were joint publications with one of the following: Tim Murphy, Gerard Murphy, Roger Smyth, Tom Laffey, Mícheál Ó Searcóid, Rien Kaashoek, Alastair Gillespie and Martha Bertman. In addition, he co-authored two highly acclaimed monographs, one in 1974 with Rien Kaashoek, entitled *Locally Compact Semi-Algebras*, which collected and reworked some of the results obtained by themselves and others up to that time, and the second in 1982, with Bruce Barnes, Gerard Murphy and Roger Smyth, entitled *Riesz and Fredholm theory in Banach spaces*, which dealt with areas in which, at the time, the authors were world-acknowledged experts.

Trevor's colleagues in TCD will be better able to comment about his teaching ability, and his successes as a teacher; it's not something that we ever discussed in any detail, but I never heard him decry it as an unwanted burden or complain about his individual teaching load. It was simply a duty and a responsibility that he accepted with his accustomed equanimity and professionalism. My suspicion is that he quite liked teaching, and interacted very positively with students of every ability, tailoring his courses to suit their needs and abilities. I could see him especially engaging with large classes of engineering students, say, and challenging them in a provocative manner to excel at their examinations to prove him wrong!

Recently, Robin Harte shared a remark he received from a former economics student of Trevor's, which shows Trevor's playful side to teaching classes of undergraduates. Apparently, on one occasion when he was teaching elementary trigonometry to students of economics – although quite why he was doing so is beyond my ken – he felt it necessary to advise them not to cancel the 'x' on the right side of the formula; and went on to say that, if they were budding engineers he would also have to advise them not to cancel the 's'! So, on the one hand, he was implying that they might be dumb, but, on the other, that they were not quite as dumb as he thought the engineers were, which would amuse the economists. Of course, one could imagine him saying the same thing to a class of engineers, thereby deriding the economists. It would appeal to his sense of humour to play one group off against the other.

Trevor supervised two students at Ph.D. level, Roger Smyth and Ed Bach. But the fact that he had only two research students in his lifetime isn't a unique experience for an Irish mathematician, and shouldn't come

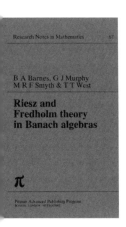

'The red book'– and 'the blue book'

as a surprise: funding opportunities in Ireland for such activity was always very limited, and students wishing to pursue Ph.D. degrees often tended to go abroad.

The DIAS symposia held twice a year were the meeting places for Irish mathematicians of every stripe, which meant that talks often only appealed to a very small proportion of the audience, and the talks given at one were selected by vote at a previous meeting. In addition, as the 1960s drew to a close, the Irish mathematical community was expanding to cater for the ever-increasing numbers of students going to university here. But these symposia also served a very useful social function, and, in particular, gave people attending them from different universities an opportunity to discuss common problems. The younger mathematicians especially were able to air their views in convivial surroundings on issues affecting the growth and development of their subject, and the need to form some kind of association to foster their aims and aspirations took root.

Trevor and I undertook to survey the mathematical community with a view to seeing what could be done to progress these hopes. One idea to emerge from our analysis of the results was to hold summer schools in different areas of the subject at regular intervals of time. Also, when we presented our findings at a public meeting to examine what the structure of such an association might be, we were persuaded, mainly by Professor Rev J. McConnell, of the Royal Irish Academy (RIA), to form it not as a new entity, but rather as an offshoot of the RIA National Committee for Mathematics, something that he would support. True to his word, he persuaded the Council of the RIA to go along with his proposal to establish such a sub-committee, one of whose aims would be to organize mathematical summer schools, a new concept at the time. This led to the establishment in 1968 of the RIA Symposium sub-committee under Professor McConnell's chairmanship; Trevor was appointed its secretary.

Under his very capable direction the first such school was held in the summer of 1969 in TCD on group representations and quantum mechanics. It was a marvellous success, educationally and financially, and people from far and wide flocked to it. It was followed in quick succession by another school held two years later in UCC on complex function theory, and another in 1972 in UCD on numerical analysis. UCG hosted a summer school on group theory and computation in 1973, and, during the following year, TCD ran a symposium on spectral theory, while the DIAS, in partnership with the London Mathematical Society, organized a conference on probability in physics, and UCD held a second conference on numerical analysis. Two subsequent conferences were run in UCD in 1976, one on numerical analysis and another on group theory. The sub-committee was also responsible for coordinating visits of prominent mathematicians to Ireland from Europe and America. Within a short space of time the committee had more than fulfilled its objectives and justified the trust placed in it when it was set up; and much of its success was due primarily to the indefatigable efforts of Trevor. However, though certainly it had achieved its initial purpose, a cause of some disappointment to its members was its failure to hold similar meetings in QUB or Coleraine University because of the political climate then prevailing in Northern Ireland.

During the 1970s staffing levels in mathematics departments in all Irish universities expanded. It became manifest that the time was fast approaching for the need for a larger body of Irish mathematicians, independent of and not subservient to any organization, to cater for the needs of the mathematical community at home and abroad, whose officers would be democratically elected. I set forth my views on this in a discussion document, which was circulated at the end of 1975. At about the same time Trevor independently prepared another document, which set out cogent reasons why it made sense to form a body fully representative of Irish mathematicians that would be able to formulate effective mathematical policy for the future development of mathematics in Ireland. These ideas were subsequently thrashed out at a meeting held in TCD during a DIAS symposium, and led to the establishment of the Irish Mathematical Society (IMS). Trevor and John T. Lewis were asked to prepare a draft constitution for the new society, which they presented at the first annual meeting, where it was unanimously adopted. Thus, with Trevor's assistance, the IMS was born. I was elected as its first president.

In the late 1960s when money was scarce and staffing levels were low, in an effort to inform and stimulate us, Trevor initiated a visiting lecturer scheme, which operated between UCC and TCD whereby if one college invited a foreign mathematician to visit, he or she would also be expected to visit the other's campus, and expenses would be shared between the colleges. This worked well for many years.

At Trevor's funeral, Tom Laffey recounted a few pertinent things about Trevor's early days in TCD. Apparently, he was instrumental, together with the active support of Maurice Kennedy, in starting a joint TCD-UCD seminar, which met regularly to study one or more modern topics: still active, the seminar is run weekly during term time. He and

Maurice Manning also played a part in regularizing to some extent the presence of the Hungarian mathematician Geza Freud, who in 1974 turned up in Dublin looking for asylum.

This is something in which I may unwittingly have played a part. I had met Freud earlier that year at a meeting at the Mathematical Institute in Oberwohlfach – incidentally, at the end of World War Two this institute was saved from destruction by the advancing Allied army because the leading battalion contained John Todd, a mathematician from Northern Ireland, who knew the significance of the building. (Together with his wife, Olga Taussky, who supervised Fergus Gaines for his Ph.D. at CalTech in the 1960s, Todd is published in the *Proceedings of the RIA*.)

Freud sidled up to me in the library at Oberwohlfach, explained that he was anxious to defect, and asked for my assistance. He wanted me to arrange an invitation for him to visit the UK or Ireland. I communicated his wishes to Lionel Cooper who was there at the same time, and thought no more about it. Although I can't be sure, my suspicion is that Cooper invited him to London, whence he made his way to Dublin. He had visited Dublin in 1972 to participate in the UCD summer school on numerical analysis, which was his specialty. According to Tom Laffey, Maurice Manning and Trevor arranged a visa for Freud, which enabled him to stay in Ireland as a visiting lecturer while he straightened out his affairs. I don't know for how long Freud stayed, but he did attend the second UCD conference on numerical analysis, and gave a paper there. He eventually made his way to the USA, where he settled.

Trevor was very proud of his membership of the Royal Irish Academy and conscious of its influence north and south of the border. He did everything in his power to further its aims and objectives. Shortly after being elected to the Academy, he set about increasing its membership of mathematicians and, year in, year out, he campaigned to enlarge their number. He took a personal interest in Section A of the *Proceedings of the Academy*, which he promoted assiduously, encouraging his colleagues to publish their research results in it. He was keen to extend its readership by changing its format whereby it was published in volume format, containing a small number of articles, rather than publishing the individual articles in pamphlet-like form. The format he proposed meant that librarians could display it more easily, unlike the pamphlets, which were impossible to stack on shelves. By urging the Academy to publish as a book the collection of papers presented at the spectral theory conference he organized in 1974, he showed what could be achieved by adopting his ideas. The Academy eventually came around to his way of thinking in 1980, and revamped the editorial process as well at that time. (Now, of course, the *Proceedings* are also published electronically, and the earlier issues don't necessarily arise.)

Trevor's generosity, which he demonstrated in many different ways towards his fellow mathematicians and others, is legendary, and will not easily be forgotten. For instance, a trawl through the visitors' book at Charleston, his home on the outskirts of Midleton, reveals the names of a large number of mathematicians from Ireland and beyond who spent periods there, many more than once, and some with their families. And countless more of us, in search of a bed for a night in Dublin, will have experienced the basic accommodation he provided in his ascetic bachelor rooms in the Rubrics of Trinity College!

Anthony O'Farrell, Ursula Nagel, Trevor West, Lisa O'Farrell and Rainer Nagel at the Westfest dinner, 2005.

Charleston Visitors' Book, 1988.

Cork County *vs* Cambridge at the Mardyke cricket grounds, Cork 1960.
Cambridge: D. Allen, T. Mc Rea, C. Reed, B. Dukes, T. Winkworth, G. Stratford, G. Cappock,
A. Winkworth, S. Mosey, A. Davies, D. Nichol and T. Cope.
Cork County: Ian Lewis, Tom Kiernan, Pat Dineen, Paddy Riordan, Jim Fitzgerald, Rodney Thompson,
Barclay Wilson, Trevor West, Raymond Murphy, Jim Kiernan, Des Cashell, Umpire Ian King.

Cork County *vs* Peterhouse, Cambridge, in 1961 in the same grounds a year later, 1961.
Cambridge: Chris Reed (Captain) Bruce Coleman, Trevor West, Geoff Coppinger, Colin Croott,
Charles Woodhouse, Tony Montriou, John Heatherington, John Cope, Michael Davies, D. Nichol,
Michael De Morgan, Martin Staniland.
Cork County: Ollie Barriscale, Paddy Riordan, Jim Kiernan, Pat Dineen, Dan Duggan, Tom Jackson,
Cyril O'Donnell, Des Cashell, Raymond Murphy, George Vardy (Captain) Tom Kiernan. Umpire: Bill Keegan.

Reflections on a Friendship

We first met at Cambridge, in April 1961, in the pavilion at Fenners. We were on the same side in the Freshmen's Trial and were sitting together waiting to bat. Neither of us won cricket blues but instead started a friendship that lasted all our lives.

I would have been struck by his Irish accent. With the open, friendly enthusiasm he never lost, I expect he told me about his cricket in Cork and at Trinity College Dublin, that he was doing a Ph.D. in maths and that he was at St John's. This was the same college as Mike Brearley, who was captaining our team in that game, but who, unlike us, went on to play for Cambridge and to captain England.

Hearing I was at Peterhouse, Trevor said that his family in Cork had put up some of the Peterhouse cricket side when they were in Ireland the previous year. This was the link that kept us in touch. Peterhouse were having another Irish cricket tour that summer and Trevor joined us. His family again hospitably put up a few lucky Petrean cricketers, of which I was one. This was at Charleston, the large Edwardian country house built by Trevor's step-grandfather in 1911, in Ballinacurra, County Cork, about which Trevor was to write, some forty-five years later, in one of the best of his many books, *Malting the Barley*. Trevor always had a deep sense of family. He said he wrote that book in 2006 to fulfil 'a most important familial obligation'.

It was a privilege, perhaps not fully appreciated at the time, for us young, callow English undergraduates to meet Trevor's parents, his aunts and his brother John. His mother Dorothy, an Oxford graduate, headed the family's historic malting business, and was very much the matriarch; his father Timothy was a long-time successful headmaster of nearby Midleton College (where the rest of our team were billeted) with a passion for cricket and rugby, and his younger brother John was later a distinguished international rugby referee. I can still remember hearty breakfasts in the large dining room at Charleston with Trevor, John and their father leading great chat on cricket, rugby, Ireland and much else besides.

Our friendship grew through cricket. Trevor, a postgraduate, was three years older than me, but this did not matter. We spent hours at Cambridge in the nets bowling to each other over the next three years. I can still picture facing Trevor's tidy, underrated and decent off spin. His encouragement about my cricket never stopped. In the summer long vac terms we merged our two college cricket sides, Peterhouse and St John's, organizing together many fixtures with visiting teams. This was my first glimpse of Trevor's gift and knack of bringing people together through sport, later evidenced by his astonishing near fifty-year leadership and championing of Dublin University sport.

I had never met anyone like Trevor. He welcomed me and my Peterhouse room-mate Michael Davies, a keen cricketer who had also been in that house party at Charleston, into his Cambridge social life. We got to know his postgraduate Irish housemates, R.E. (Robin) Harte and J.A. (Tony) Taylor (Trevor often used initials and surnames when referring to friends), and a well-connected, talented American couple, the Hufbauers. They made an eclectic, interesting household in Barton Road, Cambridge, with Trevor the life and soul and catalyst. It was a new world for Michael Davies and me. About forty years later Trevor was delighted when Michael was knighted on his retirement as Clerk of the Parliaments.

Our finest joint cricketing triumph was Peterhouse's famous one-wicket win over Dublin University at College Park on 21 June 1961. Peterhouse was a small college not noted for cricket. Trevor was proud of the then strong Trinity side of which he had been a member the year before. He was worried before the match that we might be hammered, so that epic Peterhouse win meant much to us both. Trevor never stopped reminding me about it for the rest of our lives. That it took place in College Park, a ground and a pavilion that Trevor later helped save, made it doubly special. Trevor took 4 for 40 that day, including the wicket of his brother John, Trinity's wicketkeeper. And John dropped me before I scored. Such is the charm and uncertainty of cricket.

It was apt that after Trevor's Thanksgiving Service at Trinity in December 2012 many of his friends returned to the same pavilion for a final pint to share memories of someone who had meant so much. At that service John had spoken movingly with affection and humour and Trevor's friend, Seamus Heaney, who was to die a year later, sent a poem. Another friend, Mary Robinson, former President of Ireland, was also there. Many years previously she and Trevor had worked together as Dublin University senators in Seanad Éireann, and she was now Chancellor.

I am lucky to be one of countless friends whose lives Trevor enriched. He became like family to all my family. He would just pitch up, often with little or no warning. He knew he was always welcome. The phone would ring and the conversation would go: 'It's Trevor here.' 'Where are you?' 'At the station.' We'd then collect him from Guildford or Woking Station (from the Heathrow bus) and he'd stay for however long he wanted to fit in with his busy itinerary. In this pre-Maura Lee era, Margaret, my wife, often would do his washing and remembers more than once taking him down to the shops to buy a jacket if it was cold as he usually travelled light with the same small bag and sometimes left even his duffel coat behind. He was best man at our wedding and godfather to our middle daughter Philippa in whom he took always a particularly close interest. His speeches at our and her weddings and other family occasions became part of family folklore. When Philippa got engaged he told her fiancé Will that he was delighted he was making an honest woman of his goddaughter.

Our son Tim can happily remember being shown by Trevor how to wind the clocks at Charleston and, aged eleven, going with Trevor to find Horace Plunkett's grave at St Mary's church, Byfleet. This was when Trevor was researching his outstanding biography *Horace Plunkett: Co-operation and Politics*. Recently among the books in my late mother's small house in Chester Row, Belgravia, I found a copy with Trevor's hand-written words 'To Peggy with love Trevor, St Patrick's Day 1988'. A favourite with all the family, Trevor would often stay there when he needed a bed in London.

He sent us over the years copies of all his books. His warm handwritten messages in all of them track our friendship. Thus in *The Bold Collegians* he wrote 'Charlie and Margaret, with love and affection for Thirty Years of Friendship, Trevor Nov 91'. I cherish and keep all these books together, and enjoy dipping into them. They reflect the astonishing breadth of Trevor's interests, life and ability. They tell us much about Trevor. *Malting the Barley* is an exceptional social and economic history of 200 years in southern Ireland (as well as a tribute to his mother and his step-grandfather, John H. Bennett). His *Midleton College, a Tercentenary History 1696–1996* is a tribute to his father and explains why Trevor himself served as chairman of the school governors for twenty-four years.

Trevor had an open, warm, infectious optimism. He was gregarious and inclusive, perceptive and of course, as befits a lifetime Trinity maths don, highly intelligent. For us English friends his Irishness and humour made it good just to be with him. He was without any side. He had quite simply the gift of friendship, which, with many others, I was lucky to enjoy for over fifty years. He allowed no pomposity or humbug and this helped me, especially at Cambridge as a young, diffident undergraduate, fresh from an English public school.

We were complete opposites. Trevor said I needed lightening up and he never stopped trying to do just that. And he could get away with it. He would never let me forget howlers. For example, having no cash on me for the collection at church in Midleton, when standing next to his father; or for a dropped catch, when he was standing in as umpire for a game at Guildford; or for my not taking off my cap during the national anthems at an England v Ireland match at Twickenham.

He had a habit of calling in (often unexpectedly) at my law firm in Lincoln's Inn Fields when he was in London. He was amused and fascinated by my firm, Farrer & Co, and its connections. I think he approved without actually saying so, while gently chiding me for advising what some perceived as the establishment or in his words 'the great and the gormless'. On one visit I was called up by reception and told that a Dr West, an Irish professor, was in the waiting room to see me. There I found Trevor, a bowler hat perched between his famously large, wiggly ears. It was obviously not his. Before I could tell him to take it off, its owner, a long-time landed and titled client, walked into the room to collect it with the firm's senior partner. I could have dug a hole. But Trevor, without batting an eye, simply apologized in an extra-strong Irish accent, saying he had mistaken the bowler for his own and moved swiftly to choose another from the hat rack. They were not to know Trevor never wore bowlers.

On another occasion we were at Wembley for an England v Republic of Ireland international and (probably because Trevor was then an Irish senator and I did much sports law work) we were guests of the FA at a post-match VIP meal – or feed, as Trevor would describe it. Many well-known sports people, not just from football, were there. We were on the same table as a leading athlete and former world champion about whom there had been gossip, albeit never proven, about performance-enhancing drugs. Trevor feigned ignorance of all this and, pretending not to recognize the athlete, started the conversation with, 'Tell me, what do you think of this drugs nonsense?'

He had a gift for getting words and phrases exactly right and always supported friends and family. I well remember him ringing me in the office on the Friday afternoon before his brother John's first international as referee in 1974: 'Charlie, watch John at Twickenham at the Wales match tomorrow. It'll all be up to the referee.' And it was. John famously disallowed a Welsh try, which would have changed the result, after an exciting race to touch down between England's David Duckham and J.J. Williams of Wales with John many yards behind. Trevor delighted in telling me about the white sticks with Welsh postmarks John was to receive. He was also of course very proud of John's successful, long career as a sought-after and respected international referee. On another occasion Trevor came especially to Guildford cricket week to watch a young Irish cricketer, Ed Joyce, playing for Middlesex against Surrey, whom he described as the best batsman Ireland had ever produced. Almost inevitably Joyce was given out LBW first ball. Trevor spent the rest of the day in the beer tent. Another good memory is of Trevor coming to Henley Royal Regatta, whose solicitor I then was, to cheer on the Trinity eight. He was diligent, indeed raucous in doing just that, a pint in hand, but with his back to the river except when Trinity were racing – they won that year to Trevor's delight as he fulfilled his duty as a popular DUCAC Chairman, championing Trinity's rowers.

Trevor could break down all barriers. He had time for everybody and remembered names. No wonder his important but unsung linking role in the early stages of the Peace Process by talking to some of the unionist hard men was praised in his obituaries. A Southern Protestant, he was accepted and trusted by all sides as a true independent who simply loved all Ireland, with no prejudice or baggage. Although Trevor and I talked about just everything, he only alluded briefly to being 'in the North' and visiting Long Kesh, never going into detail. Typical of his modesty, he underplayed his role.

His marriage to Maura Lee brought him evident happiness as his friends enjoyed the striking changes to his former bachelor lifestyle. He suddenly appeared smartly turned out. Maura Lee encouraged him to keep on his beloved rooms at Trinity, although he had told me that under Trinity's rules when he was elected a Fellow he would never have to retire! When Margaret and I were fortunate to revisit Charleston once more in 2009 with Maura Lee looking after us all, we saw how content Trevor was. He and I walked again round Charleston's grounds and went back together to the Mardyke, Cork County's cricket ground, where my favourite touring club, Free Foresters, were playing Cork County. In the pavilion Trevor delighted in regaling the new young Free Foresters about his only innings for the club more than fifty years ago. I had put him up to play as a candidate against Sussex Martlets at the Saffrons at Eastbourne and he

Cork County *vs* Cambridge at the Mardyke cricket grounds, Cork, 1960.

Cricket at TCD with the Museum building in the background.

ran out his partner, an elderly Forester stalwart, in a classic mix-up. Trevor's calling went 'Yes. No. Sorry, Colonel.' Not the ideal man for a candidate to run out in a club where both honorary secretaries, who were watching, were also retired colonels. But Trevor for ever after told the story with relish and emphasis on his run-out victim's name, Colonel Aeneas Perkins.

Charleston and the Mardyke had not changed. On this last occasion we also both happily recalled Peterhouse's Cork visit in 1961 when our friendship took root. I did not see Trevor again and our frequent catch-up Sunday evening phone calls, which Maura Lee helped Trevor continue as long as possible, progressively became more difficult as his memory deteriorated.

Trevor's many impressive tributes and obituaries described him as a teacher, mathematician, writer, politician, historian, and sportsman. He was all of those things. But, for me, it was his gift of unchanging friendship, humour and constant encouragement that mattered most.

The beginning of his friend Seamus Heaney's poem *Markings* could have been written for and about Trevor:

> We marked the pitch: four jackets for four goalposts.
> That was all. The corners and the squares.
> Were there like longitude and latitude.

Lester Connor, Trevor, and Carolyn Hufbauer in Washington D.C. *circa* 1990.

Cambridge and Beyond

In 1961 as newlywed American graduate students, Carolyn and I rented a flat in the same Victorian mansion as three Irishmen, also graduate students: Trevor West, Robin Harte and A.J. Taylor. They shared the flat with an Englishman who later worked for the British Coal Board, while the three Irish 'lads' were all destined for academic life. The four men had the upstairs flat, we had the ground floor, and a married couple occupied the basement.

The house, 17 Barton Road, in the Newnham neighbourhood of Cambridge, later became noteworthy because its owner, Sir Francis Crick, along with James Watson, won the Nobel Prize in 1962 for their joint discovery of DNA in 1953. Sir Francis rarely put in an appearance, leaving landlady chores to his wife Odile. The mansion had a few horse chestnuts and less memorable trees along the Barton Road side, and an extensive lawn in the back garden, rolled flat by the gardener, with a grassy mound covering a World War Two bomb shelter at one end. Our living room had a large window overlooking the garden and a sunny conservatory on one side, filled with plants. These pleasing features provided the setting for our graduate years in Cambridge.

We did not take up residence until December 1961, when Trevor and his roommates had already been ensconced for a year. As *de facto* leader of the Irish gang, Trevor immediately made us welcome with tea and stronger drink. We soon discovered that Trevor and Robin were partial to Guinness brews – only much later did we learn that Trevor's mother was a malster to the Guinness firm.

Since the upstairs flat was in constant disarray, the Irish gang came downstairs to socialize rather than vice versa. As Californians, we were not accustomed to the damp cold of a Cambridge winter, and we kept the gas fires going most of the day and evening. Often we would sit near the living-room fire to study; the trick was to face away so as not to fall asleep. Cold didn't faze Trevor and his friends, but they enjoyed the warmth of our flat.

Trevor and Robin were maths Ph.D. students at St John's College, while Tony Taylor was a classics scholar working on Linear B at Clare College; his studies were not going well and he slept long hours. In those days, a Cambridge Ph.D. was pretty much a 'do it yourself' proposition, with limited guidance from the supervisor. Maths is difficult at best, not given to casual conversation, and Trevor was much fonder of cricket than economics, so we didn't talk much shop at 17 Barton Road.

Come spring 1962, we frequently played croquet on the mansion lawn. Trevor had the advantage of long practice at Midleton and Trinity College; he was the player to beat. Robin, an inveterate smoker, would seldom dress before noon, so he played morning croquet in his red dressing gown, often puffing while lining up a tricky shot. But at Trevor's urging, and to keep in the good graces of Mrs Crick, Robin was fastidious about his cigarettes, and would put the butts in an empty tin.

Among his many accomplishments, Trevor was a great raconteur. As mentioned, another married couple occupied the basement flat at 17 Barton Road. The husband apparently worked some distance from Cambridge, and during late afternoons the wife was visited by a 'Corporal S.' who would arrive on his bicycle, park it against a tree, stay a few hours, and then pedal off. One afternoon, Trevor had the clever idea of hoisting the corporal's bike into a horse chestnut tree, about twenty feet off the ground. The corporal emerged from his tryst at dusk, searched frantically for his bicycle, but never looked up. After ten minutes or so, panic set in and he ran off, never to be seen again. Of course the Irish gang were discreetly watching from their upstairs flat, laughing their heads off. Another story illustrates Trevor's frugal ways, though he was raised in comfort. In 1962 Trevor visited a local Cambridge dentist, seeking relief for an aching front tooth. The dentist told Trevor the tooth would cost one pound to pull and five pounds to fill. Much to our amazement, Trevor chose the pliers, and ever after wore a bridge for the missing tooth!

We visited Trevor and his family in Midleton the summer of 1963, enjoying the hospitality of his mother Dorothy, father Tim, and faithful aunt Margaret. My wife Carolyn had just finished her History Tripos at Cambridge, which included writing a six-hour exam on a 'special subject', the Anglo-Irish settlement of 1922. Feeling she knew a lot about Irish history, Carolyn made the mistake of expressing sympathy for the poor Irish, oppressed by the nasty British, Trevor's Anglo-Irish family. They politely corrected some of her 'facts'.

Later that summer Trevor accompanied us on the train ride to Southampton to board the ship for America. After five days on board, with his Irish accent still echoing in her head after listening to his hilarious tales during the train ride, Carolyn phoned her sister Annie from the dock in New York. Annie responded, 'Why Carolyn, you sound so Irish!'

Trevor's second teaching post after Cambridge was at the University of California Los Angeles (UCLA), beginning in the fall of 1965. Arriving in September, Trevor's first stop was Boston to meet old family friends, and then he came to our home in Albuquerque, New Mexico, for the christening of our new son, Randall, born on 14 July. Trevor and another Cambridge friend, Tom Ray, were the godfathers. After the Episcopal Church ceremony on 6 September we all rode the train to the nearby ghost town of Lamy, with Randall sleeping peacefully through the entire journey. Trevor described his new godson as 'well behaved and growing fast after a slow start'. Trevor was a conscientious godfather, and in the years ahead, wrote to Randall frequently and entertained him during visits in the United States and Ireland. Tragically, Randall died shortly after his twenty-fifth birthday.

In October 1965 there was a big celebration in La Jolla, California, honouring Carolyn's father, the distinguished scientist Roger Revelle, for the new college at the University of California San Diego named after him. Roger was later world-renowned for his discovery that CO_2 concentrations were responsible for climate change. At the time, Trevor – never reverent – described Roger in a letter home as a 'big noise'. Trevor had met Roger in Cambridge and was invited to the celebration. As Trevor had just bought a used and well-worn Studebaker for $100, he decided to drive south on the 101 freeway. I happened to be in Los Angeles for a lecture, and we two got together for the three-hour drive to La Jolla. About a third of the way down, Trevor's Studebaker spewed smoke plumes and then the engine burst into flames. Navigating heavy traffic, Trevor pulled to the side. A passing police car doused the fire and called a tow truck. The truck arrived forty minutes later and the driver said it would cost $50 to haul the Chevrolet to a repair shop, or instead surrender the wreck to the tow company. After a moment's thought, Trevor signed it over and said farewell to his brief experience as a California driver. We then rented a car and made it to La Jolla where the celebration was in full swing. The Studebaker was not a total loss because, as Trevor wrote in a letter home, 'the bloke who sold it to me (and who is on the Maths Dept staff) is so upset that he's going to give me most of my cash back'.

Sometime in the fall of 1965 Trevor broke his ankle in a soccer game, and had to cope with a cast and crutches for several months. But that did not stop his exploratory travels. During the Christmas holiday Trevor visited my mother, Arabelle Hufbauer, in Berkeley, California. He arranged for his parents to send Arabelle, an architect and artist, about five yards of coarse Irish linen to be used for her oil painting. She was delighted with the material and became very fond of Trevor and his amusing stories.

While at UCLA, Trevor lined up a position in the mathematics department at Trinity College Dublin, which became the base for his entire professional career. Before leaving the United States he persuaded his parents, Timothy and Dorothy, to meet up with him in San Francisco, then stop for a while at our New Mexico home before returning to Ireland. By the time Trevor and his parents reached Albuquerque, in June 1966, it was pretty warm. After a life in County Cork, the senior Wests were not used to heat and outdoor excursions proved a trial. One excursion was the tramway ride up Sandia Peak – the longest tram in North America, swaying in the wind and traversing deep gorges. Trevor was relaxed, told stories and joked along the way, but the tramway was all the excitement Timothy and Dorothy could take.

We visited the West family in Midleton in December 1969, on our return to the US from two years in Lahore, Pakistan, together with our four-year-old son Randall and eleven-month-old daughter Ellen. To entertain Randall, Trevor's father got down under the table and barked like a dog, to the indulgent smiles of Trevor's mother. Ellen had come down with a nasty flu bug just before our departure from Pakistan. Alas, we shared our exotic flu strain with the entire West household.

During the summer of 1969 or 1970 Trevor joined the extended Hufbauer family at their cabin near the small town of Petrolia a few miles inland from the mouth of the Mattole River on California's remote 'lost coast'. The Hufbauer great-uncle T.K. 'Boss' Clark was the proud owner of the largest and most valuable ranch for miles around and led an excursion to the huge ocean-facing bluff where he fattened his cattle. However, Trevor, who got along famously with the aged Boss, concentrated instead on collecting the wild strawberries along the way. We also remember that on another excursion Trevor was the only one brave enough to strip down to his fishnet shorts and dive into the frigid Pacific, and my brother Karl recollects that Trevor had a unique way of playing hide-and-seek with Karl's three children on the beach strewn with driftwood. When Trevor was the seeker, he would announce that he had found one or more of them with a barrage of pebbles and little sticks. When he was the hider, he would manage to stay out of sight by scampering over and around the logs that had drifted ashore. This technique was a huge hit with the children, (the 'white mice' aged nine, seven and four), and when the game was over, he would charm them with stories.

About two years later Trevor more than reciprocated the Petrolia hospitality by welcoming to Ireland Karl and his entourage: Sally, his wife, their 'white mice', Beth, Ben, and Ruth, Karl's mother, Arabelle, and her travelling companion, Mary Jo Anderson, granddaughter to 'Boss' Clark. Upon meeting their ferry from England, Trevor greeted them with a plan for their week-long visit: after two nights and one full day getting acquainted with Dublin and its pubs, they would all squeeze into a rented Ford sedan, drive to Galway, overnight there, then embark on the day boat to Inisheer, the smallest and southernmost of the three main Aran islands. Karl, who was mindful of his group's number and completely unaware of the existence of the Aran Islands, thought it was indeed a 'mad' plan. But just as Trevor predicted, all worked smoothly.

The visit to Inisheer with Trevor was the ideal ending for the five-week European journey of the Hufbauer family. They were brought to shore from the boat by small wooden currachs and walked to the homes that would be hosting the large party. First they explored around the harbour, noticing that all livestock and crops were in small enclosures surrounded by hand-stacked limestone walls, and later clambering around the ruins of abandoned church properties. Toward the end of their stay Trevor guided the party around the entire island, pointing out that most of the paddocks on its windward side had been deserted as the population declined with emigration since the mid nineteenth century. Each evening after dinner with our various hosts and getting the white mice to bed, he would organize an excursion to one of the island's few pubs for the 'black lemonade'. Although big waves made for a difficult departure from Inisheer, with Trevor's encouragement all the party and a cow made it into canvas-covered currachs that were rowed safely to the boat by sturdy islanders, the first leg of the Hufbauers' long journey back to California.

In the 1980s Trevor turned to history to write an authoritative biography of Horace Plunkett (1854–1932), founder of the Irish co-operative movement and a leading politician. Trevor's book, *Horace Plunkett: Co-operation and Politics*, was published in 1986. As a young aristocrat, Plunkett took up ranching in the Bighorn Mountains of Wyoming (1879–1889) and for his research Trevor travelled several times to Plunkett's stomping ground to dig up old newspaper accounts, land deeds and letters. When

Croquet in New Square, TCD.

we were living in Washington DC, Trevor stopped on his way back from Wyoming and regaled us with tales of ranching life a century earlier: boom and bust, drought, cattle rustling, hangings were all part of the saga. Trevor was not only a frequent guest but he was also a great host. On several occasions, travelling to and from conferences, Gary would stay for a visit at Trinity College or rest and relaxation at Midleton. Trevor would ensure that a cricket or rugby match was on the agenda, and then in the evening a round of his favourite pubs. Very knowledgeable about the region around Cork, he would take us on excursions to Kinsale, Blarney Castle and other sights, and recount the history going back centuries. As these vignettes recall, Trevor West was not only a most memorable personality but also one of our very best friends along life's journey.

University of California, Los Angeles soccer
coach Jock Stewart attends to Trevor West's
injured knee at a UCLA soccer match in 1965.

Letters Home

It seems typical of Trevor West that when he wrote home to Midleton during his post-doctoral year at the University of California Los Angeles his requests should include copies of the Edinburgh Maths Journal, *a publication on the rules of rugby, and the price of Aran sweaters in a shop on the Grand Parade in Cork. It is also typical that, as recorded through Michael Mortell's scrutiny of those letters, he should quickly have identified like-minded academics and sportsmen, several of whom were academic sportsmen, and several more of whom were Irish, of Irish extraction, graduates of Irish universities and above all graduates or postgraduates of Dublin University. Michael Mortell of course combines three of these attributes in himself: an academic, a sportsman and a graduate of University College Cork. His contribution here tracks Trevor's journeys and activities from 1965 to 1966, including a meeting with Professor Jim Carney of the Institute for Advanced Studies (Celtic): 'a very friendly soul'.*

By 20 October 1965 Trevor had played two games of cricket at UCLA without, as he writes, distinguishing himself. The wicket is concrete, and

> the strip is matting over grass and is ok if the grass has been rolled – if not it's worse. The grass texture isn't strong enough to stand up to wear – it's hard enough making it grow at all. There are some good players here, about 2 per team. Alfie Cooper (Clontarf) who got one Irish cap as a quick bowler now plays for the U.S. team as a bat. But he is 500 miles north of here …

With the cricket season finished Trevor plays soccer on what he describes, in a letter to his brother John, as a pretty international team: American, Algerian, Irish, Argentinian, Hungarian, Columbian, German, Italian, German, English, Scots – 'It's quite a good side, if we only had a decent centre-forward …' In a game against CalTech he was marking Paul Rispin, a UCC graduate whom Trevor remembered from cricket at the Mardyke in Cork. Michael Mortell was also playing with John Gallivan, a physics student from UCD – 'the boys are all doing Ph.Ds'. Another Irishman in the maths department at UCLA was John Hickey of UCD, 'the current Irish 6-mile champion. He spends a great deal of time running.' Already, however, Trevor has been injured, a bang on his leg resulting in a bruise under the kneecap: sent to the training room he discovers that 'they have equipment there that one wouldn't find in a hospital at home.' He prices the whirlpool and sonic ray treatment together as costing close to £1500: 'Can you imagine any other place with equipment like that?'

Michael Mortell's scan of these letters finds accounts of journeys from California to Miami, from Vancouver to New Mexico, with a stopover in New Orleans for a visit to Basin Street and Canal Street. The trip to Miami was to give a seminar at the invitation of the distinguished mathematician Paul Halmos, 'a renowned figure in functional analysis'; there was a conference in Chicago and another seminar at the University of New Mexico; his friends the Hufbauers lived in Albuquerque. 'He slept on the beach in Monterey,' writes Mortell, 'and sent home a book by Steinbeck. Brian (his brother) and he met in San Francisco and he was with W.B. Stanford in Berkeley.'

To Trevor "Paddy" West
for his Outstanding Leadership –
Presented by the UCLA Soccer
Team and Coach —

Although the soccer is going well and Trevor has been performing capably at full back or half back there is no one to score a goal: 'Oh for my friend McCarthy the holy centre forward from Banbridge … ' As Mortell reports, early in November 1965 his football career in UCLA came to an end when he fractured an ankle in a game against 'a fairly robust and unskilful team'. Something of the same kind took place at an annual challenge game between UCLA and CalTech: four of the six Irishmen at CalTech were from UCC, three were on the CalTech team and of these Paul Rispin, hoping to finish up after four years in America, broke his leg badly and was put in thigh-high plaster for twelve weeks. 'I felt very sorry for him,' writes Trevor, ' I'm hoping to get my plaster off tomorrow.' Two others at CalTech are Dick Scott, 'whose mother is chemistry professor at UCC', and Bob Jeffers from Carrigaline.

'It seems,' writes Mortell modestly, 'that we ended up on the UCLA sports field playing hurling …' Trevor's version is slightly fuller, having spent the weekend at CalTech with Mortell. This County Cork hurler is

> a very nice lad and a very keen rugby and soccer player. He played rugby on Friday, soccer on Saturday and on Sunday we came back to UCLA with another fellow from Newcastle West and hurled on the UCLA sports field. I stood in the one spot and Mick could put the ball on me from 50 yards with great accuracy.

He expects to meet a Father Keohane from Midleton soon, but also notes in this letter the death of his friend Robin Wilson of Queen's maths department, his predecessor at MacBrayne Hall at the University of Glasgow. 'All his friends will be terribly sad. He played wing forward for Ulster several times and had been a schoolboy cricket interpro.'

On 20 March 1966 Trevor's letter to his parents thanks them for the safe arrival of shamrock and tells of enjoying himself thoroughly at the GAA dance organized by Mick Mortell and Fr Donal Keohane. But he is keeping in touch with events at home:

> I see that Ireland had a great win on Saturday against Wales. It reminds me of the game when Jack Kyle dropped his famous goal – I was with James under the East Stand and we went berserk. I read a report of the game on Tuesday morning 15 March at 10 a.m. in the Sunday Times of 13 March – express service. Of course the blowing up of the Pillar got a great deal of publicity. I also saw the Irish Times with the Budget – it seems severe – the Irish economy must be under a strain.

He assures his parents that he has been working hard and that he has a research student too who has just got his Ph.D. 'He's a lieutenant colonel in the Army and should be visiting Ireland in July.' Whether this was a portent of a colonel's visit to Midleton and to Charleston the letters don't say. However, as Mortell points out, Trevor was also watching for employment opportunities back in Ireland, and the final line of this letter hints at the future: 'The grapevine says that David Spearman is the new Applied Prof in Trinity.' When a Trinity maths lectureship was advertised that same month, Trevor applied and was appointed.

119

The Bold Collegian

The card for Trevor signed by members and coach of the UCLA soccer team.

UCLA soccer coach Jock Stewart.

A gathering of TCD Junior Deans, 2005.
Back row: John Gaskin, Fred Faulkiner, Fred Allen, Petrus Florides,
Anne Denard, Jane Grimson, Sean D. Barrett, Libby McElroy, Brendan Kennelly
Paddy Jackson, Brendan Tangney and Margaret Woodburn.
Front row: Trevor West, Clarissa Pilkington, R.B. McDowell and Ivy Crawford.

To Catch a Thief

I find it difficult to remember how I first came to know Trevor, or, as we often called him, TT. I think it must have originally been through some sporting activity at TCD, probably cricket. With himself, and a few others who enjoyed the game but weren't prepared to give it the commitment required to play for one of the university teams, we formed a team called the Trinity Farmers. To join, all a prospective member had to have was a pair of whites and a cloth cap, no other type being permitted. TT was a great organizer and arranged some very amusing matches – we used to play the staff and other such scratch teams.

Having got to know each other we started to look around for other outlets for entertainment. It must be remembered that in the fifties there were no exams at the end of term, only at the end of holidays. This timetable freed us to enjoy to the full any term-time activities in which we wanted to partake, although it did make rather a mess of the holidays. Enjoying to the full could be interpreted as engaging in harmless pranks. When I say harmless I mean ones that caused no damage. We always thought that the painting pink of the statue of the mathematician and former Provost George Salmon in the Front Square, for example, was a step too far. It cost the College a fortune to have it cleaned.

We considered that unrestricted entry to all parts of the College was essential. The main obstacle standing in the way of this goal was the fact that most of the doors were protected by Yale-type locks. While it is possible to pick such a lock it was delicate and time-consuming work, not to be performed when being tracked by a porter. Mortise locks, on the other hand, were far easier to deal with as we had a collection of useful skeleton keys, and it was this latter fact that led to a discovery that was to make most of our future escapades possible.

One night we were looking for a ladder and thought that the most likely place to find one was in the Clerk of Works yard. This yard was situated in the corner of Botany Bay at the end of the bathhouse and was accessed by climbing over the wall. On the other side we found not only a ladder, but also the Clerk of Works office, protected only by a simple mortise lock. Inside was the great find: all the Yale keys for the doors in

Front Square with the Examination Hall to the left, scene of the phantom organ recital.

College neatly labelled and hung in rows. There was also a key-cutting machine; we had, however, to provide our own blanks. During the following weeks we managed to copy virtually every key to every College door. These we coded and bunched together by area. When I left College they were in the safekeeping of TT. We never found the key to the Campanile but eventually we managed to fabricate one from one of those old-fashioned cast-iron monsters. Possession of this made it much easier to scale the outside of the tower. I believe I still have it somewhere.

Thinking back on the things we did in College one wonders how time was found for work. The answer of course was that in those days, other than attend lectures, the majority of students didn't find time. There was no immediate exam pressure during term-time as exams were always held in September. I have never fully understood why the timings were changed and I can't even remember when they occurred. My memory is so poor as to when things happened that I have divided those pranks I can remember by location rather than by time.

Most of the escapades were carried out by a small band of worthies, most of whom, alas, are dead. There were Brian Clarke, a gold-medal physicist, aka 'Shifty'; Trevor West, aka 'Slick'; Jas Poynton, aka 'Slim'; Mike Philcox; and Neville Avison, aka 'Turd'. We tried not use our own names in case we were overheard. A whole range of others were co-opted when available.

An early attempt to disrupt Commencements nearly went seriously wrong. Just before they began we inserted a crow-scarer in through one of the curved windows. A word about crow-scarers: these were a series of powerful bangers attached to a length of slow fuse; the flame crawled slowly up, igniting the bangers as it went at approximately ten-minute intervals. We placed a length just inside the window, which could be levered outwards, lit it and retired to await results. What we had neglected to do was to fix the string to the inside ledge. The result was that after the first explosion the string of bangers jumped off the ledge and fell down on top of one of the large framed pictures. We were lucky. It fell from there to the floor where it was quickly dealt with. Had it lodged behind the picture it could have done serious damage and it was gross irresponsibility not to have foreseen such a result.

The second attempt at disruption in the Examination Hall was more successful and was suggested by TT. I always consider this prank as one that showed the depth of talent available. It involved finding the turntable, amplifier and loudspeakers of the Gramophone Society, which were in the process of being thrown out to make way for more up-to-date equipment. When we got the equipment to our rooms we tested it and found rather to our dismay that the amplifier – one of the old sort with valves – was not working. It being late at night there would have been no possibility of a visit to Peats Electrical Suppliers. Brian Clarke rousted out a physics colleague, Billy Hipwell, and we all trooped down to the physics department where we managed to get a replacement. Having got all the bits and pieces working we hauled them up to the top of the organ.

The next step was to get a power source. After some experimenting we led a wire from one of the top offices over the roofs and in through openings into the hall above the organ. The connection was made in one of the attic spaces of the buildings on Front Square. One was able to access this space via a trap door in the ceiling. We connected the two wires in parallel inside the ceiling rose of one of the lights, the idea being that we simply had to switch on the light to start the music. We then camouflaged the wire as best we could. We connected up the equipment and set the record to be played, Bach's *Passacaglia and Fugue*. Rather than play the full twenty minutes or so of the 10" LP we tried to leave the needle on the gap of the record and just play the fugue. As it turned out we actually left it on the last few bars of the *Passacaglia*. This inadvertent misplacing actually made the effect on those assembled below more striking. These last few bars of the *Passacaglia* boomed out, followed by a pause, which allowed the presiding officials to get themselves together and restart the ceremony only to be plunged in confusion again when the fugue started up.

It should be recorded that the whole thing very nearly never came off. Once Commencements started we gave it a few minutes then went to the room and switched on the light. We then rushed down hoping to enjoy the ensuing confusion, but listening outside the door we heard nothing but the uninterrupted drone of the ceremony. Feeling badly deflated with a grievance against the eagle eyes of the security staff, who we assumed must have found and removed the wire, we mooched disconsolately around Front Square, cursing our luck when the thought occurred that it might be worth checking our connections. Back we went, switched off the light, climbed up into the attic and had a look. As far as we could tell everything seemed in order, but just to be on the safe side we undid and remade the connections, switched on the light and more in hope than in expectation went back down to Front Square. Oh the joy. We didn't even have to go to the portico to listen. We could hear the organ, which had been silent for years, booming out from where we were. We watched as Dr McDowell, followed by porters, rushed up the stairs to the balcony only to come running down again exclaiming that there was no one in the organ.

If we hadn't had to make the second visit to check the wiring there might have been more serious repercussions. While we were up there we found a handkerchief with the name tape of Neville Howard Avison prominently visible. As it was the College authorities took it in good spirit. While perhaps they knew who might have been responsible there was little they could have done without proof positive. Later on that day Basil Chubb, my tutor, implied congratulations on the choice of music – Bach organ music as opposed to 'Jailhouse Rock' – by returning to me the record, which I still have.

On another occasion a film production team was filming in Trinity – I believe it was something called *Shake Hands with the Devil*. As part of their equipment they had a long rubber-tyred chassis, which they used to mount the camera for moving shots. When they finished they removed all their equipment but for some reason the chassis was left. I don't know who came up with the idea but it was thought a good place to put it might be on top of the Exam Hall. A party was got together. From memory there must have been about twelve of us, all, I remember, scholars (except Ronnie Wathen, my room-mate, who was needed for his ropes and strength and who rather let the side down, being only a sizar). It was generally accepted that the only way to get the chassis up would be to run it up the wall and the only place where this could be done with some hope of avoiding detection would be the Provost's Garden. We duly trundled through into the garden, went up to the roof, dropped a rope down, hitched up the chassis, returned to the roof and with a belay round a chimney started hauling it up, the wheels running up the curved wall at the back of the Exam Hall.

All proceeded according to plan until it reached the overhang of the roof ledge and there it stuck. Try as we might we couldn't manhandle it over the obstruction. In the end there was nothing for it but to double belay it and make it fast while we went away and thought about it. It being late, TT suggested that we leave the chassis where it was and come back the following night with some bars to lever it over the overhang. The only vote against this plan came from Ronnie who didn't want to risk losing his rope. He was an avid mountain climber and took his ropes very seriously. As it wasn't one of his best he eventually capitulated to the common good and there the chassis remained, suspended high in the air. Luckily it was only visible from the Provost's House itself and not from the rest of College. Apparently no one must have looked out the windows, for when we returned the next night armed with scaffolding bars, kindly presented by the Clerk of Works, there were no porters lying in ambush.

The chassis was levered over with no trouble and run to the front of the roof where it was placed with one pair of wheels over the ridge tiles. I believe there was a picture in *The Irish Times*. It was removed the following day, although it had to be dismantled to get it down. We were aggrieved to hear that we were being blamed for damaging the tiles. As we always prided ourselves in never causing collateral damage we were somewhat annoyed. We had taken great care not to damage any slates even to the extent of bringing up light planks to distribute the load as the tyres were rolled up the roof. We would have liked to assure the authorities that any damage was caused by the heavy feet of the dismantling crew.

One never appreciated officialdom's attempts at imposing their writ. Consequently the appearance of 'No Parking' signs in Front Square tended to be met with a certain amount of disfavour, as an unnecessary restriction of collegiate liberty. It should be remembered that in the fifties few students had cars. One night TT and a few of us set off to deal with the offending article. This article was in fact a free-standing sign about four foot high and weighing at least a hundredweight due to its very heavy base. Climbing on to the roof of the exam hall a rope was let down and tied to the sign, which was hauled up and swung into the pediment. What has imprinted this episode on my mind was the narrow escape we had from being discovered. As I remember it I was sitting on the bottom ledge of the pediment assisting in manoeuvring the sign into its final position when from across the square, out from his rooms, came R.B. McDowell. He came across Front Square from no. 8 jingling his keys and passed almost underneath us. We remained frozen with the sign partly on the ledge but still half-suspended from the rope. Mercifully he never glanced up, for had he done so he would certainly not only have seen us, but more importantly would have recognized us, it being about 4 am on a rapidly lightening summer morning. Sadly the Clerk of Works with his new expanding scaffolding had it down by lunchtime.

As all and sundry thought it a shame that the Howth tram was going to be closed we thought we might mark our displeasure by stranding the last tram at the top of Howth Hill. We understood that the last tram would run from Howth up the Hill and down to Sutton. On this basis we thought we would remove a rail just below the summit on the Sutton side and then when the train reached this point and was forced to stop we would remove a second rail below the summit on the Howth side, thus stranding the tram at the top. To do this after having selected the places for the rail removal we needed a large crowbar, which we borrowed from my future father-in-law, a large enough spanner to open the rail bolts, a sledge to knock out the wedges and most importantly a couple of red warning oil lamps usually found in those days in the vicinity of road works. Strangely these proved difficult to source and we had to spend quite a time driving through Dublin looking for suitable lamps that we could take without endangering passing traffic. We eventually got what we wanted and set off for the Hill. I can't remember when we thought the last tram was scheduled to depart, possibly about 10 pm. With whatever time firmly fixed in our minds we removed one of the rails and set out the lamps on the Howth side of the break about ten minutes before what we had worked out to be the ETA of the tram at our position and there we sat in anticipation of the fun to come.

Of course we had got it all wrong and either the last tram wasn't coming from Howth, or the company had put on an extra one, for the next thing we knew was that we heard a tram approaching from the Sutton direction. I suppose I could say that there was consternation all around with the thought of an impending derailment. I forget who it was exactly but one of us – I would like to say myself, but it was probably TT – had the presence of mind to grab the warning lights and put them on the Sutton side of the break. I remember touching the rails as the tram approached and getting a slight shock. I suppose the system used the rails as an earth return. The tram braked and people got off to see what the trouble was and after a certain amount of milling around all boarded the tram again and it set off back down from whence it had come. In the confusion my girlfriend Joanna and I climbed on board and rode it part of the way back down towards Sutton.

The sequel to this event, which I regret must be counted as a failure, was the prosecution of a perfectly innocent bystander, one William Dick. As I understand it he had heard about what we intended to do and had driven up in his father's car to see the fun. His car was spotted and when he drove down to the road crossing below to see if there was any further action it was seen again and someone took its number and reported it to the Garda, who then contacted his father, who in turn made William go along to the Garda and explain his (non-existent) role in the matter. The outcome as I heard later – the holidays intervened and I was away – was that whatever William told the Garda didn't wash and he was paraded before a district court judge who fined him £5. This, I thought, was a bit hard, especially as he had nothing to do with it.

Like all graduates I emigrated to England in search of a job so I rather lost sight of Trevor until I returned in 1966 (although I became very popular with his parents by staying with them at Midleton and giving them all a dose of 'flu, ending up in bed there for a week). Once back in Dublin I would go to town on a Friday to the Neptune Gallery and always cut through Trinity, calling often as not to see Trevor either in his rooms or at the top of 27, the DUCAC rooms. He consulted me over the security of the new Berkeley Library in connection with a Picasso exhibition that Trinity were staging. I suppose his thinking was, set a thief to catch one.

Sheet music for 'Non Nobis, Domine'.

Non Nobis, Domine

Trevor retired as an academic in 2004 after thirty-eight years in the maths department and stepped down as Chairman of DUCAC in 2009 after forty-three years of service; one year as a DUCAC Executive member, nine years as the Hon. Treasurer and thirty-three years as Chairman. He was blessed with many gifts and talents, none of which he wasted. Gifted with a brilliant intellect, he was curious about everything, read and researched widely, thirsted for knowledge, and had a way of analyzing situations, visioning, seeing the broader picture and thinking outside the box. He had a gift for friendship, which was classless, and treated everyone equally. This chapter explores some of these gifts and talents and also discusses the passion and values that Trevor shared with staff and students.

Trevor had a wonderful ability to hold people's interest and was great at making contacts. As Michelle Tanner, Director of Sport in TCD recounted, Trevor had an innate talent to connect with people through sport; he would quickly find a connection and tell a story of relevance to that person: 'He was a man with old-fashioned ideas but was always open to modern thinking,' a view endorsed by engineering graduate and first Sports Scholar, Conor Fennessey, also a member of Dublin University Boat Club: 'Trevor was a modernist, tolerant, passionate and recognized the world was changing.'

He was a true networker and advocate for sport. In the early 1990s Trevor 'connected' with Guinness regarding funding for sports scholarships. The establishment of a sports scholarship system for Trinity had been mooted a few years previously, but it wasn't until 1993 that DUCAC grasped the nettle and the first Guinness sports scholarships with a value of £600 per year for four years were awarded to Junior Freshman students including Anya Bowers, Jan Cunningham, Zanya Dahl, Conor Fennessey, Ray McIlreavy and Jan Perrin, representing rugby, hockey and rowing.

The scholarship scheme is still going but has evolved over the twenty-two years and today other organizations including the GAA fund the scheme. Almost 400 sporting students have received sports scholarships to date, which are awarded on the basis of high performance, potential development and involvement in particular sports along with academic excellence.

A few years after setting up the scholarship scheme Trevor got in touch with Ken Ryan of KPMG. Ken's son Neil was the captain of the rugby club. Ken worked with Trevor, Terry McAuley and others to develop a strategy for sport for Trinity, which provided a blueprint for the appointment of a Director of Sport and the development of sports facilities in College and at Santry Sports Centre. Trevor had the vision to develop the sport facilities both on and off the pitch and to develop the Pav – the sports bar – for social occasions. For those students who didn't wish to partake in club games he championed the development of the new sports centre with a swimming pool. Prior to the opening of the new pool the DU Swimming Club and recreational swimmers used the Markievicz Pool on Townsend Street.

Trevor was a wonderful servant of TCD. He gave himself to the benefit and betterment of College and its collegiate life with particular focus on its sportsmen and women. In the spirit of the motto 'a healthy mind in a healthy body' he was an advocate of a holistic education; he promoted the importance of sport to student development in higher education and in preparing students for life, not only for their degree.

He was a Renaissance man with a Renaissance talent. Unprompted, 'Renaissance' was used to describe Trevor by many of those I spoke to in recent months. He embodied the characteristics of a cultured and human life. He was a professor who loved teaching mathematics yet he researched and wrote a biography on the founder of the co-operative movement, *Horace Plunkett: Co-operation and Politics,* published in 1986. He was a Senior Fellow on the University Board yet as a sports historian he wrote with passion about the development of sport and sport administration in TCD in his book *The Bold Collegians,* published in 1991. He wasn't the academic in an ivory tower, he was very much in touch with the student body. He had a determined streak, and like a good politician was good at smoothing ruffled feathers and very good at getting his message across, both written and verbal. Trevor was at best described as a conservative radical but not a radical conservative. As a radical he was not afraid to challenge or push out the boat and accepted that change was needed.

However, as a conservative he saw the point of tradition and the importance of the institution as linking the past with the present. As Peter Barrett, Captain of DU Hockey Club (1979–1980) and Chaplain from 1994 to 1998 remembers, 'In a university that was getting bigger and increasingly more anonymous Trevor was a point of reference, a point of continuity, and a point of unity.' Like the Oregon maple tree in Front Square that moves with the wind and changes with the seasons, he was a very rooted person. Elaine Smith, history and politics graduate and now chef at Per Se restaurant in New York, treasures her College experience in which Trevor played a huge part: 'I fondly remember visiting him for a chat and a KitKat in his DUCAC office, or running into him in College Park, or having coffee together and a wander around the Science Gallery.'

His conservative radical viewpoint was evidenced in how student sport in TCD changed in the 1980s and 1990s. Thomas Aquinas's famous dictum that 'the sea unites peoples, the land divides' could be adapted for Trevor as 'sports unite where politics divide'. Trevor encouraged the development of sporting links with Northern Ireland schools including Bangor Grammar School, Campbell College, Dalriada, Methody, Portora and Victoria College and many students from these schools came to Trinity to study and play their sports including Cathryn Curran (hockey), Mark Pollock (rowing) and William Robb (rugby).

Trevor was very good at celebrating success. As Irish people we don't celebrate success enough and often focus on the things we could have done better, but not Trevor. In the DUCAC academic sporting calendar we did lots of celebrating. First there was the ceremony for the announcement of the new sports scholars, held in November in the Pavilion Bar, where proud parents and school staff celebrated the success of the new scholars. Next celebration was the Service for the Gift of Sport, which took place in College Chapel in April (Trevor was a great supporter of College Chapel). The format for the ecumenical service was devised by Trevor and Peter Barrett. The first service was in 1996 and all TCD chaplains were in attendance: Peter Barrett, Ken Lindsay, Katherine Meyer, Paul Murphy and Richard Sheehy, and it has been an annual event ever since. Trevor especially chose 'Non Nobis, Domine' as the sporting anthem. His friend Dr Cyril White provided Trevor with the history of the hymn, whose words were written by Rudyard Kipling in 1934 and set to music by Roger Quilter in 1936. 'Non Nobis, Domine' was adopted as the Olympic hymn to be sung at the opening ceremony of the XIV Olympiad in London in 1948. On that occasion 1200 voices were conducted by Sir Malcolm Sargent. In College Chapel in April 1996 TCD's new sporting anthem was sung by about twenty voices of the Chapel Choir. Trevor distributed the words of the hymn to all present in Chapel and we joined the choir in singing

Trevor presiding at the annual Sports Commons.

Non Nobis, Domine
Not unto us O Lord
The praise a glory be
Of any deed or word

Sporting Commons was the next event. As Trevor said, 'DUCAC always put on the best parties in College', booking 150 seats on Commons for invited guests and successful teams who decorated the Dining Hall with their winning silverware and plaques. When the meal ended and fellows and scholars left, coffee was served and the fun began. Trevor stood on his chair and without a microphone asked each team in turn to stand while he bellowed out their winning honours. The evening would end with all invited to join Trevor in the Pav for a pint. Trevor kept his 'Chairman's Tankard' behind the bar and into this was poured a Smithwick's. Trevor's tankard was made by Alwright & Marshall in Fade Street and was an exact replica of the David Webb (Botany) tankard.

Other celebratory events that took place during the 1990s included the visit of the Sam Maguire Cup to Trinity on two occasions. First, Joe Brolly brought the cup to the DUCAC office in House 27. Joe played Gaelic football for Derry and was on the team in 1993 when Derry beat Cork in the final to win the Sam Maguire for the first time in their history. Three years later 'Sam' was on Commons, accompanied this time by members of the Meath football team, the cup winners that year. On Sunday, 29 September 1996, the day of the final replay against Mayo, the Meath team had held a light run on the rugby pitch in College Park that morning. If I remember correctly it was Seán Barrett, an avid Meath supporter and friend of the Meath manager Seán Boylan who had organized this. Trevor was a big fan of GAA and around this time he negotiated with Nicky Brennan, chairman of the Leinster Council at the time, for the introduction of a TCD development officer for Hurling and Gaelic Football.

In 2004 the Pavilion hosted a reception to celebrate a hundred years of women in Trinity at which the book *A Danger to the Men?*, edited by Susan M. Parkes, was launched. Maeve Kyle, who won fifty-eight international caps for hockey and was the first woman to represent Ireland in athletics at the Olympics in Melbourne in 1956, and Jane Grimson, Vice-Provost of Trinity at the time, spoke at the launch. Trevor and Maeve were very close. Trevor's vision was the opening up of sport to all and especially women's sport, whether in teams or as individuals.

In 1988 Ronan Tynan participated in the paralympics in Seoul, Korea, with much success. He was awarded a College Pink that year, the highest accolade given to elite sportsmen and women who brought honour to Trinity at either national or international level. Trevor organized an evening to recognize and celebrate Ronan's achievements and presented a vase, which at the base had three rings: gold, silver and bronze, representing the medals Ronan had won in Korea, and revelling in Ronan's sucess. Ronan explains:

Trevor West's Alwright & Marshall tankard. Like the botanist David Webb, Trevor left his tankard to TCD's silver collection.

> I believe, though, that what Trevor enjoyed most were our evenings at the Pavilion Bar. There he would ask me to sing, and he would listen and encourage me even more. Trevor was a wonderful human being and a wonderful representative for all that Trinity stands for. I was truly honoured to know him and above all, honoured to have him as a friend.

Hugh Tinney was an honours maths student who represented Trinity in tennis on the winning colours team in 1979. He left Trinity before completing his degree in order to study the piano in London. Trevor never taught Hugh 'sums' but loved telling people that Hugh was his student. Their paths crossed many times since those College days, latterly through music. Both Hugh and his sister Ethna, a student of modern languages, represented Trinity in Colours and intervarsity tennis: ' I knew of him also through my mum, Sheila Tinney, associate professor of maths and physics at UCD. We always got on well. I enjoyed his quick intelligence, low-key approach and humour and of course his polymath-wide range of interests.'

To mark Trinity College's quatercentenary in 1992, RTÉ radio aired a series of programmes, which Maura Lee produced with Brendan Kennelly as the presenter. In all, twelve programmes were made on various topics reflecting life in College, including history, science and distinguished alumni. Brendan was very insistent that RTÉ make a programme on sport. Maura wasn't enthusiastic but to keep Brendan on side she agreed. An interview was arranged by Brendan for Maura to meet with Trevor in the Senior Common Room and after less than ten minutes of chatting to Trevor, whose enthusiasm for sport was infectious, Maura realized that a programme on sport was what was needed and it would be full of colour!

A recording date was set for a Saturday morning. Brendan conducted the interviews with Trevor, Tony Hanahoe and Hugo MacNeill. The content of the interview was wide-ranging, thoughtful and very amusing. In opening the programme Brendan set the scene when he stated 'Sport is one of the most important extracurricular activities to be carried out in the university since its foundation.' The panel discussed the ways in which sport prepared young students for life after College, how it helped with self-development and fostered companionship; how it taught students about self-discipline and knowing limitations; about losing matches and learning to lose with dignity. Trevor also spoke about his belief that sport crossed all barriers.

Under Trevor's chairmanship DUCAC played a significant role in the quatercentenary year. A major capital project was undertaken with the complete refurbishment of the Pav. Women's changing rooms were incorporated and the footprint for the original men's changing rooms was increased. Upstairs, new patios were laid and work was carried out on the steps. DUCAC contributed £1m towards the project, which was finished in time for the 1991–92 year. On Friday, 29 November 1991 DUCAC hosted a quatercentenary dinner in the dining hall, and many club intervarsities were held in College that year. At the end of April 1992 the Irish Universities Athletic Association (IUAA) gave special permission for the track events of the IUAA championships to be held in College Park to mark TCD 400. This was the last time the IUAA championships were held on a grass track.

Roger Dodd, now living in California, was a member of staff of the maths department in the 1980s and 1990s and remembers Trevor's kindness to him when he first arrived at Trinity and also remembers a perfect gentleman: 'I am a cricket fan and a sure sign of the approaching new season was the figure of Trevor, mounted on the roller, rumbling very slowly across the cricket field – this has remained one of my abiding memories of Trinity.'

In May 1992 on the night of the Trinity 400 Ball, Trevor was seen standing guard on the cricket crease due to a big tent full of revellers in College Park, which were causing him intense anxiety as a three-day international cricket match was due to be played against Wales starting in July. Trevor had the world and his wife helping to get the wicket perfect. He was determined it would not be ruined by stiletto heels that evening. His all-night guard duty paid off and the wicket remained intact, College Park looked great; and Ireland drew with Wales.

That same July 1992 there was an academic procession from the Examination Hall to St Patrick's Cathedral and back again to College, the streets closed off, the academics wearing their colourful regalia. Among them Trevor walked with his great friend Brendan Kennelly who at the time was doing a commercial for Toyota on TV and was a household figure. As Trevor recounted afterwards, loads of 'auld ones' were stopping Brendan along the way because they recognized him from the adverts. Remarks about Toyota cars were flung at him, to which he responded with literary and witty gems, although the funny thing is that Brendan didn't even drive. Trevor said he could have sold half a dozen Toyotas that day.

Although Trevor celebrated the success of others in the spirit of *Non Nobis Domine* he did not expect to receive praise himself. However, DUCAC hosted a dinner for Trevor on the occasion of his thirtieth anniversary in office. At this dinner John Luce, Public Orator in Trinity, Professor of Classics and previous Chairman of DUCAC, read a piece he had written in Latin, 'In Praise of Trevor West':

> O West, you are a star! You are the champion of our sportsmen and women!
> The farmers who cull the rich cornlands of fair Midleton may rightly sing your praises.
> There is your native seat, and after passing through your father's school, you came to Dublin, destined to win Trinity's highest honours.
> I pass over those mathematical numbers that you are wont to handle so skilfully. O muse, strike up a different strain!
> With what an agile foot you used to propel the inflated leather!

And then how many full pints you used to imbibe with a crowd
of friends in a neighbouring hostelry!

When elected a fellow, you set your hand to weightier matters,
checking the misdemeanours of the young with lighthanded
authority, and working unceasingly for the promotion of sport.
With the gods on your side, this is the thirtieth year since you
were duly elected to the DUCAC Executive, and soon as chairman, ever conscious of the common good, you were never to
deny their desired grant to the sports clubs!

Time would fail me were I to try to list all the ways in which the
sporting fraternity is in your debt.
Those students who pursue their courses as holders of athletic
scholarships rejoice in your initiative.

Now you are setting even grander schemes in motion, and in
a second sports hall, we may at long last come to view a
swimming pool.
O West, you are good company, and a good-hearted comrade
to all in college, and you devote yourself tirelessly to the
development of sporting facilities on our campus.
Among the Bold Collegians, none more bold than you!

Geraldine McAuley and I in DUCAC loved when spring arrived every
year as Trevor would bring us gifts of Charleston daffodils each week to
adorn the office. He would pick these the previous evening, wrap them
in a recycled *Financial Times* and these bundles would make their way to
DUCAC via the early Cork train. They always survived the journey. In
the autumn he would bring bags of apples from the Charleston orchard,
once again on the train from Cork to Dublin. On rare occasions he would
bring a slice or two of Tessie Finn's wonderful coffee cake to the office –
it was mouthwatering!

Much of Trevor's generosity to students and others was anonymous.
On many occasions during my eleven years working in DUCAC Trevor
had helped students financially, also pointing them in the direction of the
Minchin bursary and Taverners' Cricket bursary. The Minchin, established in 1982, is open to undergraduate students (except, ironically,those
reading mathematics or physics). The bursary is awarded annually to students meeting the criteria of 'academic merit, athletic prowess and financial need'. The Taverners' Cricket bursary on the other hand is open to
all students. It was established in 1993 by the Museum Players and other

Cathy and Pat Doyle with Charles
and Margaret Woodhouse at Trevor
West's seventieth birthday party.

Taverners' cricketers as a result of funds raised during Trinity 400 the previous year. It is awarded annually 'to a needy student, preferably one who has demonstrated sporting prowess within the University'.

On a personal note Trevor was very kind to me. In the summer of 1991 I was unwell when pregnant with my second daughter and was hospitalized for many months, during which Geraldine covered for me in DUCAC. Trevor used to visit me each week at Mount Carmel and arranged that the new Apple Mac computer from the DUCAC office was brought to the hospital. He would arrive and mischievously announce to the nurses that Dr West was here to see me. The healthcare staff were convinced he was a medical doctor! When my pregnancy settled down in the third trimester I was allowed home to rest and there Trevor would update me on DUCAC news and on the progress of the rebranding of DUCAC, the new gold shamrock logo, newly designed stationery, the DUCAC ties and scarves and the jacket cover for *The Bold Collegians* designed by the late Giancarlo Ramaioli of The Graphiconies. In December 1991 Clíona was born and in the spirit of celebration Trevor invited my husband Pat, Clíona and me to the January 1992 meeting of the DUCAC Executive. Trevor attended the christening and the party, which followed at our house. He was loved by my relatives for his boyish appearance and the ease in which he fitted in and by my nieces and nephews when he introduced them to his 'ear-wiggling' party trick.

Trevor has a rich tapestry in terms of his legacy. He rejoiced in the success of DUCAC and its clubs and encouraged the widest possible participation for the sheer enjoyment of sport and the friendships it engendered. He saw himself as part of a collegiate life that had been going for over 400 years, a life of knowledge and endeavour, and he believed it was his duty to continue, develop, improve – and maybe leave his mark – and pass it on to the next generation. He had an infectious collegiate spirit, was a wonderful representative for sport and for all that Trinity stands for. Bold and determined, with the courage to share his vision, in many respects the title of *The Bold Collegian* is a fitting description of TTW.

I was truly honoured to have known him, to have learnt from him, to have worked with him, to have been inspired by him and to have had him as a friend.

Gusty Spence (PUP) with *right to left*: William (Plum) Smith (Red Hand Commando, aligned
to the UVF), Gary McMichael (UDA), David Irvine (PUP/UVF), David Adams (UDA) at
the announcement of the ceasefire by the combined Loyalist military command, 13 October 1994.

Meeting Gusty

An Independent Dublin senator from 1970 to 1982, an accomplished mathematician at Trinity College and a respected author and sports enthusiast, Trevor West was President of the Irish Association for Cultural, Economic and Social Relations and played a very significant role in the Northern Ireland peace process. Although born and raised in Cork, he had a good understanding of life in Northern Ireland, having spent many summer holidays as a youth with his uncle in Belfast.

Trevor was a devout member of the Church of Ireland while his uncle was a Presbyterian who enabled his young nephew to meet Unionists and gain a greater understanding of their thinking. Through his holidays in Belfast Trevor had come to know the geography of the city streets and had ventured into Loyalist working-class areas. Ulick O'Connor related how he once asked Trevor 'What street is this?' 'Oh,' Trevor replied, 'this is the Shankill Road.' Ulick was shocked and immediately exclaimed 'Let's get out of this.' But Trevor assured him that everything was all right and so it proved to be.[1]

Trevor became aware of the downward drift towards violence at an early stage but could not turn away from the complex problems of the North. Instead he tried to help change things for the better. He was aware that aspects of the Irish State were having a negative impact on the people of Northern Ireland. He had been Senate election agent for Mary Robinson (later President of Ireland) and in August 1971, he, with other senators including Robinson herself, signed a letter to Stormont and Westminster politicians expressing concern about violence in Northern Ireland. The senators insisted there could be 'no lasting peace or security' while a large section of the population were unable to give their consent. A new system acceptable to the minority was seen as essential because the alternative could lead to an 'escalation of sectarian strife to the dimensions of civil war.'[2]

In December 1973 Trevor called for a debate on the historic Sunningdale Agreement and was supported in this by Mary Robinson. By July of 1974 the Stormont Institutions had collapsed, leading to a critical situation. He then asked the government to outline its policy on reconciliation.

1. *Sunday Independent,* 18 November 2012

2. Letter from senators at Seanad Éireann, 30 August 1971

In the course of the debate that followed Trevor referred to two strands of thought by the Irish government and opposition:

> The government ... pointed out that Irish unity was at present out of the question and that moves or warlike noises made by the Republic in that direction could precipitate sectarian civil war. On the other hand, the Fianna Fáil party ... underlined the aspiration to Irish unity by consent – a non-violent aspiration to unity – and claimed that the government was not doing enough to persuade the minority in Northern Ireland of the rightness of this aspiration.[3]

Trevor then emphasized: 'We now realize that a relentless pursuit of unity by any means whatever will inevitably involve Northern Ireland and the Republic in sectarian civil war.' His views were a recognition of the fears then being expressed in the North. He said most people in the Republic would like to see unity, 'but the Loyalist Ulster Workers' Council strike has sharpened our perspective'. He therefore advocated 'joint responsibility for any new Administration in the North', with a 'considerable degree of autonomy'.[4] This was close to what has actually been achieved although as yet there is no effective mechanism for decision-making that could help avoid the deadlock resulting from the mutual veto at Stormont.

By 1976 Trevor supported peace moves on the streets by taking part in a demonstration in Cork.[5] In January of the following year he responded to comments by 'Cromlyn' in the *Church of Ireland Gazette*, saying that 'Northern Protestant fears ... are often not appreciated in the rather too homogeneous Republic' with its Catholic 95 per cent majority. Northern Unionists had a much smaller majority and were very much a minority on the island. As for Protestants in the Republic he quoted 'competent observers ... talking in terms of their final extinction'. [6] But Trevor West perceptively rejected this on the grounds that radical changes were already taking place in the Republic in which Irish Catholics, 'are coming to value the open-mindedness and liberal standards, which are an essential part of Protestantism'.[7]

Trevor was also aware of growing reactionary forces in NI that stood in direct conflict with the open-mindedness and liberal traditions referred to. This retreat was partly a consequence of the IRA's campaign of violence, which in theory was fought against the British but in practice was experienced as a war of attrition against Unionists who felt betrayed on all sides. In an election address that same year Trevor West emphasized the proud 'tradition of independence' among fellow university senators. They were outside the political parties and were therefore able to play 'an essential role in molding public opinion'. In the same address Trevor spoke of being a regular visitor to the North where despite the violence 'life goes on as normal'. He advocated policies that would bring people of differing traditions together and emphasized the need for separation of Church from State in the Republic. He advocated legalizing the sale and distribution of contraceptives, the introduction of civil divorce, integrated schooling and care for the environment.[8]

That election address was given in 1977, the year in which Trevor West would also make a very significant practical move on behalf of peace in Northern Ireland. It so happened that he knew of a TCD student who was a former Young Unionist associated with Loyalists in Belfast. The student had appeared in a television debate during the early 1970s. Trevor heard him expressing strong views on Northern Ireland and was so impressed that he contacted the student. They met together on a number of occasions. The student soon realized that Trevor was serious about wanting greater understanding of the North in order to help in some way. He advised Trevor that to understand what was really happening he should speak with Gusty Spence, a leading Loyalist then in the Maze Prison (also known as Long Kesh).

The student was perceptive because Gusty Spence had played a central role in early Loyalism by leading a small UVF group based on Belfast's lower Shankill Road. Gusty had related how Unionists, including a former army colonel in County Tyrone, had initiated him into the UVF in 1964/5. The UVF was intended as a province-wide organization with Spence leading Loyalists in Belfast's Shankill Road area. He was considered an ideal candidate, having served with the British army in Cyprus during the EOKA campaign. EOKA was a Greek Cypriot paramilitary organization, against which Gusty had been directly involved in military operations.

Spence's family was strongly Unionist with a tradition of British military service. He was born in 1933 and reared on Belfast's Loyalist Lower Shankill Road during the hungry thirties. His brother Billy Spence was secretary of the West Belfast Imperial Unionist Association and Gusty had an intimate knowledge of Unionist Party workings on the ground. He had worked for Unionist candidates during elections, which included organizing a group of people prepared to steal votes by impersonating electors.

These factors made Gusty Spence an ideal candidate to lead the Shankill UVF. Many Unionists at that time had highly exaggerated fears

3. Seanad debate,
11 December 1973
and 28 May 1974.

4. *IBID*, 3 July 1974.

5. *IBID*.

6. *IBID*, 1 September 1976.

7. *Church of Ireland Gazette*,
28 January 1977.

8. *IBID*.

of the IRA, which were being stimulated by certain politicians and demagogues. Right-wing Unionists were convinced that O'Neill's reforms were going too far and that the prime minister was weak on the NI constitutional position as part of the UK. This, in Gusty's view, explained the motivation for the re-formation of the UVF. The idea was to oppose O'Neill's reforms by fomenting 'incidents' that would impel O'Neill to bring in stricter security measures. However, Gusty insisted, it had not been intended that the UVF should engage in killings.

Despite this by 1966 the small Shankill UVF sought to kill a leading republican who was not at home when they called. They found other easy targets, young Catholic men drinking in a public house near the Loyalist Shankill Road. The result was that Peter Ward, a young Catholic from the Falls Road, was cruelly murdered. Shortly after this, Gusty Spence and others were charged with the murder although Gusty always denied the killing. In the absence of convincing evidence he was released but rearrested and convicted, with others, of conspiracy to murder. He went to prison with a strong sense of grievance about the injustice of the situation but found some consolation in seeing his punishment as a form of poetic justice. He had never denied being in the UVF but resented that the episode had come about at the instigation of Unionists who were seeking to expose O'Neill's weakness through violent incidents.

During RUC questioning it became clear to Gusty that they saw him as part of a conspiracy that also involved politicians right up to cabinet level at Stormont. Once incarcerated in Crumlin Road Prison, he began a serious re-think of the historical circumstances that led to his imprisonment. He became an avid reader of Irish history and came to the view that the real starting point of the conflict was the plantation of Ulster in the early seventeenth century. His commitment to reading was confirmed by other prisoners and by a prison officer who said Gusty was often seen deeply engrossed in books. He was hungry for knowledge and read voraciously on a variety of topics.

While in Crumlin Road Prison he led a campaign for better conditions and for a time went on hunger strike. When moved to Long Kesh Prison he was faced with even more uncongenial conditions in dilapidated Nissen huts. He became commanding officer of both UVF and UDA prisoners and immediately set about improving things. He created a strict military regime to keep up prisoners' morale and throughout his time in prison was involved in other significant developments. He made contact with leading republicans, which set the scene for future negotiations and inspired others with new possibilities. The prospect of talking with republicans seemed unthinkable at that time yet he also formed a friendship with the future Cardinal Tomás Ó Fiaich. This became public after they exchanged Christmas cards. It also became public that Gusty Spence had sent a letter of condolence to the widow of Joe McCann, an unarmed republican from the Markets area of Belfast, shot dead in central Belfast by British soldiers.[9]

The discussions that Gusty Spence helped to initiate in prison were so effective that some people began to refer to the prison as Long Kesh University. Gusty encouraged Loyalist prisoners to follow the same path of learning and questioning that he had taken himself. He was so successful that a number of these prisoners gained degrees and doctorates while in prison or shortly after their release. These were young men from the back streets of Belfast and other places who had often been rejected by the selective educational system.

Gusty encouraged his fellow Loyalists to think for themselves and question taken-for-granted assumptions promoted by demagogues or handed on from the past. He would ask each prisoner as they arrived 'Why are you here?' Their response usually began with an outline of the specific circumstances that led to their conviction. But Gusty insisted they go further to consider the wider factors including historical circumstances. In this way he tried to stimulate critical thinking among the men. In the end there were seminars on prison issues but also on social, educational, political and other matters. Progressive documents were forwarded to the UVF beyond Long Kesh, which were sometimes rejected even though similar 'new thinking' had begun among UVF men in the community.

Gusty's views changed radically during his long years in prison. He rejected sectarianism and the lack of vision among Unionist politicians yet remained Unionist at heart. He could see that O'Neill's reforms had been necessary but inconsequential as they should never have aroused the kind of fears that followed. He knew that some Unionists politicians had hyped up fears over what amounted to little or nothing. He accepted that local government elections should not be based on property qualifications, which in any case had affected Protestants and Catholics alike.

To have introduced universal franchise in local elections would have been common sense, but many Unionists saw the demands as a ruse to undermine the Northern Irish state. Gusty also rejected discrimination and wanted all legitimate nationalist grievances removed. He was not

9. Joe McCann died on 15 April 1972.

blind to the fact that some republicans wanted more than the removal of wrongs and were prepared to force Unionists into an all-Ireland state. This had the effect of strengthening the spirit of resistance and intransigence among Unionists.

During much of this time he was a voice crying in the wilderness. He and some friends who supported him were being demonized as communists especially when they began to reach out to the more progressive republicans. In 1974, with his encouragement, the UVF leadership beyond the prisons went further by meeting with senior figures in both wings of the IRA. These meetings took place in the Irish Republic. Martin McGuinness was present at some and was astonished to see UVF men placing themselves in the care of the Provisional IRA leadership. They were ordinary working-class people 'like ourselves' who showed amazing courage by meeting the Provisional IRA in a remote part of the Irish Republic. Loyalists did not flinch at IRA men standing guard with machine guns. Some limited progress was actually made in the discussions on reducing violence.

However, when the UVF leaders returned to Belfast the 'super-Prods' in their midst 'wouldn't wear it' so in the short run the whole experiment was abandoned. Some Unionists, hard-line Loyalists and members of British Intelligence continued to demonize Spence and leading progressive UVF men as communists. But senior Loyalists were critical of Unionist politicians and wanted a better society for everyone. Elements in MI5 also sought a military victory over the IRA and could not accept the idea of a negotiated way forward. They feared that progressive Loyalists were aligning themselves with one or other wing of the IRA. In this they were wrong because these leading Loyalists were intelligent, committed Unionists, even if they were highly critical of the Unionist parties.

Gusty Spence valued the prospect of a new relationship between the people of Northern Ireland and between them and the people of the Irish Republic. Leading UVF men wanted genuine change and a better life for all. Many had experienced similar and in some cases greater deprivation and disadvantage than nationalists. But progressive Loyalists were vulnerable to charges of sell-out and leftist politics from those Unionists who had done nothing to encourage the 'new thinking'. They preferred to damn Loyalists who never got the credit for the risks they took and the courage they had shown. Given the vulnerability of progressive Loyalists to charges of betrayal, they urgently needed support from whatever quarter it could be mustered. This was the context in which Trevor West could play a positive role. He began by contacting a relative of Gusty Spence who obtained for him a family ticket, which meant that Trevor was able to visit Long Kesh in 1977. He travelled with Ulick O'Connor, who was keen to meet Gusty after reading his 'beautiful letter' to the widow of Joe McCann. Trevor explained what happened when they arrived at Long Kesh:

> On entry we were taken by bus to various compounds and at each stop had to stick our arms out horizontally, as in an airport departure lounge, to facilitate the search. On the third such occasion we faced an immaculately attired individual who, I thought must be the prison governor only to hear the reassuring words, 'At ease men. I'm Gusty Spence.'[10]

Gusty Spence's 'immaculate attire' was testament to his efforts to instill military discipline and good order among the men while also tidying up conditions in the prisons. His objective was to raise morale among the men. Martin Meehan, a well-known republican prisoner incarcerated in an adjacent hut, admitted that they too were following a similar military regime. But Meehan objected to republicans following British military discipline even though some republicans had been in the British army.

When Gusty Spence met Trevor West he was greatly impressed, not because he was an Irish senator but because

> I found him absolutely open-minded. I found him warm, aye, indeed affectionate. He was extremely quick on the uptake. When I was making points, which would be obscure to many people, Trevor was on them like a terrier. He certainly encouraged me to keep on hammering away. It was a good, uplifting experience.[11]

Trevor and Ulick were 'flabbergasted to meet such an organized, humorous, optimistic, articulate and well-informed individual, whose enthusiasm for Irish history seemed to know no bounds.'[12] Spence wanted to know what Southern Irish people thought about Northern Ireland and was convinced that Unionists needed to get a glimpse into the lives of ordinary people in the Republic: 'I remember saying to Trevor, "Do you want to have a positive influence?"' He suggested that people in the North needed an insight into the lives of ordinary people in the Republic:

> The people of Northern Ireland don't know you; they don't know you at all; they don't know what makes you tick, they don't know your social habits except the stage Irishman thing. If I were the Irish government, I would get two big boosters, put them right

145

The Bold Collegian

10. Undated speech, delivered late 1990s.

11. Interview with Gusty Spence, 18 April 2000.

12. Transcript from Trevor West's notes, 14 April 1999.

on the border and beam RTÉ into homes in Northern Ireland.[13] Gusty Spence lived to see his idea come to fruition, thanks at least in part to Trevor West. Today RTÉ is widely available throughout Northern Ireland but at that time this was a radical suggestion to come from any Unionist. Most Unionists probably saw the Irish Republic as an alien, aggressive neighbour prepared to resort to violent or perhaps more subtle means to take over the north. The words of Unionists who hyped up these fears were unwittingly backed by the violent activities of the IRA. These things helped to foster fearful perceptions. Some Unionists wanted no contact whatever with the Irish Republic, which claimed jurisdiction over the whole island. But Northern Ireland was for many Unionists the very basis of their security while the IRA was widely regarded as a servant of the Irish state. Gusty saw things differently. He told Trevor that the Unionist sense of Britishness had to be accommodated rather than see the last vestiges of British heritage in Ireland being removed.

The Sunningdale Agreement of 1973 was undermined largely because of the insistence on the Council of Ireland, which was interpreted by many Unionists as an embryonic united Ireland. Yet Sunningdale had come at a time when leading progressive Loyalists had begun to reach out a hand of friendship to their nationalist neighbours. Some UVF men were therefore ambivalent about the Ulster Workers' Strike in 1974 because they had been preparing the ground for negotiating a new dispensation of peace and harmony.

Trevor West realized that Gusty Spence had been a constructive force within the prison and that his work could continue in the wider community if he were released. He had spent almost nineteen years – from 1966 to 1984 – in jail. Some suspected he had been kept in prison precisely because he was such a force. Trevor West recognized the injustice in this and played a crucial role in Gusty Spence's eventual release in December 1984. Trevor had contacted the politician Paddy Devlin, who previously helped get improvements for prisoners inside Crumlin Road Prison, and made Paddy aware of the injustice of incarcerating Gusty Spence beyond accepted limits. A short time later Gusty introduced me to Paddy Devlin who explained what happened when Trevor phoned him:

> Trevor West asked did I know anything about Gusty Spence? I said, 'No, I'm not in contact with him.' Trevor explained, 'He's been in there nineteen years. A life sentence is supposed to be sixteen years yet he's still there.' I said, 'Well I'll contact Jim Prior and the both of us will go and see him.' I contacted the secretary

of state, who arranged the meeting. Both of us made the case
to the secretary that Gusty had been in for about nineteen years
instead of sixteen.[14]

Secretary of State James Prior was surprised to be told this, but he agreed
to check it out and promised that if what they were saying was found to
be true, 'I'll let him out.' Trevor paid another visit to Gusty in the Maze
before he later contacted Lord Gowrie, minister responsible for prisons
in NI. After a chat with Gowrie and his assistant, both of whom had family connections with Horace Plunkett, whose biography Trevor had written, Trevor recalled his argument that the prison authorities had been
well aware of the constructive role Gusty played inside and *ipso facto*, what
a force he would be for sanity if released. 'I then put John O'Connell – a
colleague of mine in Leinster House – in touch with Gusty and he was
equally impressed.'[15]

Gusty Spence was eventually given temporary parole and then permanently released before the end of 1984. The very morning of Gusty's
release he went to Paddy Devlin's home where Paddy and his wife Theresa
welcomed him with tea and toast. He thanked them profusely for their
kindness. Sometime later I was privileged to accompany Gusty to meet
Paddy and Theresa at their home and I will never forget their hospitality.
On another occasion Paddy Devlin told me that he realized how close he
was to Gusty Spence's political thinking. They both wanted a new society
in which the underdogs got a fair go. In fact Paddy went further, saying
of Gusty Spence: 'I had more in common with him than I had with anybody else. The only other one that would have fitted into that triangle
would have been Sam McAughtry. The three of us used to have discussions … I reckon that that would have done an enormous amount of
good if it had come out.'[16]

Paddy Devlin had gone through a similar experience in having been
in the IRA and in prison. Like Gusty, he seriously re-thought many things
and developed a new vision for a better future. Both men worked tirelessly, especially for the marginalized working classes in both traditions.
Gusty was able to play a central role in the moves that followed towards
peace. I can never forget my time in Stormont Buildings on the day of
the Good Friday Agreement. Thanks to Gary McMichael of the UDP, who
Trevor West had also met, Billy Mitchell of the PUP and Ann Carr of the
Women's Coalition, I was free to wander round the corridors of the building where I met many of the negotiators from all sides. I sat with Gusty

13. Spence, *op. cit.*
18 April 2000.

14. Interview with Paddy
Devlin, 24 March 1999.

15. Transcript from Trevor
West's notes, 14 April 1999.

16. Paddy Devlin *op. cit.*,
24 March 1999.

Spence in the bar while he smoked his pipe. There was even talk about the colour of the smoke and what this might mean in terms of reaching agreement.

Trevor West continued to contribute to mutual understanding between the main traditions in Ireland and between the two islands. His knowledge of Gusty Spence's role must have given him encouragement. During 1980 in an article in the *Sunday Times* he referred to the close relationship between England and Ireland. Trevor said there was surely no pair of comparable sovereign states, after an entanglement of over a thousand years

> who still dispute a considerable proportion of territory; which have endured 2000 deaths, the burning of an embassy; the assassination of an ambassador, a shadow cabinet minister, and a member of a royal family in a decade of violence, and which have, in spite of all, maintained friendly relations at every level.[17]

Trevor referred to the special relationship in which 'each nation has a definite stake in the prosperity of the other'. Their differing electoral systems had proved remarkably stable and he referred to England's cultural influence in Ireland as 'so immense as to seem at certain points, to be all-pervading'. Ulster was the main obstacle to Anglo-Irish harmony, which could not be regarded as just an internal problem by either side. No solution could be worked out by either government acting alone. He insisted that just because Sunningdale had collapsed did not mean that 'the spirit in which that conference took place was not the right one.'[18]

Lord Donoughue of Ashton, senior advisor to prime ministers Harold Wilson and James Callaghan during 1974–1979, wrote positively about Trevor West's view that 'better relations between Westminster and Dublin [were] a necessary precondition for peace in Northern Ireland'. As one contribution towards this goal they organized a soccer match between the two parliaments. Bernard Donoughue wrote about working with Trevor during the IRA hunger strike:

> Trevor acted as a mediator with me when I was in Number 10 in 1978 trying to solve the IRA hunger strike at Long Kesh Prison and, with the help of the Irish trade unions, made progress. But the inflexible Home Office blocked any settlement, repeating to me the tired mantra that 'we never negotiate with terrorists'. Of course we later did after many more deaths.[19]

Subsequently I spent many hours at Gusty's home enjoying his chat and the good company of him and his wife Louie. Gusty Spence's voice remained a vital element in encouraging moves towards peace on all sides. Senior Loyalists like David Ervine, Billy Mitchell, Jim McDonald and others had begun developing their politics at the feet of Gusty Spence. They went out from Long Kesh as missionaries to all and sundry inspired by a new message: peace was possible. Gusty gave much-needed encouragement to many people who were seeking to overcome the difficulties to a better future. Trevor West had helped liberate him from Long Kesh so he could continue this work. Since those days Northern Ireland has changed radically; even if many problems continue to haunt us, things can never be the same.

I cannot forget Trevor's kindness to me personally. I was involved in research into my family history in Louth and Monaghan when Trevor welcomed me to TCD where I was free to use his study and other facilities over a number of days. I continued to enjoy meeting him occasionally at his beloved Linenhall Library in Belfast and on at least one occasion at the home of Gusty Spence. He was always generous, kind, compassionate and a never-failing source of encouragement and hope.

Trevor West placed a copy of my QUB dissertation *The Ulster Volunteer Force Negotiating History* (1991) at TCD library. He, more than anyone else, strongly encouraged me to write a seminal work on Gusty Spence.[20] I deeply appreciated his encouragement. Without him, Gusty Spence's life story might have remained a largely closed book. In the wake of his passing on the 30 October 2012, senators paid heartfelt tributes to Trevor West on 6 December 2013, expressing their appreciation for his contribution to relationships throughout this island in so many ways. Some senators specifically referred to his work towards the release of Gusty Spence. Much remains to be done but Gusty Spence's contribution to peace in Ireland has been enormous – thanks mainly to Dr Trevor West.

The Bold Collegian

17. *The Sunday Times*, 5 October 1980.

18 *IBID.*

19. *The Times*, 13 January 2013.

20. Garland, Roy, *Gusty Spence* (Belfast 2001).

Brendan Kennelly, Hugo MacNeill, Trevor West and Tony Hanahoe in Front Square, TCD, 1991.

The Ideal of a University

There is always a temptation when writing about an individual to overstate their qualities and their good points, especially when asked to contribute to a collection such as this. Trevor no doubt had his shortcomings like the rest of us. However, I can genuinely say that no one I met ever embodied the concept of the university in all its richness, oddities, diversities and splendour than TT.

I have to admit that I loved university life. Well, I did spend enough time there: four years at Trinity, three at Oxford and one at UCD. What understanding parents I had – and a tolerant and patient bank manager. Would I have liked to play rugby in the professional era? I am afraid not, although I would have loved to train like a professional athlete and play for Leinster in the European Cup. However, that was more than outweighed by having two lives: one of international rugby and the other of work and study. I would have found it impossible to have given up university life and the friends made there.

That's where Trevor comes in. In some ways this is quite an easy contribution to write. Trevor was a person of genuine substance and a very good friend. On the other hand it is not so straightforward. One does not want to write a hagiography or a mere gathering of special moments that are of little relevance or even interest to a broader audience. This is also situated in a collection of pieces, most of which are written by other friends. With the best will in the world, someone coming from outside the 'circle' may find their attention wandering. Therefore the modest intention is to focus not only on the character of Trevor himself but also to illustrate that many of the things that fired his enthusiasms have been and hopefully continue to be of direct and continuing relevance to a wider community.

What marked him out for me in the first instance was that he existed so comfortably at the confluence of so many strands of Irish life: Trinity professor, senator, author writing about Horace Plunkett and the co-operative movement, quiet worker for peace in Northern Ireland through his work with Gusty Spence and Loyalist paramilitaries, historian of Midleton College, organizer of soccer matches in prisons, distinguished scholar, passionate promoter of student sport across the island … and so on and so on.

Trevor really did embody a very strong sense of what a university education was supposed to be about. Developing the ability to think independently and not cram for exams. Easy to say, not so easy to do. He brought Brendan Kennelly (Professor of Anglo-Irish Literature) to talk about poetry to his engineering class. He was very generous about the academic achievements of many of his peers in other fields, a trait not always widely to be seen in academic life. As Yeats highlighted in his poem 'The Scholars', where he observes a divergence between the spirit of the work and the way academics behave: 'Lord what would they say? Should their Catullus walk that way?'

I have told the story in other places (including in the history of Trinity rugby) about his late-night 400-metre race with Brendan: half past two in the morning; the College athletic track; dim light from the Kilkenny Design Centre; the professor of mathematics, senator in Dáil Éireann and chairman of DUCAC *versus* the poet and professor of Anglo-Irish literature. Trevor's early lead reined back by the former Kerry minor footballer who took a lead into the bend at the Pavilion Bar. The last desperate throw of the dice – the mathematician cutting across the infield bisecting the final bends. Crashing into the cricket nets while the poet came triumphantly down the home straight, arms aloft in victory. No, this is not a fabrication. It did actually happen. I accept I was the only witness. Typical Trevor. Typical Brendan. He spoke proudly about his victory over the 'Professor of Sums' as he called him. Do our universities still produce such rounded characters?

Does this concept of roundedness matter for students? I think it does. Firstly it is of value in its own right. However, it has other implications. It was brought home to me a couple of years ago during the recruiting season with a multinational organization. Students from all over these islands applied for jobs. I had been involved in recruiting for a long time in two such large organizations, which attracted many of the strongest candidates. It had always been a matter of pride for all us Irish in these companies that the Irish graduates had held their own with those of any other university and were better than most. However, a few years ago the relative strength of the Irish candidates began to decline. This could be because the best graduates were seeking alternative careers, but there was a very clear pattern and a large disconnect between the CVs submitted and the individuals sitting on the other side of the table. Stellar Leaving Cert and college grades on the one hand; pre-packaged answers and little orignality of thought or expression on the other. The first few times I thought this was an abberation, but the many more that followed made me less sure.

One of the many great things about the Trinity Foundation Scholarship is that every ten years you get invited back for the Scholars' Dinner (when the new fellows and scholars are elected). My most recent event was 2009. As always there was a wonderful atmosphere in the Dining Hall where the excitement of the newly elected mingled with the renewing of old contacts by those on their ten-yearly trip. There were two newly elected scholars to my right and they were clearly and justifiably delighted with their election. But what was somewhat disappointing (if one has the right to be disappointed whilst eavesdropping) is that a significant part of their chat was how they had carefully and analytically structured their exam technique to get the marks and grades they required. There was hardly a reference to any interest, passion or excitement about the subject they were studying or what lay ahead of them in that regard. Maybe that is an unfair comment. Most people have to think about exam technique to some extent or another, but maybe it is not. The element of balance appeared to be lost. With technology continuing to replace most process functions the requirement for independent thought, originality and judgement will only become more important.

The Trinity connection with Oxford and Cambridge is particularly rich in the sporting arena. Trevor played a very important role in building, nurturing and sustaining these relationships. I remember him being the single Trinity representative on the touchline at Grange Road in Cambridge or Iffley Road in Oxford. Many of us were to go on to study at these universities and to compete in various shades of blue. Trevor was always on hand with practical advice and very useful and relevant introductions. When I talked of going to Oxford he absolutely demanded I meet his great friend John Kelly (editor of Yeats's letters and professor at St John's College) and his wonderful wife Christine (a formidable academic in her own right). We have been friends ever since. Building 'networks' came naturally to Trevor; his reward was not a material one but rather the pleasure and satisfaction of making genuine friends and bringing them together.

Trinity's historical connection with Northern Ireland has weakened in recent times. This is due to a number of factors including the fact that the UK's UCAS system has a scoring model that makes it very hard to achieve high marks in the CAO points system in the Republic. This is a real pity as there is relatively little understanding of Northern Ireland in the South and correspondingly little interest. Bringing people together in a university setting is one of the most powerful ways of promoting genuine understanding and actually making real friends. Seamus Heaney used to recount the story of a young English journalist being assigned to Belfast during the period of the troubles. One night while having a drink with a group of older colleagues he shook his head and admitted that he was really confused with the situation. 'That's absolutely fine,' replied one of his older brethren approvingly, 'if you're not genuinely confused by the situation, you don't understand it at all!'

Trevor really got the North. He loved difference and his great curiosity and passion led him to spend the time there and develop a genuine understanding and deep friendships. He did this in a very careful and thoughtful way. His stature as a leading Southern Protestant who held positions of considerable influence in the Republic gave him a credibility and a trust that he used with many leaders of Northern Loyalism, and to very good effect. Here again his sensitivity and the absence of a personal agenda enabled him to make real impact in a careful and understated way. It is positive that Trinity has been looking at ways in which to make it more possible for students from Northern Ireland to come to College. Trevor would have approved.

He had an important role in setting out the history of Trinity sport and *The Bold Collegians* gave him real satisfaction. Perhaps at times a little formal in tone, with every character given their full range of initials in advance of their surname, it is a great story of sport in an institution that has spanned centuries. I had the privilege of chairing a group reporting to the governments in Dublin and Belfast, which recommended we bid to host the Rugby World Cup in 2023. In the section on 'Why Ireland–the Legacy?' it was set out that Trinity College in the heart of Dublin was the oldest continuously playing rugby club in the world and the tradition is carried on strongly in College Park to this day. Mike Halliday's contribution to this volume highlights Trevor's belief that sport can be a complimentary companion of the academic life.

Trevor was a very kind person who was always looking to help, whether it was finding a few bob for a student running short or looking after new visitors to a College sporting match. We always remember especially when people show acts of kindness to our parents. He made a particular impression on mine and became a good friend of our family. He invited my brother Eoin – whom he puzzlingly called E.P. MacNeill, although his second name is Dermot – to join his soccer team, which contained a very interesting cast of characters. 'The beautiful game' it was not and it's lucky for Ulick O'Connor that there were no TMO officials or Hawkeye to see some of his 'tackles'.

His natural instinct was to praise and to celebrate (especially the achievements of student sportsmen and women), standing by the bar in the Pav, chairman's mug in hand, eyes closed, recounting someone's achievement. He could of course talk as much nonsense as any alickadoo in any bar over a prolonged period of time, and he frequently did. But there was never any malice. He loved the banter and the slagging as much as anyone, but there was never any edge that would demean or hurt. He had a lot to say without needing to stray beyond the crease. He had enormous generosity of spirit. Seeing people doing well gave him real satisfaction. He never had to be the centre of a gathering although he did lead organizations with authority when assuming positions of responsibility.

Despite his genial and avuncular manner he could be tough and decisive when required. It became part of Trinity folklore that when it was proposed that the rugby pitch should be built on, Trevor marshalled such an army of distinguished past students (many of whom were men of the cloth and the legal gown, thus ensuring God and Caesar were well covered) that the idea disappeared without trace.

Rugby in College Park.

Universities can be lonely places even for people who live on campus. Many academics remain single. Spending most of his life as a bachelor, Trevor was reasonably set in his ways and could disappear from a scene more discreetly than Eliot's Macavity the Mystery Cat. It was fitting – or what Kennelly might have described as the 'inspiration of accident' – that an RTÉ documentary on Trinity sport should have brought him and Maura Lee together. It was a perfect match. While his friends could enjoy the transformation of his dress sense there was a genuine and universal delight that Trevor had found someone to share his rich and varied life.

In recent times, after the financial crash, there has been much talk of the role of the citizen. Trinity itself has held a series of gatherings to examine the concept of citizenship and the life well lived. Trevor instinctively understood and lived this out. A focus on a rounded education, using sport to make an impact on the wider university and civic life

155 The Bold Collegian

(through equality of access and fairness), building an inclusive and tolerant society, the importance and rewards of real engagement with the North and also with the wider British relationship: these are and remain issues of direct and current relevance. These are matters with which Trevor engaged all his life, making an impact on us all.

DUBLIN UNIVERSITY A.F.C. 1978–79
(Irish Universities League and Cup Double Winners)
Back Row: *Dr. S. Barrett (President), H. McNeill, P. Carroll, S. Ó Nunáin, J. McDonagh, P. Jennings, A. Donohoe, E. Daly, L. Tuohy (Coach).*
Front Row: *D. O'Brien, G. Humphrey, K. le Gros, B. McSharry, J. Carpendale.*

Collingwood Cup Team AFC 1978–79.

Trevor and the Chairman's Tankard.

Westminster Wanderers, back row PC Jefferies who was kit man and coach, Ted Weldin (Commons staff), Viscount Craigavon, Bernard Donoughue, Bruce George MP, Kenneth Clarke MP, Robert Bradford MP. *Front row*: Peter Bradford, David Natzler, Bryan Davies MP (now Lord Davies of Oldham), Peter Bottomley MP (now Sir Peter), Geoffrey Pattie MP (now Sir Geoffrey), Colin Brown. 10 June 1978. *(Methodist Minister Robert Bradford represented South Belfast as a Unionist. He was assassinated by the IRA in 1981.)*

The Irish Parliamentary soccer team, which played against Westminster Wanderers in London on 10 June 1978. The match was organized by Senator Trevor West and his friend Bernard Donoughue, (now Lord Donoughue of Ashton). Representatives of the Dáil were beaten by their British counterparts 4–1. *Back row*: Liam Aylward T.D., Lorcan Allen T.D., Liam Lawlor T.D. Senator Michael Lanigan, Senator Michael Kitt, Barry Cogan T.D., Michael Smith T.D. *Front row*: Sean Calleary T.D., Mick Lipper T.D., John Donellan T.D., Senator Trevor West (Captain), Enda Kenny T.D., Bertie Ahern T.D.

Trevor West, Carol Graham, Maura Lee West and Terry McCauley, Director of Sport at TCD, at the unveiling of Carol Graham's portrait of Trevor.

Challenging Times

I first met Trevor in the 1970s in Swarthmore College, Pennsylvania, where I was then a professor of classics. His friend Lester Connors, a professor of English at nearby Chestnut Hill College, had brought him to meet me. I would later see the two of them on a regular basis after I joined the School of Classics at Trinity in 1979. Lester was a frequent visitor to Dublin and Trinity, drawn there by his love of Irish literature and by his friendship with Trevor. They seemed to me to be two of a kind – personable, sociable, liberally educated, broadly interested in things of the mind, and fully committed to the academic life.

I came to know Trevor over the years as a congenial colleague, a dedicated teacher who cared deeply about the welfare of students, a diligent researcher who left his mark on several areas of mathematics, and a full-time participant in all facets of life of the College. He was a doer, an activist in the best sense, eager to engage, and his commitment to the welfare of his students was unstinting.

During my term as provost I often called on Trevor's advice and his astute sense of the College's mood, and he was particularly helpful to me in dealing with one of the most serious challenges that I faced in the course of my provostship. In July 1995 the Minister of Education, Niamh Breathnach, brought forward proposals regarding the governance of universities, which, in Trinity's case, would have dismembered its charter. It would have deprived the College of its status as an independent, self-governing university by creating a board with an external chairman and mostly composed of ministerial appointees. The board rejected the proposals in their entirety. There followed months of negotiations with the Department of Education. The talks were courteous and constructive, and eventually agreement was reached that there would be only two external representatives on the board and only one would be a ministerial nominee. But both would have to be acceptable to and formally appointed by the board. It was also agreed that all who attended the board would have full voting rights.

I felt these proposals were acceptable. They preserved the College's autonomy and the integrity of its charter, and enabled what I considered a necessary change to the composition of the board to make it more representative of the College community and give it the benefit of some external input from members in whom the board had confidence.

But there was disquiet, especially among some of the fellows, about accepting any change to the board, and also about reducing the role of the fellows by giving all who were appointed to attend the board full voting rights. I was anxious to allay any worries and maintain the greatest possible consensus and Trevor helped me in this. He saw the merit of the proposals concerning the board, but he appreciated the sincerity of those who had concerns. He was a good intermediary, and undoubtedly helped avoid any major division on this issue within College.

When I presented the proposals to the board they were fully approved and despite some temporary setbacks we were subsequently able to make the necessary changes to the charter by means of a private bill, written and sponsored by the College in accordance with the provisions of the College's charter. The Universities Bill became law in June 1997. I should add that, alongside people like Trevor, the registrar of the day, David McConnell, and the three Trinity senators, Mary Henry, David Norris and Shane Ross, significantly contributed to the result. It was an important outcome. It not only preserved Trinity's autonomy as a self-governing institution under its charter, but it reaffirmed the principle that changes to the charter could only be made on the College's initiative and through the mechanism of a private bill.

I had the pleasure of working with Trevor on one other major project during my term as provost, a new indoor sports centre. The traditional Trinity educational ideal embraced the view that a rich extracurricular life was an important adjunct to the academic regime in extending the student experience and strengthening social and leadership skills. Sport featured strongly in the College's array of extracurricular activities, and it was Trevor's particular passion. He was himself an active and versatile sportsman, and he was at the centre of the College's sporting life for decades. By the 1990s, when student numbers were rising rapidly, the sporting facilities of the College were inadequate, outdated and no longer fit for purpose. The proposed indoor sports centre was an urgent priority. Trevor devoted himself to achieving it, not least by assisting, with Ken Ryan of KPMG, in the production of a report entitled *Sport in Trinity – A Strategic Plan for the Next Decade*, which had been commissioned by the university in 1996. It was prepared and presented by KPMG in association with the Trinity Foundation.

The project was ambitious and expensive and, as usual, the big challenge was finding the money. Students voted to accept a new sports capital levy, but it was clear that a big donor would be required to make the project viable. I was more than happy to help with the fundraising effort as I fully supported the view that a vibrant extracurricular life was a necessary element in Trinity's drive for academic excellence, and I also believed that sport should be an integral part of the extracurricular activities available.

I turned once more to Chuck Feeney, whom I had met during my first week as provost, and who proved to be my strongest supporter and the College's largest donor during the entire period of my provostship. Without him the College's large-scale building programme and extensive acquisition of neighbouring properties in the 1990s would not have happened. Chuck – one of the world's richest men – used his foundation, The Atlantic Philanthropies, to distribute his wealth to best advantage to make the world a better place. He was a strong believer in education as the most effective way of improving the lives of people, and Trinity was a major beneficiary in the 1990s, as were some other Irish universities. As he was also a believer in sport as an effective educative force that should be an important part of the life of young people Chuck showed immediate interest when I mentioned the sports centre to him. When the foundation approved – on his recommendation – a grant of $10.5m (almost €9m) the project became feasible. It would take many years to complete, but Trevor's tireless efforts to make it a reality finally bore fruit, and the building was opened in 2009, a boon to students and staff. It stands as an impressive monument to Trevor's vision and tenacity, but it represents just one of the many ways in which he served his alma mater well. He will be remembered as a distinguished and deeply loyal graduate, who exemplified all that was best in the Trinity liberal educational ideal.

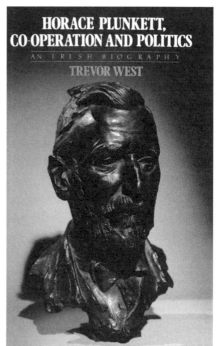

Portrait of Sir Horace Plunkett by Sir John
Lavery. (Dublin City Gallery, The Hugh Lane
Gallery)

Cover of Trevor West's jacket biography
of Horace Plunkett.

Trevor West and Horace Plunkett

Trevor West's involvement with the co-operative movement arose out of his deep interest in Horace Plunkett. It appears that this interest was sparked when Trevor read Plunkett's book, *Ireland in the New Century*. Although the founder of the co-operative movement in Ireland, which inspired similar movements in other parts of the British Empire, Horace Plunkett's name may not be as well known as those of the many who died in the cause of Irish freedom. Nor is he as well known as many of his contemporaries in the Irish literary revival. However, Plunkett's contribution to the host of challenges that faced Ireland in the early years of the twentieth century is immense and deserves greater recognition.

His contribution spanned the formation, almost single-handedly, of our co-operative dairies, and addressed the immense complexity of the political questions of the time. Plunkett aimed to create an economic regeneration in Ireland, using education, technical skill, self-help and a commercial ethos. He overcame many challenges and continues to inspire those who take the time to learn from what he did and what he aspired to do.

The original biography of Plunkett was written by Margaret Digby in 1949, but as Trevor's interest in Plunkett developed he completed a further biography in 1986, entitled *Horace Plunkett: Co-Operation and Politics*. For over thirty years Trevor was regarded by the co-operative movement as the expert on Plunkett, and his insight, understanding and recollection of detail was very much appreciated, as was his ability to communicate his infectious enthusiasm for the subject.

However, there was much more to Plunkett than co-operatives and politics. For eight years he was Unionist MP for South Dublin, despite being leader of a strongly non-sectarian and non-political movement. He was chairman of the Irish Convention in 1917, which was formed to address the Home Rule question. He had also been vice-president of the Department of Agriculture and Technical Instruction, forerunner of the Department of Agriculture and Education, and was influential in political and business circles in Ireland, Britain and in the US.

Published in 1904, *Ireland in the New Century* was intended to be a blueprint for the economic development of Ireland. Its essential theme was summed up by Plunkett himself: 'Whenever I set out on a mental excursion into Irish political, sociological or economic questions, no matter where I start I always come back to education as the condition precedent of all progress in Ireland.' (*DATI Journal* 1901/2) This approach fascinated Trevor, who was intrigued by Plunkett's drive, commitment and energy. He must also have identified with Plunkett, who had much in common with him in terms of background, education and a family tradition of service. When Plunkett's book was reprinted in 1983 Trevor wrote the foreword, noting:

> Plunkett aimed to change the current state of Irish opinion from its obsession with politics to a consideration of the ways in which his countrymen could work together in a revitalised Ireland. His great achievement had been to persuade Protestant and Catholic, unionist and nationalist to combine for their country's good; thus his view of Irish history, his discussions on the state of Ireland in his own day and his optimistic view of the possibilities for Ireland's future have an enduring interest and importance.

Ireland in the New Century is divided into two sections. In the first part Plunkett sets out his views on Ireland and its institutions, Anglo-Irish history and politics, Irishmen and the character of the nation. He critically surveys the agencies that moulded the Irish character, the political parties, the Catholic Church, the educational system and the Gaelic revival. In the second part he sets out a detailed description of the work, past, present and future of the co-operative movement and of the Department of Agriculture and Technical Instruction.

It is easy to understand Trevor's fascination with Plunkett's analysis and the views expressed. He must also have identified with the opportunity to generate economic development through rural regeneration by farmers working together through their co-operatives. At the time that Trevor read this book, he had been in the Senate for a number of years, and would have experienced the rapid development of agriculture following Ireland's accession to the EEC in 1973.

Plunkett's co-operative movement initially struggled in the face of scepticism from the peasant farmers he was trying to help, as well as from the private merchants who had been exploiting these same farmers. The eventual success of Plunkett's co-operative strategy can be seen today in many of Ireland's successful co-operatives and companies, which are our major food exporters.

An outline of Plunkett's background and achievements may give some insight into Trevor's interest in this exceptional individual. Horace Plunkett was from a leading Anglo-Irish family, the Dunsanys, who have been major landowners for many generations and remain so to this day. The Plunketts were heirs to three peerages of Louth, Fingall and Dunsany. He was educated at Eton and Oxford at a time when there were many social reforms, such as the legalization of trade unions, the secret ballot, the Education Act and the first Land Act. Many in Oxford at the time were major advocates of these reforms, and this may have stirred the social conscience of some of their students.

Plunkett acknowledged that during this time he took on a strange, somewhat vague idealism. In his reflections there are hints about the socially destructive effects of the Industrial Revolution, the anticipation that industrialization would spread to agriculture, and that rural change could be beneficial if it occurred in the right way, and that he would try to bring about this change in Ireland. After completing his education he returned to Ireland, where he looked after his father's estate. At the time tuberculosis was endemic and had claimed the lives of his mother when he was four years old, and later his brother and sister. Horace and his other brother were also threatened with TB and were advised to move from the lowlands of Meath to a drier and more bracing climate.

His brother went to southern Africa, but died from the disease on his return journey. Horace headed for the western United States, probably influenced by friends who had been there before, as much as by the possibilities of making fortunes from cattle and gold. He spent about half of each year in the decade from 1879 to 1889 in the USA. During his time there he was astute in business, worked hard and was involved in cattle-ranching, real estate and transportation ventures. He returned to Ireland permanently in 1889, the year his father died.

Trevor travelled to Wyoming on a number of occasions to learn more about Plunkett's experiences in the frontier cattle country in the 1880s. During these visits Trevor became friends with Larry Woods, who subsequently wrote a book in 2010 titled *Horace Plunkett in America – An Irish Aristocrat on the Wyoming Range*. In his introduction, Woods referred to Trevor's own book:

> [He] wrote a carefully researched study of Plunkett, filling in many of the answers to questions raised by Digby. Yet my good

friend Trevor was puzzled by some aspects of the western part of Plunkett's story, and there are sources in the United States that illuminate some of those aspects. Hence, this effort.

Plunkett observed the scope of the agricultural potential from the USA, particularly beef and grains, and the impact that this might have on Europe and his own Ireland. This threat was greater in light of recent innovations in refrigeration and developments in transportation using rail and steam shipping. Ireland was not prepared for this competition because of low agricultural efficiency, tiny farm structures and poor product quality being put on the market. Plunkett decided that this needed to be addressed. He believed that if farmers used better farming methods, and supported this by being better organized in processing and marketing their produce, that it would lead to a better living standard for the rural population. Thus he coined the slogan 'Better Farming, Better Business, Better Living.' The 'Better Living' was his real objective, and the other parts of the slogan were the means by which to reach it.

To achieve this he realized that the farmers needed to organize. Technical innovations in Scandinavia had transformed butter-making and their butter was taking over the British market. In leading the campaign to introduce co-operation to Irish agriculture he foresaw a movement that would put aside political differences and be a movement for economic regeneration of rural life, and ultimately for regeneration of economic life on the island of Ireland.

This movement was based on a self-help philosophy, which included democracy, education and a strong business ethic. The first co-operative was formed in 1889, not by Plunkett, but with the assistance of the Co-operative Wholesale Society (CWS) from Manchester. However, Plunkett was successful in forming the second co-operative creamery in 1891 and by the end of the year there were fifteen dairy co-operatives. As the number of co-operative creameries increased, the need for an organization to promote and support the co-operatives was recognized, and this resulted in the formation of the Irish Agricultural Organization Society in 1894. Shortly afterwards in 1897 he set up the Irish Agricultural Wholesale Society, for the supply of inputs and supplies to co-operatives. The success of the co-operative movement on Ireland then spread to England, Wales, Scotland, Australia, New Zealand, South Africa, the USA and further afield.

A further major area of contribution by Plunkett was in governmental organization. When Plunkett was elected as Unionist MP for South

Dublin in 1892, he felt that it would strengthen his influence and help his economic and industrial work. In this role he was instrumental in pulling together a broad-based Recess Committee, of which he was chairman, and which produced a report in 1896. This report was adopted and had the dramatic effect of removing agricultural issues from Westminster and made the Home Rule case for the development of Irish agriculture.

A further consequence of the Recess Committee report was the creation of a new model in administration, which, for example, linked voluntary and statutory bodies in a co-operative rather than a competitive way. One of the recommendations of this report was the creation of a Department of Agriculture and Technical Instruction (DATI). This was realized in 1900 and Plunkett was its vice-president for seven years, acting as administrative head and having ministerial status by representing the department directly in Westminster. This new department was Ireland's first independent government ministry, which supervised farming and vocational education in the whole island. Its task, as Plunkett saw it according to Trevor, 'was to put the benefits of modern science at the disposal of the Irish farmer'.

It was during this time that Plunkett wrote *Ireland in the New Century*, urging Irishmen from all political and sectarian opinion to work together, in a campaign of national regeneration. It analysed the range of economic, social and political problems that affected Ireland at the turn of the century, concluding that the root of the problem was 'character'. Plunkett's criticism of the Catholics and the influence of the Catholic Church drew the fire of the Catholic Nationalist element in the political arena and the co-operative movement was damaged by implication. This frank expression of views was typical of Plunkett, but by putting this in print he drew hostile criticism from the clergy and gave ammunition to his opponents, which ultimately made his position at DATI untenable. He resigned in 1907, while the controversy caused by his book created difficulties for the co-operative movement as public funding was reduced.

Throughout his life's work Plunkett devoted a lot of effort to the Irish political situation. He was operating in an environment where views were polarizing on Home Rule. His challenge was how to hold the movement together when, for example, he and some of his associates such as R.A. Anderson were unionists, while others, such as Father Finlay and George Russell (AE), were nationalists. Since 1908 he strongly opposed partition and was concerned that the issue of Home Rule was distracting action

The Bold Collegian

from the social and economic challenges facing Ireland, challenges he believed must be faced by local self-government and co-operation, the best basis for political self-government on a national scale. His objective at this time was that the Irish question in Ireland must be settled in Ireland by Irishmen. As chair of the Irish Convention, which was trying to reform the Irish political structure, Plunkett tried to promote All-Ireland dominion home rule. However, discussions became tied up in Land Act issues, and Lloyd George, under pressure from Tories and Carson, imposed partition.

In 1903 Plunkett had purchased a property at Kilteragh, in Foxrock, south Dublin, which became a focal point for many important contacts and where he entertained the leading political and literary personalities of the time. Visitors included Roger Casement, Arthur Griffith, W.B. Yeats and Lady Gregory. Michael Collins dined there four days before he was shot. At Kilteragh Plunkett developed a model farm and demonstrated a scheme for supporting dairying with fodder crops in order to sustain autumn calving and so provide an all-year-round milk supply for an export market.

Plunkett was a regular return visitor to America where he had a major influence in Anglo-American relations and worked to encourage the US to join the First World War and support Britain. He acted as a vital link between the British and American governments.

Part of Trevor's research for his Plunkett biography included contact with the Irish Co-Operative Organization Society (ICOS), the umbrella organization that represents agricultural co-operatives in Ireland. Previously known as the Irish Agricultural Organization Society (IAOS), which Plunkett had founded in 1894, the library archive at the ICOS head office in Merrion Square, Dublin contained the annual reports, papers and correspondence of the organization from its earliest days. One of its resources was the collection of editions of *The Irish Homestead*, which was first produced in 1895. Edited by George Russell (AE), these included articles and reports written by Plunkett, and Trevor in turn wrote about Plunkett in the journal of the ICOS, *Co-op Ireland*, in 1981 and 1982. His article about Plunkett's social philosophy in the *Year Book of Agricultural Co-operation 1981* was published by the Plunkett Foundation in the UK and as a consequence he was invited to speak and write about Plunkett in different parts of the country. With the publication of his biography there was a renewed interest in Plunkett with many reviews and commentaries from interested parties. For example a letter from Charles Lysaght, the lawyer, author and journalist who had worked for the Department of Foreign Affairs and for the Law Reform Commission, was highly complimentary:

> Your work seems to me to be up to the highest standard of historical scholarship. It is remarkable for a person who has been trained in a discipline far removed from history to be able to write a history book of such a standard. You have gone through all the primary sources. Your summing up at the end is a real *tour de force*.

A review by Lieutenant General M.J. Costello, general manager of the Irish Sugar Company, included Costello's own comments on matters that Plunkett had advocated and envisaged. One of these was the opportunity to encourage a vigorous country life in America, which would balance urban development. That this opportunity was missed has resulted in 'decay of rural areas and the blight of cities overcrowded, decaying centres of unemployment and crime' according to Costello. In the context of the political and security situation in Northern Ireland at the time of the review, Costello felt that this aspect of Plunkett's views might be regarded as simplistic, but was not as simple-minded as those who pursue the opposite course.

Authorities outside Ireland also responded to Trevor's book: 'As I go forward with my work on the pioneers of the Irish co-operative movement,' writes Jim Kennelly, professor of international business and management at Skidmore College in New York State and author of *The Kerry Way: the History of the Kerry Group 1972–2000* (2001), 'Trevor West had something to do with it. There are few works on Horace Plunkett and the co-operative movement where the authors do not reference Trevor's contribution to their own research.'

During Plunkett's efforts to create agricultural co-operatives, his role in setting up the DATI and later his political role leading to the Irish Convention, he regularly entertained all of the most influential political and economic figures of the time and Lady Fingall was involved in these schemes, acting as hostess at Plunkett's dinner parties and as the interior designer for his home at Kilteragh. Daisy Fingall was the wife of Plunkett's cousin Lord Arthur Fingall, and when invited to write the foreword to the reprint in 1991 of *Seventy Years Young / Memories of Elizabeth Countess of Fingall*, Trevor remarked that the relationship between Lady Fingall and Horace Plunkett was, 'the thread which holds this book together. It lasted (probably unconsummated – he was an exceptionally fastidious man) without ever rupturing the friendship with his cousin, the Earl.' He believed that Plunkett remained unmarried because of the fascinating Daisy, with whom he was unquestionably in love, and who much later in life assured a younger acquaintance, 'My dear man, I never slept with either King Edward or Sir Horace Plunkett!'

Plunkett was well aware of the unremitting drudgery and toil that many women had to face on the farm; his ideal of achieving a better standard of living for the farming community included the life of women. In 1910, together with Daisy Fingall, Emily Lawless and other co-operators, he founded the United Irishwomen (which became the Irish Countrywoman's Association in 1935). Plunkett summarized their aims as

> firstly, to attend to women's business in the life of the community which no man, least of all an old bachelor like myself, can understand; secondly, to see that farmers attend better to the business of their organization and make them as helpful to women and the household as they are to men on the farm; thirdly, for Irish women to take up their rightful part in the building up of a rural civilisation in Ireland.

Trevor used his knowledge about co-operatives and what they have done for the economy and local communities and in the Senate debate on the economy on 1 October 1982 he spoke on the merits of co-operatives, and how this approach might be part of our industrial policy:

> In our industrial policy to increase employment, people now see the limit to the attraction of multinationals to this country. In a time of recession they do not have any obligations to us. They come here because the benefits from the State are high: in other words the taxpayers' money is used to fund their enterprises.

> However, their commitment to Ireland is limited. In the long run it would be more advantageous for us if, instead of attracting multinationals, we tried to encourage our own enterprises. In areas where large capital sums are required to set up industries it could be done along co-operative lines.

> It would be much better if we could provide the enterprises ourselves. Perhaps the Government might consider the possibility of industrial co-operatives filling the gap that exists in terms of employment and towards which we have directed many efforts to attracting the multinationals.

It is of interest to look at the agricultural sector. In the early 1960s, when the boom was on, it must have appeared to outside capitalists to have been the most attractive investment in Ireland. The reason Irish agriculture remains in Irish hands is that so much of it is run on a co-operative basis. Clearly there would have been great incentives for investment in that area by foreign capitalists and the multinationals, but fortunately for us the co-operative system has ensured that the control of our agriculture has remained in Irish hands.

He reminded the Senate of the need to go back to the basic co-operative ideals, to the ideal that the benefit the members got was not in payment of a dividend but in more efficient marketing, in higher prices, in educational benefits and in the economic and social benefits they got by taking part in the co-operative enterprise:

When thinking of setting up industries on co-operative lines we need to examine the ideals of our co-operative movement which forms such a large sector of the agricultural industry. The total turnover of co-operatives is something in the region of £1,400 million to £1,600 million a year. After all, some speakers recommended all-out nationalization; other people are entirely free enterprise philosophers, and the co-operative comes midway between the two. It has the benefit of collectivization without the element of compulsion. One Senator mentioned the stark fact that the compulsory collectivization of agriculture in Eastern Europe has not been successful and the Eastern European governments are trying to re-introduce incentives to increase output, production and efficiency. Therefore, compulsory collectivization is not the answer.

However, we still have a great deal to gain from the co-operative movement and the ideals which inspired the co-operators, the Rochdale pioneers and their famous philosophy, and this is one important way of generating capital from small investments and dealing with the unemployment problems. The Government should encourage that sort of move – it would require legislation and certain incentives – with our own people and our own resources rather than spending time, effort and money on inviting the multinationals to try to solve the problem.

For its centenary in 1994, ICOS produced a book to mark the occasion and to record the main events over the century. *Fruits of a Century* was edited by Maurice Henry, with Trevor West and Pat Bolger as assistant editors. Maurice Henry had been editor of *Co-op Ireland* and had many years of experience in agricultural journalism. Pat Bolger had produced a definitive history, *The Irish Co-operative Movement – its History and Development,* in 1977. A close friend of Trevor's, Bolger had been an agricultural adviser, county development officer in Donegal and worked for ICOS. These three experts of the co-operative movement collaborated to produce a memorable book. Trevor's contribution drew on his knowledge and understanding of Plunkett and on his own many years of contact with co-operatives.

Plunkett believed that the creation of the IAOS had supported the formation of co-operatives throughout the country to organize farmers, and followed this with the formation of the Irish Agricultural Wholesale Society (IAWS) in 1897. The IAWS was set up to supply farm inputs, such as animal feed ingredients and fertilizers to the co-operatives for onward supply to farmers. It was a co-op owned by other co-ops and grew rapidly to become one of the largest businesses in the sector.

Because of his expertise in Plunkett's career and work, Trevor was well known to both the Chairman of the IAWS plc, Jim Moloney, and the Managing Director, Philip Lynch, who saw the importance of recognizing Plunkett's legacy. The IAWS co-op shareholders were the co-ops themselves, both large and small, and many of these could trace their origin back to Plunkett's time. Having been reared in Ballinacurra in East Cork, Trevor was very familiar with farming and agri-business, which is so important to that area. The family farm grew genetic strains of barley and its dairy produced milk for the local village. He knew Con O'Leary who was the manager of Imokilly Co-op in East Cork, which became part of Mitchelstown Co-op, and is now part of Dairygold Co-op. His capacity to share his expertise was important to co-op management who wanted to educate their members about Plunkett's work and the advantages of co-operation. (Trevor went on to share this in seminars and presentations, and was much in demand.)

One of Trevor's neighbours near Ballinacurra was Denis Lucey who was chief executive of Dairygold and later became chairman of IAWS plc and subsequently chairman of Aryzta. They became friends and both had a strong interest in business, co-operatives and current affairs.

Late in 2006 Trevor wrote *Malting the Barley: John H. Bennett – the Man and his Firm*, which was the story of this well-known malting business. It had been run by Trevor's mother Dorothy since 1935, when her stepfather, John Bennett, died. This book was something that Trevor had wanted to do for some time, to record the achievements of this long-established family business, which grew and malted barley on contract for Guinness. When Dorothy West retired in 1969 the family sold their shares to Guinness.

Among the sources that Trevor consulted in his research for the Plunkett biography were the Plunkett diaries and papers. Horace Plunkett kept a daily diary from 1 January 1881 until 19 March 1932, exactly one week before he died. These detail his travels to America, the setting up of the IAOS, his political career, his time at DATI, his efforts at forging links across the political divide and his chairing of the Irish convention. On his death the diaries were left to the Plunkett Foundation in Oxford but they are not easy to decipher and have been a challenge to anyone interested in studying them. In their original form they were of limited value to scholars because it was sometimes difficult to read the handwritten script and interpret some of the abbreviations.

In the early 2000s, however, Kate Targett, who had worked at the Plunkett Foundation and has a strong interest in Plunkett began to transcribe the diaries. She embarked on this task when she was working for the Plunkett Foundation and was subsequently encouraged by Jim Moloney (IAWS) and John Tyrrell (ICOS) to continue this work. Funded by the Golden Jubilee Trust and IAWS, the job of transcribing, annotating and indexing the fifty-one volumes took about four years to complete. It was prepared in a Word document, which makes it very accessible.

During this transcription process the diaries were located in the Plunkett Foundation library in Oxford. Kate visited Ireland on a number of occasions to check on details she had found in the diaries, and for which she needed to seek a second source for verification. On several of these visits she met with Jim Moloney, John Tyrrell and Trevor to update them on her progress, to bounce ideas and to seek confirmation of information or possible other sources to cross-check her interpretations. Trevor revelled in these conversations and sharing this knowledge with others who were as interested and passionate about Plunkett as he was. While this was going on, Jim Moloney and John Tyrrell, with Trevor's support, began to discuss the possibility of having the diaries repatriated to Ireland. The effort to have them returned to Ireland was not straightforward, because

173

Left to right: editors Maurice Henry and Trevor West, with Northern Ireland Minister for Agriculture Baroness Denton, John Kelly (Agriculture Adviser AIB) and editor Patrick Bolger at the launch of the Co-operative Centenary publication *Fruits of a Century* at Lurgan Town Hall, 10 October 1994.

Dermot Burns with Trevor at the launch of *Malting the Barley*, 2006.

the Plunkett Foundation also felt a close link with Horace Plunkett, and the diaries were important to them. When eventually the Foundation decided to offer the diaries for sale and ICOS and IAWS encouraged the Irish National Library to purchase them, the negotiations failed as the parties were unable to agree on a price. Instead, the Golden Jubilee Trust and IAWS decided to purchase the diaries and papers because of their significance as a record of Plunkett's achievements.

Following the sale agreement, the consent of the British Museum for the transfer of the diaries to Ireland was obtained, and the diaries and papers arrived at Plunkett House in Dublin at 10.30 am on 8 May 2007. This, coincidentally, was the exact date and hour at which the new Northern Ireland Assembly was convening for the first time. Plunkett had put so much effort into mediation between unionists and nationalists during his life that this coincidence surely would have amused him. The diaries have since been transferred to the National Library of Ireland.

Announcing Scholars outside the Examination Hall at TCD:
Provost John Hegarty with Trevor West, Roger Stalley, James
Lunney, Sheila Greene, Sean Duffy, Eunan O'Halpin, Michael
Gleeson, Denis Weaire, Jane Grimson. John O'Hagan and
Joseph Mockler (Mace Bearer).

The College Man

Trevor West was the epitome of the College man who served Trinity loyally and steadfastly for fifty-six years. There are few areas of College that did not benefit from his commitment. He cherished and wanted to enhance Trinity's traditions. He brought the team spirit of Midleton College, where his father was headmaster, with him to Trinity, and supported students in all their community activities, actively encouraging their participation in clubs and societies. Fittingly his portrait hangs today in the boardroom of the new sports centre.

A portrait is not the most important memorial to Trevor West however. His contribution is far wider and has many aspects. For example, he deserves immense credit for his strenuous efforts to save College Park and the rugby field from builders and their supporters within College. Such a destruction of a beautiful green space in the heart of the city would be unthinkable today, but for several decades many in College governance promoted buildings, underground car parking, office blocks and retail on and around College Park. The ideals of Trevor and his environmentalist friends, who were then few in number, now command much more support in College and the wider community. The emphasis on concreting over our valued green spaces was reversed. For the 2014 season the provost and the president of Malone Rugby Club officially opened the restored rugby field after a year off for reinstatement.

By keeping the bulldozers at bay, Trevor saved College Park. The enhanced rugby field and the new park at Botany complement College Park in a remarkable inheritance, which generations of Dubliners will appreciate and generations of provosts and fellows will protect as staunchly as Trevor West did in his time. However, he remained on good terms with his opponents on the College Park issue. Expressions of outrage were replaced by reasoned debate and good decisions resulted with harmony retained.

Political and diplomatic skills honed over twelve years representing College in Seanad Éireann were valuable in Trevor's roles as a board member and chair of the fellows. He gently but firmly guided College away from such proposals as the removal of pews from College Chapel under re-ordering, proposed in the 1970s; modernizing rather than restoring the common room after the fire of 1984; cutting a road tunnel through House 38 in order to bypass the Narrows, proposed in the early 1990s; restricting the access of the Hist and the Phil to the Graduate Memorial Building; and a proposal curtailing and replacing the election of the provost by an appointment by a committee so small that only one Fellow would be a member. Trevor was skilled at building broad coalitions across College against such proposals, even on occasion recruiting some of the original proponents of the project to come over to his side.

On Trinity Monday 1958, Trevor was elected to Scholarship. In the Provost's House the following day he made the declaration and in 2008 he celebrated five decades as a scholar of the College. He was praised by Sir Anthony O'Reilly on his installation as pro-chancellor. Trevor was 'the most famous man in Ireland – the only man to have two rugby stands named after him: the Upper West stand and the Lower West stand'.

Scholarship brought Trevor to Commons and rooms. Both became lasting features of his College career. Commons became the preferred venue for hospitality for visiting teams and forty years ago he instituted Sporting Commons where our successful sports teams were honoured. It began with West standing on a table barking out the names of the successful teams and their coaches. Today it has evolved into one of the best sports awards dinners you will find anywhere.

As a senator he was very proud of the TCD tradition of representation in the parliament at College Green from the early 1600s, at Westminster after the Act of Union, and in Leinster House. He believed that the minority in the Republic should play a fuller part in public life and should bring that experience to promoting peace in Northern Ireland. He visited Loyalist prisoners in Long Kesh and the victims of Remembrance Sunday bombing in Enniskillen, and from 1980–82 he was president of the Irish Association for Cultural, Economic and Social Relations, a body dedicated to promoting better relations between North and South. He especially valued his links with Trinity graduates in Northern Ireland and the role of the sports bodies in rugby, cricket and hockey as all-island bodies.

As chairman of Trinity Week, Trevor welcomed his fellow mathematician, President de Valera, to the Races in College Park, which were then the highlight of Trinity Week. As chair of DUCAC, he welcomed Taoiseach Jack Lynch to College Park for the planting of an ash tree to celebrate the centenary of the GAA.

His acquaintance with the wider College community informed his time as Junior Dean. In the tradition of R.B. McDowell and Brendan Kennelly, he enjoyed the company of students and had a benign attitude towards their antics. In the smaller College of that era, West reached amicable agreements with students brought to his attention by enquiring after uncles, fathers, older brothers, all known personally to Trevor. 'Very good choice as Junior Dean, Kennelly,' R.B. McDowell said to his successor in the post. 'You know all the rules; you've broken most of them.' Stories of West as an undergraduate suggest that this comment could equally apply to Trevor's appointment as Junior Dean.

It has also been said that a good lecturer returns in Michaelmas Term with the enthusiasm of a person who has discovered the subject over the long vacation. Trevor had that enthusiasm as Junior Dean and chair of DUCAC. He personally shared the happiness of sporting success achieved by Dick and Donal Spring, Johnnie Robbie, Joe Brolly, Alan Kerins, Hugo MacNeill, Brendan Mullen and so many more. Enjoying the success of others he was delighted to learn that his former pupil Patrick Prendergast had been elected provost. He was proud of DUCAC as the oldest staff-student committee in College and admired his predecessors, brothers Harry and William Thrift, and father and son, A.A. and J.V. Luce. 'It went from Thrift to Luce and then it went West,' he liked to remark.

Trevor would have been an enthusiastic supporter of the new residences on the site of Oisín House beside Pearse St gate. His closest friend in the residential College community was Brendan Kennelly and Cork-Kerry banter was normal when they met. In Rubrics he was among a strong residential community, which included R.B. McDowell, David Webb, George Dawson, Jim Lydon, John Gaskin, Fred Falkiner and James Whiston.

In the summer his first choice of place to visit was the Yeats School in Sligo. There he formed lifelong friendships with Seamus Heaney, Lester Conner, James Simmonds, John Kelly, Desmond Maxwell, Maurice Elliott, T.R. Henn, Canon Tom Wood and the local committee. Many of the Yeatsians used to call into the College on their return home from Sligo as Trevor's guests in Commons. I recall Archibald Cox, law professor at Harvard and prosecutor in the Watergate case and a very tall man, looking bemused at Dublin Airport when invited by Trevor into my Morris Minor for transport to College. He must have wondered if the Watergate plumbers were in any way connected with such travel arrangements. Trevor's international friends included Bernard Donoughue of the UK

Cabinet Office and Kader Asmal, Minister of Education in South Africa and former colleague at Trinity. Trevor and Kader both cheered for Ireland in an under-20s match between the two countries.

A predecessor of Trevor's who sat on the first Pavilion Committee was parliamentarian and sportsman Edward Carson. He represented Dublin University at Westminster and played hurling for College. Carson's favourite hymn was 'O God our Help in Ages Past', published in Dublin in 1749. In verse 5 we read that:

> Time, like an ever-rolling stream
> Bears all its sons away;
> They fly forgotten, as a dream
> Dies at the opening day

Few students in College today ever met him. As the chapters in this book illustrate, his contribution to many aspects of College and Ireland were immense and have enhanced many aspects of both. When he celebrated thirty years as chair of DUCAC, his predecessor Public Orator J.V. Luce was asked to compose an oration in both Latin and English. A distinguished classicist and eminent sportsman who scored the first televised international goal in hockey for Ireland against England, J.V. Luce captures so much of what this chapter aspired to do. May his poetry and my prose combine in tribute to one of finest Bold Collegians:

Laudatio Ad Hesperum

Hespere, tu sidus, tu deliciae lusorum
Nostrorum! De te licet exultare colonis
Urbis qui pulchrae Mediae sata pinguia carpunt
Patria ibi sedes, doctus ludoque paterno
Dublinium ivisti, laturus praemia nostra.
De numeris taceo quos tu tractare perite
Saepe soles. Aliud mi nunc, Musa, incipe carmen!
Quam pede tu celeri corium pulsare solebas
Inflatum! Calices quot plenas deinde bibebas
Vicina, turba comitum comitante, taberna!
Ascitus Socius graviora negotia temptas,
Imperio miti iuvenum peccata coercens,
Nec non te ludis augendis usque laborans.
Dis tibi propitiis annus tricensimus hic est

Ex quo Concilii Lusorum iure minister,
Et mox praefectus, communis conscius usque,
Remigii nunquam sociis optata negabas.
Deficiat tempus si cuncta expromere coner
Quae tibi debenus. De te laetantur alumni
Munere de ludis qui fructi studia pergunt.
Nunc maiora moves, in gymnasioque secondo
Est ut nos tandem piscinam conspiciamus.
Hespere, tu comis, tu nobis usque sodalis
Ingenue cordis, circum confinia Campi
Deditus impense ludos ad proficiendos.
Studentes inter fortes tu fortiori exstas!
Lusori celebri cyathos tollamus, amici.

Sean Barrett, James Whiston Ph.D. and Trevor West at College Commencements, December 1975.

Letter from Seamus Heaney to Sean Barrett, 22 December 2012.

191 Strand Road, Dublin 4, Ireland   Fax: (353-1) 260 0807

22 December 2012

Dear Sean,

You were kind to send greetings on the occasion of the named professorship, and to let me have the service sheet in memoriam Trevor. I was moved and gladdened to find 'Markings' included, all the more so because it was read and — I am sure — chosen by you.

Meanwhile, you keep busy and cogent in the Senate. With fond wishes for a happy Christmas — Seamus

Gusty Spence.

A Remarkable Career

This obituary was published in The Sunday Independent, *18 November 2012.*

Trevor West, who died recently, had a remarkable career, the impact of which has not yet been fully realized. It was clear when Trevor came up to Trinity College Dublin that he was regarded by the faculty as having unusual mathematical skills. In a university which had produced Nobel Prize-winner Ernest Walton and Rowan Hamilton, the inventor of quaternions, this was praise indeed.

Later perhaps his development as a mathematician was held back by his involvement in public life as a senator representing Trinity and his singular devotion to the needs of his country in trying to improve conditions in Northern Ireland. There is no doubt, however, that his political involvement contributed greatly to the benefit and welfare of the country. Trevor had a great love of sports and was an outstanding player on the Trinity First XI cricket team as well as playing both soccer and rugby. He was able to put this passion for sport to good account when an effort was made by developers (assisted by people who should have known better) to attempt to turn the Trinity rugby pitch into a building area. Trevor's response was to send many thousands of letters on Senate writing paper to former Trinity graduates, which shortly put an end to the disgraceful plan. He also played on a touring soccer team I put together where he soon became immensely popular and made lasting friendships with international players such as Liam 'Rasher' Tuohy and Paddy Ambrose. After being elected to the Senate as Trinity representative, he continued the tradition of his predecessors W.B. Stanford and Owen Sheehy-Skeffington of initiating and supporting legislation not previously considered by a predominately nationalist and Catholic body.

His work in Northern Ireland is virtually unknown. But Trevor West had a significant effect in bringing members of the Northern Ireland Protestant community forward in relation to the political divide. One connection he had with Belfast was particularly useful. Though Trevor grew up in Midleton, Cork (his father had been a headmaster of Midleton College), an uncle who was resident in Belfast controlled much of the tram system there. Trevor had spent many of his boyhood summers travelling free throughout Belfast like a young deer let loose on a fertile pitch.

This may have given him an understanding of the Northern temperament that was to prove invaluable in the part he would play later in bringing the two communities together.

I remember one day walking in the middle of a street in Belfast as the footpaths were crowded but there was little traffic on the street. I said to Trevor: 'What street is this?' 'Oh,' he replied, 'this is the Shankill Road.'

'Holy Christ, let's get out of this,' I said.

But Trevor insisted all was right. And it was.

He would succeed in getting the confidence of a section of the Northern Ireland Protestants that no one from the South had succeeded in doing up to this. It was Trevor who introduced Paul O'Dwyer, President of the New York City Council, to Northern Irish leaders who wielded power. Andy Tyrie, commander of the UDA, and John McMichael were invited by Paul O'Dwyer to New York to work with legal experts to initiate a framework that could lead to a new world in Northern Ireland.

Paul was the ideal person to negotiate this leap forward. He had left Ireland as a very young man after taking part in the anti-Treaty side in the Civil War, and had become one of the most admired figures in American politics, known throughout the country as one of the great civil rights leaders and an honest politician of much skill. I had introduced Trevor to Paul and it was a delight to see them together. They both had astute political brains, were hungry for justice and, though coming from different backgrounds, were held together by their Irish temperament trained on the wheel of experience. In an article I wrote in 1977 for the *Washington Post*, I had this to say about what we used to jocularly refer to as the 'O'Connor-West Plan':

> What is important at present is the growing grass roots acceptance of the idea of shared community. The Protestant is becoming aware of how much closer he is in temperament to his Catholic fellow Ulstermen. The Catholic community is coming more and more to see that it has in common with the Protestant qualities of shrewdness, reliability and industry, which are not as marked in the easy-going south.

A major influence on Trevor had been Sir Horace Plunkett, who was the force behind the Irish co-operative movement. Trevor's first book was a biography of Plunkett. It was Plunkett's analysis of the weakness in the Irish political system and his plan for the development of our agricultural output and national assets that appealed to Trevor. He put enormous time and energy into writing this seminal work, which should be reprinted.

Trevor wrote several other books, including the splendid *Malting the Barley*, all of which reflected his own particular view of the Irish condition. Trevor had a magnetism that was not apparent under his almost boyish appearance and witty conversation. With just a slight move of the head, he would say what he was after and then usually would get his way. When he failed to get into the Senate after eight years in 1976, one could only feel ashamed of the Trinity electorate.

Trevor was very private about the work he was doing in relation to Northern Ireland. I have a picture in my mind of an event that reveals this aspect of him. I had gone up to Northern Ireland with Trevor in 1978 to have a meeting with John McKeague, commander of the UVF, and Andy Tyrie of the UDA. Afterwards we were having tea in the Belfast Park Hotel. The little old lady who was serving us was an expert at fielding comments and coming back with witty replies. As I looked round the laughing faces, I thought, here were two Northern Ireland Protestants, a Belfast priest (Fr Des Wilson), a Dublin Catholic (me), a Cork Protestant (Trevor), a Mayo lawyer from America (Paul O'Dwyer) and a Protestant Belfast working-class woman – all joking with one another because we had in common an Irish sense of humour and the levelling of class consciousness which it can bring about.

It was Trevor's achievement to have made such meetings possible and it would play a significant part in creating a situation where the dominance of the bomb and bullet has been replaced by a working parliament.

Later, reflecting on his experiences with Trevor West in Northern Ireland, Ulick O'Connor remembers meeting people from widely different backgrounds when in Trevor's company: Gusty Spence was one, Andy Tyrie, commander of the Ulster Defence Association (UDA) was another with whom I became acquainted. From the nationalist side Fr Des Wilson shared with Trevor in bringing people from completely opposite sides together. Fr Alec Reid, the Redemptorist priest, more than any other was a vital figure with influence on both sides.

As a result of his family background and tradition Trevor had arrived at a unique understanding of the Northern Ireland unionist position as it stood at this time. I went to a number of meetings in Northern Ireland with him in which there were Irishmen of completely different backgrounds, but with similar temperaments, who could clearly create a solution if certain circumstances were put in place.

A visit to Gusty Spence in Long Kesh, which I made with Trevor in 1978, was an indication that a new mind-set was coming into shape in

Northern Ireland. Gusty was one of the very able people who had decided that the way to peace in Northern Ireland could be achieved other than by violence. It turned out that he was acquainted with Cardinal O'Fiaich who thought highly of him and used to visit him in prison.

Gusty: 'I'm very fond of His Eminence.'

Ulick: 'Why?'

'He's straight.'

'Gusty, I don't call him Your Eminence. I am a republican. I don't like titles. Tell me, what you do talk about?'

'That's between me and him. Sometimes we talk about tobacco. One day he broke his pipe and I gave him a new one with baccy that we grew in here. Then I got a message from him: "Will you send out more of that strong tobacco?"'

Trevor not only drew the best out of people but those who were totally against his views were the better off for hearing them. He had a magnetism and depth, which were immediately apparent from his youthful appearance and witty conversation. When he found out that the Trinity College rugby pitch was to be replaced by buildings, his only comment was a slight grunt. His reaction to the plan that could destroy the Trinity landscape entirely was to write to thousands of graduates throughout the world to let them know what was happening. When I asked him a month later what the reaction had been to his letters he just nodded and said 'Good'. The rugby pitch is still there.

Trevor's biography of Plunkett explores the influence of the Anglo-Irish in an emerging Ireland. It is essential to read if one wants to understand the growth of Irish politics to the present day. Also, it can tell you a lot about my dear friend Trevor.

NAME	ADDRESS	
Pat Finucane	11 Fortwilliam Drive Belfast (777909)	Thanks for the rest, Trevor. All the more pleasant for meeting Les + John.
Cruelly murdered 12 Feb 89		WACKO JACKO AND WEST THE BEST!
Katherine Finucane	11 Fortwilliam Drive	From JACKSON to Charleston! Slán
John Finucane	11 Fortwilliam Drive 98 Heath St. Hampstead, London N.W.3.1.O.P.	Heartfelt Thanks for rescuing me so gallantly
Kate O'Toole	Eyrephort, Sky Road, Clifden, Co. Galway	from the madding Crowds at the Michael Jackson concert.

Visitors' Book, Charleston, 1988. The Belfast solicitor Pat Finucane and his family were visiting Cork to attend a concert by Michael Jackson.

The brothers Brian, Trevor and John West at Charleston.

West Decomposition

Growing up, Trevor may have been our uncle, but he didn't do avuncular. He spoke to children the way he spoke to adults, as if addressing an undergraduate who'd made a particularly stupid mistake on a test. This kind of teasing could seem mildly intimidating but it was not malicious. In tone and content it was the sort of slagging bright nineteen-year-olds would throw at each other after lectures in the 1950s, and, bar some individual modifications, the vocabulary of hectoring remained unchanged into the twenty-first century. At various stages of adolescence I was called a moonbeam, a goon, a fool, a baluba, and above all an idiot. These epithets were delivered in a distinctive drawl combining both mockery and affection.

While disconcerting to a ten- or twelve-year-old, I somehow grasped that by treating me like a freshman he was paying me a compliment: that he was taking me seriously by not taking me seriously. The fact that he continued to talk to me as if I'd failed elementary algebra long after I left college I put down to nostalgia and habit. It's certainly true that I became used to being introduced with the words, 'Have you met my idiot nephew?' But that was partly because the range of epithets and honorifics conferred on people was so extensive. Our cousins were 'the McPoons'. A visiting American lecturer was always presented as Lester P. Icarus Conner. Bernard Hickey, an Australian mature student who became a professor of English literature and the Australian consul at Venice, was Hickballs or *Il Bollice*. His own wife Trevor addressed directly by her full name, often in the form 'Maura Lee, you're so cross!'

For a man who married late and lived most of his life in the confines of universities it's unsurprising that many of his social skills bore the stamp of a precocious undergraduate experience. Rather than arresting him in a state of perpetual adolescence, this preserved in him the many good qualities of college life. As any graduate knows, a lifetime teaching does not inevitably confer a love of students, but in Trevor's case he was utterly unafraid of, and interested in, young people of all abilities, including those who rivalled his own intellectual powers. While he enjoyed people giving as good as they got he was not by nature confrontational or cruel. He wasn't keen on rhetorical argument or superfluous debate. His preference in repartee was for a couple of traded insults followed by disconcerting laughter; his mode of administration was briskly consensual and direct.

Socially generous and gregarious, one of his great compulsions and pleasures was to make connections and introduce people – with or without epithets. It was in this context that the compliments would flow, but at one remove: 'Your father, amazing man,' or 'Terrific guy, just terrific,' or 'She's a remarkable lady and I would have known her through the Mackintoshes.' Unusually for someone so distinguished in a specialized field, he recognized and cherished life outside the bubble. In this he would have thought he was simply following the collegiate model – a university allows for excellence in many areas or departments – but his support of sport in Trinity was beyond the norm, as was his insistence that his engineering students be lectured in literature by Brendan Kennelly.

He brought the same cross-disciplinary approach to politics and history and, for all that Trinity was a conservative and narrowly defined section of Irish society, he canvassed and represented people outside of his own comfort zone both nationally and on an all-Ireland basis for his whole life.

He never talked about his achievements, he certainly never congratulated himself on them in all the years I knew him. He was scrupulously modest in celebrating the achievements of those nearest and dearest to him as well – of his brothers, for example, of whom he was extremely proud, but whose virtues he would extol only to others. Yet to call him modest is not quite right. His appetite for excitement was vast, his enthusiasm often manic and larger than life. He was particularly fond of myth-making. His favourite adjective was *famous* and it applied not to Nobel prizewinners or monuments but to common-or-garden excursions of all kinds – trips, visits, ordinary nights out that may or may not have descended into farce or chaos. He had a flair for grotesque stories that twisted and turned into improbably lurid set-pieces until you realized with astonishment that you were in them yourself; that you'd been there all along and unaware of the wonders happening around you.

Other favourite adjectives were *terrific, appalling* and *bloody funny* and there was literally no outing that couldn't be enlivened as it unfolded or in its later telling by Trevor, laughing and embellishing as he went.

He travelled widely and often impulsively. When I went off to an ob-scure school in New Mexico it was entirely characteristic of him that he would already have been out there. He came to visit me in my first term with an American friend from his Cambridge days, Gary Hufbauer. They took me and a friend to a meal in the only downtown hotel in New Mexico's Las Vegas with a fat man in a white Stetson who turned out to be a dubious local *patrón* and political honcho. By that stage I'd been told I was one of only three Irish people in the whole state, the other two being a couple from Ballyfermot who had run away to Taos, so I had some idea of how unusual it was for Trevor to know the place. Since Trevor himself was so unusual it took me several years to realize he wasn't just passing through a second time by coincidence. In 1984 New Mexico was very, very far away indeed.

At a party in his rooms before I headed off he described it to me with great enthusiasm. The room in Rubrics was full of academics and writers and sports people, most of them completely unknown to me.

'New Mexico is wonderful. The sun, the mountains. The earth is a sort of orangey red. It's the colour of those walls.'

And so it was, but I do remember thinking at the time, 'That is a very strange colour to put on your walls.' His rooms' warmth started and ended with the paint. Packed full of people on a sunny day was one thing, but a single gas fire and bare floorboards in winter was quite another. Trevor's fridge was the granite sill outside the kitchenette window, which kept a small carton of milk just above souring point for several days. The only solids he ate were served on Commons at 6 pm, supplemented by Tessie Finn's coffee cake, which he brought up each week from Cork wrapped in silver foil. Years later I remember asking him if the plugs in his rooms were the standard square three-pin ones or the ancient, black round-pin ones still found in some of the older buildings on campus

'I've no idea,' was his response.

It is entirely possible that this was the answer of a man who hadn't plugged anything into a wall in his rooms the entire time he lived there. He had no interest in electronic gadgets of any kind. As someone who was curious and enthusiastic about so many things, in the matter of technological devices he was an abstract mathematician.

Trevor was a pencil-and-paper man. Stacks of exam scripts, recycled foolscap, sheets of calculations were spread out neatly on desks or on the floor. It wasn't that he distrusted computers – in the way, for example, he had an almost superstitious fear of microwave ovens; it was that he genuinely seemed to have no use for them. He regarded simple word-processing as an arcane art only slightly less complicated than the use of Hadron colliders. He entrusted the setting of *The Bold Collegians* to Peter Ashe, a nomadic sometime lecturer in computing, who for reasons that were never entirely clear insisted on using a completely unsuitable and outdated programme designed for mathematics papers instead of a dedicated word-processing one. The extreme slowness of the process only confirmed its difficulty in Trevor's eyes and he overpaid him accordingly.

However rarified the abstract realm of his work, Trevor's physical world was strictly Newtonian. His fondness for the physics of sport is well known: ballistics, vectors, the laws of motion and of falling bodies pleased him greatly. It encompassed his love of pranks: water bombs, flying bicycles, clock hands. It informed his unforgettable party piece for all young people of any age and disposition, which was to waggle his ears. And it extended to a delight in ancient locks, keys and anything with old-fashioned levers and pulleys.

Taking a family group to a pizza restaurant in a converted warehouse in Dublin, he was thrilled by the antique spring-loaded messaging system suspended from the ceiling, which had been preserved as a gimmick. Above the tables hung small canisters on wires into which the waiters would place your order before – zing! – sending them with a satisfying whizz and clunk along the ceiling to the kitchens. As a working model of equal and opposite forces, Trevor took it as a challenge to fire off as many as possible before being asked to leave – an equal and opposite force of a different kind – but he found the whole episode deliriously, almost inexplicably, exhilarating.

If socially and recreationally he was a Newtonian, when it came to driving he was a theoretical physicist. As a student, an added attraction of staying at Charleston, the family house in Midleton, was being asked to drive my late grandmother's pale blue Fiesta to a pub or restaurant in East Cork, or take Trevor to or from the station. I say added attraction because this was before I had my license. I would go further and say that at that time Trevor was probably the only person in the world who would voluntarily sit in a car while I drove it.

The first time he asked if I could collect him from Kent Station was a significant milestone. I carefully practised hill starts on the drive leading up to the house before spinning off to meet the Dublin train. The N25 from Midleton to Cork is fantastically direct. It's basically a straight line

The Trevor West Memorial Trophy for Inter-Varsity Cricket.

Cricket bat and ball.

due west, though you may remember that as it nears the city there is a very sharp turn onto a bridge over the railway line to Cobh. I certainly didn't, even though I'd driven over it in the other direction only minutes before. Now, heading east with Trevor beside me, I took the 90° turn left at full speed, followed by an equally sharp 90° turn right a few yards later, all without changing gears. Luckily we negotiated this chicane without the extra hazard of oncoming traffic but I can still hear the sound of his nails tearing the seat covers. I knew how much I'd rattled him because he didn't call me an idiot the whole way home.

My driving improved, though shortly after I did manage to stall on both the way into and out of Cloyne. 'Jesus,' came the disbelieving mutter the first time, and 'You're some baluba,' on the way back.

An excursion he particularly enjoyed recounting was of a drive to Inchicore with Lester Connor and Alec Reid to see Michael Hartnett read. The designated driver was Lenny Abrahamson, then a physics student at Trinity, which was how he knew Trevor, and in possession of a car, which was why he was asked. Lester had got the date or time or place wrong, or Hartnett had, or drink was involved, or possibly a combination of all of the above. But there was no poet and no reading. The senior members of the party had a pint in the Black Lion. They returned to Trinity.

But to hear Trevor's version, instead of a mildly disappointing trip to a non-event in a convertible Morris Minor, they had flown across town in a sports car on a mad picaresque adventure, fighting off locals and rescuing each other from danger on their way to literary immortality. He enjoyed the story so much he insisted I meet Lenny and he introduced us on the stairs of Number 24 and told it all over again: the sun shining, the roof of the car rolled down, Alec Reid's white hair blowing in the wind, Lester slipping off his stool.

Lenny and I went on to share rooms for two years in Trinity so I am very fond of the story myself. Trevor dropped round to us one night with a collection of mushrooms in a plastic bag and an instruction.

'Cook those. They're from the provost's garden.'

He left after a cup of tea and some trademark, eye-wrinkling sighs and I duly made an omelette with the last three eggs in Rubrics. Coming back to my rooms next morning I found a note under the door saying 'Mykul. Under no circumstances eat the provost's mushrooms. They have been sprayed with weedkiller. You will die.' When I ran into him that evening I told him his warning had arrived too late. 'Then ignore it,' was his advice.

Although from the country, Trevor was not a woods and wild sort of man. His interest in plants and trees was sincere but fairly limited. His grand passion was for a humbler form of vegetable life: grass. Cutting the lawns in Charleston was no joke and in the wet summer months the stuff pushed up relentlessly. A succession of gardeners helped keep it in check but there were times when he cut it all himself with a hand-pushed lawn-mower. But domestic lawns, no matter how unruly or sprawling, were for amateurs. His real obsession was the grass in College Park – and specifically the roped-off 30 x 60-yard strip around the cricket wicket. He guarded that wicket doggedly, overseeing its cutting and aeration, its rolling and trimming. W.G. Grace may have batted on it, but if he'd walked across it in football boots he'd have had his beard yanked.

There is, or used to be, a large, wall-mounted aerial photo in the accommodations office showing Trinity on a gloriously sunny day in the mid eighties. The day the photo was taken coincided with a staff strike in College: all maintenance, portering and ground-keeping was suspended. The only evidence in the photo for this industrial action is a solitary, slim, white-shirted figure pulling the roller down the wicket towards the Pav. Even from an altitude of several hundred feet the silhouette is recognizable.

I remember an afternoon walking the long grass round the ruins of Bowen's Court, the eighteenth-century home of Elizabeth Bowen's family in Cork. Having survived the decline of the nineteenth century and the War of Independence it was torn down by the farmer who bought it in 1959. Watching the bullocks graze in the muddy granite-strewn site prompted a sober conversation about Charleston, its upkeep and expense: dealing with the bees in the attic, the teetering trees, the ever-growing grass and ivy, the demands of maintaining the grounds, keeping the slates on the roof and the rooms warm – in itself a fairly relative term in Church of Ireland households.

After his mother's death and before Maura Lee came and added considerably to the comfort of Charleston, he shuttled between his tiny bedroom upstairs and the round table in the morning room where he worked and survived on tea and Tessie Finn's coffee cake. Once I remember seeing among the pencil and paper calculations a paper published by some Chinese mathematicians whose title caught my eye. It proposed to name an operation in matrix theory *West Decomposition* after a discovery of Trevor's.

I thought it was a marvellous name. It came back to me one night when on one of his spontaneous visits he handed me a mobile phone and asked me to call Maura Lee. His hands shook too much to call up her name and I saw when I held it that the numbers were almost entirely erased from the keypad.

In his later years, at an opening night of one of our plays, Trevor greeted me in the foyer with the words, 'Christ, Michael, that was appalling,' which was reassuringly like the old days. He seemed very happy and in his element as the crowd milled about us. He was later rescued from going around shaking hands with and buying rounds of drink for strangers, which is to say everybody in the entire bar. In a way it wasn't very different from what this social and generous man had done for the best part of fifty years, but of course it was worse than a pale imitation because everyone was becoming a stranger to him.

Losing his faculties was deeply frustrating and depressing for Trevor. First words, then names, memories and certainties began to leave him. He would smack his forehead in exasperation as a thought or idea completely disintegrated. He found comfort in recalling the old days, the famous adventures, even as these too regressed further and further.

Trevor's treasured Munster Cricket cap.

Maura Lee remained a constant in both his mental and physical worlds and he circled her name and presence repeatedly in an effort to locate himself. As the boundaries between his many areas of expertise and interest dissolved he talked about things that normally he kept separate, leading to many interesting conversations and reminiscences that were new to me, as well as ones that were well worn and familiar. He became gentler as he became more frail. Visiting Cahir Castle he shook the hands of everyone working in reception and the shop, telling them well done. He greeted some startled tourists in the car park with a raised hand salute to old colleagues, 'Keep it up.'

Everyone he met was now terrific and lovely. As his nephew Eoin said, without the bite there was no spark; I can't remember the last time he called me an idiot but it was far too long ago.

195

The Bold Collegian

The University of Dublin

Chapel of Trinity College

A Service of Thanksgiving

for the Life and Work of

TIMOTHY TREVOR WEST

B.A., Ph.D. (Cantab.), M.R.I.A., F.T.C.D. (1970)
Associate Professor of Pure Mathematics (1977-2004)
Junior Dean (1974-1978)
Former Member of the Board of the College
Former Chair of D.U.C.A.C.
Member of Seanad Éireann, 1970, 1973, 1977, 1982
for the University of Dublin constituency

Friday 7 December 2012

5.15pm

To Trevor West in Heaven

St Peter groaned 'You took your time
But, now you're here, best know that I'm
Due quite a bit of leave, The Head
Has chosen yourself in my stead:
He likes an independent mind
And you've had dealings with the kind
We get in here, from academics
With Senatorial polemics
To hosts of Freshman Engineers
With focus fixed on birds 'n' beers;
It's bread and circuses, of course
So no need for the use of force
Just keep them busy at the crease
With matches that shall never cease;
Cherubim and Seraphim?
They like to work out in the Gym.
A job to keep the peace between
Archangel Orange, Archangel Green
And though Eternal are the hours
Prevent celestial Thrones and Powers
From building Student Mansions on
Elysian Fields, once gone, they're gone.
And most of all, be vigilant
Concerning every new entrant
No one is without saving grace
(and here a shadow crossed his face
the saintly voice raised to a shout)
But keep the bloody poets out!'

Df The graphs G_1, G_2 are <u>isomorphic</u>
if $\exists$ bijective $\phi : V(G_1) \longrightarrow V(G_2)$
st. $u, v \in E(G_1) \Longleftrightarrow \phi(u)\,\phi(v) \in E(G_2)$

Ex

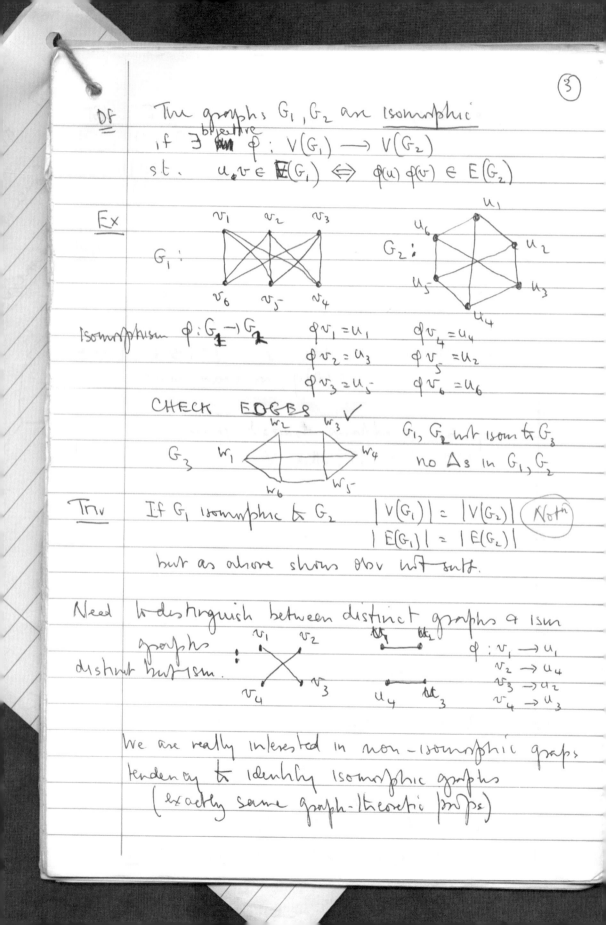

G_1 :

G_2 :

Isomorphism $\phi : G_1 \to G_2$

$\phi v_1 = u_1$	$\phi v_4 = u_4$
$\phi v_2 = u_3$	$\phi v_5 = u_2$
$\phi v_3 = u_5$	$\phi v_6 = u_6$

CHECK EDGES ✓

G_3

G_1, G_2 not isom to G_3
no $\triangle$s in G_1, G_2

Triv If G_1 isomorphic to G_2 $\quad |V(G_1)| = |V(G_2)|$ $\underset{\text{(Not}^n\text{)}}{}$
$|E(G_1)| = |E(G_2)|$
but as above shows obv not suff.

Need to distinguish between distinct graphs & ism
graphs

distinct but ism.

$\phi : v_1 \to u_1$
$v_2 \to u_4$
$v_3 \to u_2$
$v_4 \to u_3$

We are really interested in non-isomorphic graphs
tendency to identify isomorphic graphs
(exactly same graph-theoretic props)

A page from Trevor's mathematical notes.

Mary Robinson S.C. was the first woman to be elected President of Ireland (1990–97). She was a member of Seanad Éireann from 1969 to 1989 and is Chancellor of Dublin University. She served as United Nations Commissioner for Human Rights from 1997–2002 and is President and Chairman of the Board of the Mary Robinson Foundation – Climate Justice. In 2014 she was appointed the UN Secretary General's Special Envoy on Climate Change.

John West was educated at Midleton College and Dublin University and taught at the King's Hospital School. An international referee, he is a past president of the Trinity rugby and cricket clubs and a former Master of the Knights of the Campanile. Married to Cecily, he is a brother of Trevor and Brian.

Dr Paul Colton is Bishop of Cork, Cloyne and Ross. He has served on the board of governors of Midleton College since 1999 and is presently Chairperson of the Schools' Board. Originally from Cork, he is a past pupil of Ashton School, Cork, and a scholarship student of the Lester B. Pearson College of the Pacific, Victoria Columbia. He studied Law at University College Cork, theology at Trinity College Dublin and com-

pleted both a master's degree and doctorate in Cardiff University. He is married to Susan and they have two sons, both of whom attend Midleton College.

John Mc Carthy went to Trinity in 1957 and obtained a Moderatorship in Celtic Studies. He also received a Testimonium from Trinity's School of Divinity and was ordained in the Church of Ireland in 1962. His ministry ended in 1994 when he was Rector of Enniskillen and Dean of the Diocese of Clogher.

Cyril Smyth is a retired Professor of Microbiology, Trinity College Dublin, and a Fellow Emeritus of the College. He was elected a Fellow in 1986. Cyril succeeded Trevor West as Chairman of Dublin University Central Athletic Club (DUCAC) in 2009, only the fifth and current incumbent of that position. He became a Pavilion Member of DUCAC in 1989 and served as Hon. Treasurer from 1991–2001 and 2008–09. He served as Senior Dean of Trinity College from 2001–07 and was Head of Microbiology from 1988–94 and 2002–08.

Mary Henry was born in Cork and knew Trevor for over fifty years. A medical graduate of Trinity in 1965, she practised in Sir Patrick Dun's, Rotunda and

Adelaide hospitals for more than forty years. She represented Dublin University in the Seanad from 1993–2007. At present she is Pro Chancellor of College.

Michael Halliday BA Mod (History and Political Science 1971) is a history teacher and writer. He was Captain of DUCC during 1970–71 and an Irish Cricket international in 1970 and 1989.

Paul Coulson graduated with BBS from Trinity College Dublin in 1973 and is Chairman of Ardagh Group.

Richard Timoney is a professor of mathematics at Trinity College Dublin, where he has been on the staff since 1980. He was educated at Scoil Lorcáin (an all-Irish national school in Monkstown), Blackrock College (where he did not prosper at rugby), University College Dublin and the University of Illinois. He also worked briefly at Indiana University before joining TCD.

Finbarr Holland MRIA is Professor Emeritus of Mathematics at UCC where he has lectured since 1965. Author and co-author of more than sixty research papers, in 1988 he and his colleague Tom Laffey established a nationwide mathematical enrichment programme for secondary school students, which prepares an Irish team for the annual International Mathematical Olympiad.

Charles Woodhouse after Cambridge, joined the London solicitors Farrer & Co., where he was a partner for thirty years. His extensive practice included clients such as the Duke of Edinburgh and many British sports governing bodies. He was founder chair of Sports Resolution UK and President of the British Association of Sport and the Law. He captained Guildford Cricket Club and played for many clubs including MCC and Free Foresters. Trevor was best man at his wedding to Margaret in 1969 and godfather to Phillipa, one of his three children. Now living in Cumbria where he was made a deputy lieutenant, Charles is still active as a charity trustee and tree enthusiast.

Gary Hufbauer was awarded a AB from Harvard College in 1960 and a Ph.D. in economics from King's College Cambridge in 1963. He was a professor at the University of New Mexico in Albuquerque and an advisor to the Government of West Pakistan in Lahore. He served in the Treasury Department, George University, and the Peterson Institute for International Economics. He has published widely on international trade, economic sanctions and corporate taxation.

Dr Michael Mortell a distinguished scientist was President of University College Cork from 1989 to 1999. He gained his Ph.D. at the California Institute of Technology (CalTech) and is widely regarded as an exceptional applied mathematician. He has published over fifty papers on applied mathematics and is currently writing a book on nonlinear waves. He was awarded honorary doctorates by

Queen's University Belfast and the University of Limerick, and is a member of the Royal Irish Academy. He captained the UCC hurling team for five years and was a member of the Cork senior hurling team 1962–63; he was also a founder member of the Cal-Tech rugby team.

Andrew Bonar Law entered Trinity in Sept of 1955 to study economics. He was a close friend of T.T. and they both became Scholars in the same year. Graduating in 1959, he married Joanna in 1961. He formed his own industrial market research company and later returned to Ireland to become a small-time farmer and to run the Neptune Gallery in Dublin. Together with his daughter, also a graduate of Trinity, he has written a number of books on Irish maps and prints including *The Printed Maps of Ireland 1612–1850*, *The Irish Prints of James Malton* and *The Prints and Maps of Dublin* [vol. II] and is currently working on others of a similar vein.

Cathy Doyle MBA started working in Trinity in 1977 and was the DUCAC Administrative Officer from 1990–2002. She is Corporate Services Manager in the Dublin Dental University Hospital. Cathy is currently reading for a doctorate in governance.

Roy Garland has been a regular *Irish News* columnist and is the author of a biography of Gusty Spence. He was the first Ulster Unionist to address the

Forum for Peace and Reconciliation and a is former member of the Grand Orange Lodge of Research. Roy was also a former member of the Guild of Uriel, a dialogue group based near Dundalk.

Hugo MacNeill was educated at Blackrock College, Trinity, and Oxford University. He represented Trinity, the Irish Universities, Ireland, and the British Lions at rugby (and Trinity at soccer). After spending nearly twenty years in the UK, he now lives and works in Dublin.

Thomas N. Mitchell graduated from University College Galway, gaining a Ph.D. from Cornell University and a Litt.D. from the University of Dublin. His early academic career was in the United States at Cornell University and Swarthmore College. He assumed the Chair of Latin at Trinity College in 1979 and was Provost from 1991 to 2002. Appointed Chairman of St James's Hospital in 2002, he was chairman of the steering group that established the Press Council of Ireland and the Office of the Press Ombudsman in 2007 and served as the Press Council's first chairman. He currently holds positions as Deputy Chairman of The Atlantic Philanthropies and Director of Hibernia College. A Member of the Royal Irish Academy and of the American Philosophical Society, he is an Honorary Fellow of Oriel College Oxford and St John's College Cambridge.

John Tyrrell operates a consultancy business focused on the food industry, co-operatives, governance and strategy. He is currently secretary of the Dairy Research Trust and executive secretary of Nuffield Ireland Farming Scholars. He previously worked with ICOS from 1978 to 2010 and was director general from 1990 to 2010.

Sean Barrett, former Senator is Associate Professor in the economics department of Trinity College and has enjoyed a distinguished career in academic circles along with holding high-ranking positions outside of College. During his 38-year-long career in Trinity he served as Assistant Junior Dean to Trevor West and as Treasurer of DUCAC when Trevor was Chairman and President. Along with his fourteen-year tenure as Junior Dean he has served as a member of the Board of College on three separate occasions and has held key roles in many College bodies. He was elected by the College's graduates to Seanad Éireann in 2011 where he was a member of the banking inquiry.

Ulick O'Connor is an author, playwright, poet and journalist, and prominent commentator on Irish and other affairs. As a sportsman he excelled at boxing, pole-vaulting and rugby.

Michael West is a playwright. His work includes *Foley*, *Freefall* and *Dublin by Lamplight*, all with The Corn Exchange, and *Conservatory*, which was produced by the Abbey.

Iggy McGovern is a Fellow Emeritus of Trinity College Dublin. His latest collection *A Mystic Dream of 4* was published by Quaternia Press in 2013.

Appendix I
Books written by Trevor West

Horace Plunkett, Co-operation and Politics – An Irish Biography (Colin Smythe, 1986)

Malting the Barley, John H Bennett, the Man and his Firm (Charleston House, 2006)

The Bold Collegians, A History of Sport in Trinity (Lilliput Press, 1992)

Midleton College 1696–1996, A Tercentenary History (Midleton College, 1996)

150 Years of Trinity Rugby (Wordwell 2004)

Books edited by Trevor West
Fruits of a Century, ICOS (1994)

Appendix II
Trevor West Mathematical Bibliography

[64OW] P.A. Olagunju and T.T. West. The spectra of Fredholm operators in locally convex spaces. Proc. Cambridge Philos. Soc., 60:801-806, 1964.

[64W] T.T. West. Riesz operators in Banach spaces. Ph.D. thesis, University of Cambridge, 1964.

[65W] T.T. West. The spectra of compact operators in Hilbert spaces. Proc. Glasgow Math. Assoc., 7:34-38, 1965.

[66We] T.T. West. Operators with a single spectrum. Proc. Edinburgh Math. Soc. (2), 15:11-18, 1966.

[66Wla] T.T. West. Riesz operators in Banach spaces. Proc. London Math. Soc. (3), 16:131-140, 1966.

[66Wlb] T.T. West. The decomposition of Riesz operators. Proc. London Math. Soc. (3), 16:737-752, 1966.

[68GW] T.A. Gillespie and T.T. West. A characterization and two examples of Riesz operators. Glasgow Math. J., 9:106-110, 1968.

[68KWe] M.A. Kaashoek and T.T. West. Semi-simple locally compact monothetic semi-algebras. Proc. Edinburgh Math. Soc. (2), 16:215-219, 1968/1969.

[68KWl] M.A. Kaashoek and T.T. West. Locally compact monothetic semi-algebras. Proc. London Math. Soc. (3), 18:428-438, 1968.

[68W] T.T. West. Weakly compact monothetic semigroups of operators in Banach spaces. Proc. Roy. Irish Acad. Sect. A, 67:27-37 (1968), 1968.

[69KW] M.A. Kaashoek and T.T. West. Compact semigroups in commutative Banach algebras. Proc. Cambridge Philos. Soc., 66:265-274, 1969.

[70TMW] Timothy Murphy and T.T. West. Inner products in Banach spaces and supports of Radon measures. Proc. Roy. Irish Acad. Sect. A, 69:55-61 (1970), 1970.

[71W] T.T. West. Compact monothetic semigroups of operators. In Proceedings of an International Symposium on Operator Theory (Indiana Univ., Bloomington, Ind., 1970), Indiana Univ. Math. J., 20:965-970, 1971.

[72GW] T.A. Gillespie and T.T. West. Operators generating weakly compact groups. Indiana Univ. Math. J., 21:671-688, 1971/72.

[73GW] T.A. Gillespie and T.T. West. Operators generating weakly compact groups, II. Proc. Roy. Irish Acad. Sect. A, 73:309-326, 1973.

[74GW] T.A. Gillespie and T.T. West. Weakly compact groups of operators on Banach spaces. Proc. Roy. Irish Acad. Sect. A, 74:233-237, 1974. Spectral Theory Symposium (Trinity Coll., Dublin, 1974).

[74KW] M.A. Kaashoek and T.T. West. Locally compact semi-algebras. North-Holland Publishing Co., Amsterdam, 1974. With applications to spectral theory of positive operators, North-Holland Mathematics Studies, No. 9.

[75GW] T.A. Gillespie and T.T. West. Weakly compact groups of operators. Proc. Amer. Math. Soc., 49:78-82, 1975.

[75SW] M.R.F. Smyth and T.T. West. The spectral radius formula in quotient algebras. Math. Z., 145(2):157-161, 1975.

[76BW] M.O. Bertman and T.T. West. Conditionally compact bicyclic semitopological semigroups. Proc. Roy. Irish Acad. Sect. A, 76(21):219-226, 1976.

[W76ed] T.T. West, editor. Symposium on harmonic analysis and topological algebras. Royal Irish Academy, Dublin, 1976. Held at Trinity College, Dublin, Dec. 16-19, 1975, Proc. Roy. Irish Acad. Sect. A 76 (1976), nos. 21-33.

[77SW] M.R.F. Smyth and T.T. West. Invariant subspaces of compact elements in algebras. Math. Z., 153(2): 193-197, 1977.

[79MW] G.J. Murphy and T.T. West. Spectral radius formulae. Proc. Edinburgh Math. Soc. (2), 22(3):271-275, 1979.

[79W] T.T. West. Removing the interior of the spectrum—Shilov's example. In Proceedings of the Second International Symposium in West Africa on Functional Analysis and its Applications (Kumasi, 1979), pages 149-158. Forum for Functional Anal. Appl., Kumasi, Ghana, 1979.

[80MWc] G.J. Murphy and T.T. West. Removing the interior of the spectrum. Comment. Math. Univ. Carolin., 21(3): 421-431, 1980.

[80MWg] G.J. Murphy and T.T. West. Decomposition algebras of Riesz operators. Glasgow Math. J., 21(1):75-79, 1980.

[81MW] G.J. Murphy and T.T. West. Decomposition of index-zero Fredholm operators. Proc. Roy. Irish Acad. Sect. A, 81(1):49-54, 1981.

[82BMSW] Bruce A. Barnes, G J. Murphy, M.R.F. Smyth, and T.T. West. Riesz and Fredholm theory in Banach algebras,

volume 67 of Research Notes in Mathematics. Pitman (Advanced Publishing Program), Boston, Mass., 1982.

[82LW] T.J. Laffey and T.T. West. Fredholm commutators. Proc. Roy. Irish Acad. Sect. A, 82(1):129-140, 1982.

[85SW] M.R.F. Smyth and T.T. West. Barnes and support idempotents associated with ring elements. Proc. Roy. Irish Acad. Sect. A, 85(1):25-30, 1985.

[87W] T.T. West. A Riesz-Schauder theorem for semi-Fredholm operators. Proc. Roy. Irish Acad. Sect. A, 87(2): 137-146, 1987.

[89OSW] M. Ó Searcóid and T.T. West. Continuity of the generalized kernel and range of semi-Fredholm operators. Math. Proc. Cambridge Philos. Soc., 105(3):513-522, 1989.

[90W] T.T. West. Removing the jump-Kato's decomposition. In Proceedings of the Seventh Great Plains Operator Theory Seminar (Lawrence, KS, 1987), volume 20, pages 603-612, 1990.

[93LW] T.J. Laffey and T.T. West. Trace-zero matrices and polynomial commutators. Irish Math. Soc. Bull., (31):11-13, 1993.

[97MW] G.J. Murphy and T.T. West. Averaging theorems for linear operators in compact groups and semigroups. Studia Math., 124(3):249-258, 1997.

[98SW] M.R.F. Smyth and T.T. West. The minimum diagonal element of a positive matrix. Studia Math., 131(1):95-99, 1998.

[03W] T.T. West. Compact semigroups of positive matrices. Math. Proc. R. Ir. Acad., 103A(2):143-148 (electronic), 2003.

[West03] T.T. West, The Origins of the Irish Mathematical Society, Bull. Irish Math. Soc. 51:73-75, (2003).

Appendix III

Gary Clyde Hufbauer,
1315 Las Lomas Road, N.E. Albuquerque,
New Mexico, 87106

Thursday 25 June

Dear David,
I am writing this letter while trying to come to an important decision and it will do me good to get it off my chest and write things down. Anyway it will be of interest to you and your advice would be very valuable although I should make up my mind before you could reply.

I got some newspaper cuttings from Dad a week ago with an obituary of Skeff. I have felt that Skeff did a tremendous job in Ireland and Trinity during those years when many of our politicians and prelates seemed to have come straight out of the dark ages. Recently I didn't think he was so effective when those in charge seemed more sensible, I thought he chased hares unnecessarily but in the present crisis period someone outspoken and with guts is essential and people with those qualities are needed right now.

When Mary got into the Senate with, for someone going the first time, an incredible number of votes, it did cross my mind that the machine we had developed was so efficient that it could get 2 people in the next time. Of course in a by-election it would be an even stronger situation then that because the other candidate would not be competing with Mary. I had considered running myself but not really very seriously.

In the last post I got 2 letters. One from Mary asking if I was going to run and another from John Temple Lang who very generously said that he would support me if I wanted to go but said that he would go himself if not asked for my support. So I want to make my mind up in the next few days. First I think that if I ran with our machine and provided not too of many of Mary's agents were themselves candidates I would stand a very good chance – probably slightly better than John especially after the fellowship publicity. Secondly I think I would do a good job, I would not be afraid to take a stand on important issues. I would not be as good a public speaker as John but think that in many ways I would be as effective. I wonder if I would like the job as much as he would, I think not and this could be important. Of course I could be wrong here.

My mathematical career has in a sense reached a peak. I wanted to get Fellowship but also, more importantly, to have my work recognised outside Ireland. This has happened and I will continue without getting much better but I definitely want to broaden my interests. Academic life after 35 can become sterile. One of the things I want is to keep a foot on the land – vide my suggestions to you. This really would be a marvellous opportunity to get in to politics by the back door. I'm sure that when the Natl. University splits up the T.C.D., representation in the Senate will diminish. So it might be the last chance to get in this way. The most encouraging thought contrary to this is that John is someone I like and admire who would be a candidate I would really be pleased to support.

I am writing from Gary and his brother's mountain house in N. California near Eureka. Lovely mild climate, good ranch land on the coast, 10",rain. One relative nearby has 12,000 acre ranch stock and sheep mainly and this is about the only stretch of unspoilt coast in Calif. - it's pretty remote.
Write to Albuquerque and let me know your thoughts. I think I will support John but haven't decided. Apologies for the note paper, the footprints come from 2 bears and 7 children.

Love to Heather
The Hufs send their best wishes.

Trevor

205

Written in 1970 to his friend David Bird in Cork while Trevor West was staying with the Hufbauer family in New Mexico.

[1] *Cork Examiner,* 19 November 1971.

The Law Reform Commission
AN COIMISIÚN UM ATHCHÓIRIÚ AN DLÍ

ARDILAUN CENTRE
111 ST. STEPHEN'S GREEN
DUBLIN 2
IRELAND
Telephone (01) 715699

14th October 1986

Professor T.T. West,
Trinity College
Dublin 2.

My dear Trevor,

I have just completed your biography of Horace Plunkett and write to congratulate you on what is really a most remarkable achievement. Your work seems to me to be up to the highest standard of historical scholarship. It is remarkable for a person who has been trained in a discipline far removed from history to be able to write a history book of such a standard. You have gone through all the primary sources. Your summing up at the end is a real tour de force. Your writing is excellent throughout.

I have of course heard a lot about Plunkett and read about him in other books and often wondered why he did not receivemore recognition in this country. At a intellectual level he was so obviously right all the time.But the Irish National Movement was not about reason; it was about feeling and largely an expression of historical resentment at being second-class citizens and concerned largely about advancing the relative position of the Catholic Nationalist people. It is amazing how difficult it has been to create or hold the middle ground in Irish life. Everyone seems to react against compromise. I suspect this is because they think more in terms of their allegiance to particular groups in Irish society than to the merits of any policies. It is remarkable to see how faithfully developments in the North of Ireland in recent times mirror the developments in this part of Ireland in the early century.

I had not realised until I read your book how close the Convention was to producing a result. But, much as I would like to think the opposite, I do not think that any compromise it would have proposed would have held in the long run. The Irish Nationalists were not going to rest until their full demands were met.

Although a wonderful subject in history, I think you had a very difficult subject in biography. Plunkett seems to have been a wooden character and he does not come through very strongly as a personality in your pages. This must be a reflection upon him because it should be easy to project a man who has kept a diary through his life as he did. Was it that he was a bore in some way?

A thing I liked very much was your objectivity. You are very fair to all the different groups except perhaps to John Dillon and the Irish Party. The real weakness of people like Dillon was that their obsession with achieving an Irish Parliament made them oblivious to the importance of conciliating Irish people of other traditions. But perhaps they were right in their perception that the real enemy were the loyalist people in Ireland and not the British themselves. Redmond I think thought differently in the last years but by then the Irish [party had antagonised important sections of the Irish people from the Nationalist Movement. But I wonder if they would ever have been conciliated.

On one matter I cannot agree with your interpretation and that is about Horace Plunkett's private life. I think that it is not true that he did'nt get married because he wished to marry Lady Fingal. I suspect the truth of the matter is to be found in his relationship with that character Gerald Heard to whom he left all his money. But you were indeed wise to set out the facts as they are known and not to attempt to draw any conclusion on the matter.

I hope that we may meet soon for a chat about your book. Indeed I would like to be able to look through the various reviews which you have collected. Though the reviews which were complimentary I don't think they did full justice to the book's real quality as a piece of very fine scolarship in history.

Yours ever

Charles Lysaght

University of Dublin
Trinity College
Dublin 2

18th Oct 86

Dear Charlie,
Thank you for your letter with such a generous tribute. I know I don't deserve it but am particularly delighted
to have it from an old friend and one who has been through the biographical mill.

To get down to specifics. I take your point on Dillon and the IPP. Plunkett's view of them was unusually jaundiced
(2 of his chief political enemies were Dillon and Ardilaun – both related to the Plunketts in various ways) but it
was typical of the man that he made it up with JD after 1918 (and A about 1903).

I have spent a good deal of time wondering if I would have got on with Plunkett had we met. My guess is that
I wouldn't have liked him but I hope that I would have admired what he was trying to achieve particularly within
the context of the time.

I also thought a good deal about Heard. I am sure that he and Plunkett had a deep relationship, whether it was
physical in any sense I doubt but that is of little consequence. Heard did have a celebrated affair with the Kilteragh
postman (cf James Meenan on George O'Brien), he was living with someone in London when he acted as
Plunkett's amanuensis at Weybridge (employing secretaries such as Betjeman and J E Bowle later History Prof at
Oxford). The only clue I had to their relationship came in a diary entry of 23 June 1926:

Heard presented Plunkett with a memoranda on 'our relations' indicating that 'he was not happy in his present
position. He had "a friend" who had parted with him, apparently because his tie to me made the friendship less
intimate than could be tolerated by the other party. In the daytime he had been restless in mind and had talked
half in joke about marrying. Poor fellow – would that work?'

Heard wrote a particularly sensitive assessment of Plunkett as a postscript to Miss Digby's biography. He had
a large salary from Plunkett in the Weybridge period (1923–32) and came down from London twice a week and
was the only major beneficiary of Plunkett's estate (£7,000 out of £40,000).

I tracked down his executor in S. California who seemed illiterate and unhelpful (and was apparently writing
a biography). Heard's papers have been deposited in the UCLA Library. His bibliography from there is more than
30 pages but checking that carefully one discovers no apparent references to Plunkett, Ireland or the Irish Literary
Movement. For an author of 30 books I found this difficult to comprehend. It only thickened the plot. Another part
of this mystery is that someone apparently got off with Plunkett's American estate (worth perhaps $1 million in
1932). So more remains to be unravelled.

It would be a great pleasure if you could dine on Commons (6.15 pm Monday-Friday). My teaching is just
commencing for Michaelmas term. I will ring you in the Ardilaun Centre.

My deepest thanks for your letter

Yours

Trevor

Maura Lee West

This is by no means a detailed catalogue of all those who have supported this publication in one helpful way or another to whom I will always be grateful.

I greatly appreciate the time taken by Mary Robinson to write her very personal introduction.

Particular thanks go to Trevor's colleagues, friends and family who enthusiastically embraced the project and gave generously of their time to provide their contributions; Mary Leland for her editing skills and Dermot Burns for his photographic expertise. Brian McGovern's TCD photographs were also a valuable contribution.

I would like to thank David and Heather Bird and Charles Lysaght for their support and assistance.

Invaluable assistance was received from many colleagues at Trinity College Dublin including Professor Dermot MacAleese and Dr Edward McParland. My thanks also go to Mary Appied (Trinity Foundation); Curator Catherine Giltrap; Terry McAuley (former Director of Sport) and Geraldine McAuley; Trevor Peare (Trinity Library); and Michelle Tanner (Head of Sport).

Further help was obtained from Seamus Haughey and Erin O'Mahoney (Oireachtas Library), and at Midleton College Dr Edward Gash, Paula Stead and Eleanor Flynn were particularly supportive.

My warm thanks go to Sir Michael Davies (Clerk of the Parliaments, Westminster); Lord Donoughue of Ashton; Jim Fitzgerald (Cork County Cricket); Anthony and Sally O'Leary; Dr Malcolm Little and Roly Meates (IURU); Dr Murray Power (President, Cricket Ireland); publisher Colin Smythe; Dr Hugh Tinney and Dr Ronan Tynan. I am also grateful for the assistance of the Irish Co-operative Organization Society, and to Peter Stobart, Director of Music at St Fin Barre's Cathedral, Cork.

My personal gratitude to Noelle O'Lomasney and Ted Dineen at Charleston and my son Ian in Edinburgh.

No words can express my gratitude to our friend Brendan Kennelly, who little realized when he arranged a meeting for myself and Trevor to discuss a radio programme on sport in Trinity how utterly both our lives would be changed as a result. For the consequent loving, fun-filled and all too short relationship I am eternally grateful.

209

We would like
to thank our sponsors

Owen Killian
Denis Lucey
The Provost, Trinity College Dublin
Golden Jubilee Trust Fund
DUCAC, Trinity College Dublin
Cyril J. Smyth, Fellow Emeritus TCD

Excert from 'Markings' read
by Senator Sean D. Barrett
at the Memorial Service in the Chapel
of Trinity College, Friday 7 December 2012.
Reproduced courtesy of the Estate
of Seamus Heaney and Faber and Faber.

First published in Ireland
in 2016 by The Lilliput Press
62-63 Sitric Road
Arbour Hill
Dublin 7, Ireland
www.lilliputpress.ie

A CIP record for this title
is available from
The British Library.

Book design and production:
Tony O'Hanlon, Propeller

Photography:
Bernard Mc Govern
Patrick Gleeson
Mick Fitzpatrick
Billy Strickland

Reproduction:
Dermot Burns

Editing:
Maura Lee West
Mary Leland
Djinn von Noorden

Printing:
Castuera, Navarra, Spain

ISBN: 9781843516767.

4. Linear Functionals, Dual spaces   (K. & F.)

Let X_c be a N.L.S.. A map f of $X \to C$ is called a f̶
$\mathcal{r}$ is a <u>linear functional</u> if $f(\alpha x + \beta y) = \alpha f(x) + \beta f(y)$ (2
$\alpha, \beta \in C$). It is <u>continuous</u> if $x_n \to x \implies f(x_n) \to f(x$

<u>Th 4.1.</u> Let $f(x)$ be a linear functional on an N.L.S. X.
If f is cns at $x_0 \in X$ then it is continuous everywhere i̶
<u>Proof</u> $x_n \to x_0 \implies f(x_n) \to f(x_0)$
    Let $y_n \to y$. $f(y_n) = f(y_n - y + x_0 + y - x_0) = f(y_n - y + x_0) + f(y) -$
    Now $y_n - y + x_0 \to x_0$ $\therefore$ $f(y_n - y + x_0) \to f(x_0)$
    So $f(y_n) \to f(x_0) + f(y) - f(x_0) = f(y)$.

<u>Df</u>   A functional $f(x)$ is <u>bounded</u> if $\exists$ const N such th̶
$$|f(x)| \leq N \|x\| (x \in X).$$

<u>Th 4.2</u> For linear functionals the conditions of continuity a̶
boundedness are equivalent.
<u>Proof</u>   Let f be bounded by N & let $x_n \to 0$, then
$$|f(x_n)| \leq N \|x_n\| \to 0$$
    so $f(x)$ is cns at 0 & by Th 4.1   everywhere in X.
    Conv. Assume $f(x)$ not bdd. Then given n $\exists x_n \in X$ s.t
$|f(x_n)| > n \|x_n\|$. Put $y_n = x_n / (n \|x_n\|)$, $\|y_n\| = \frac{1}{n}$ $\therefore$ y̶
But $|f(y_n)| = |f(x_n / n\|x_n\|)| = (1 / n\|x_n\|)|f(x_n)| > 1$, so $f($̶
is not cns at 0

<u>Df</u>   Let f be a cns. lin. fnal the <u>norm</u> of f is
$$\|f\| = \sup_{\|x\| \neq 0} \frac{|f(x)|}{\|x\|}$$

Geometry:

Let X be a N.L.S. and H a closed subspace of X ($\neq X$̶
but such that ~~such~~ $\exists x_0 \in X$ such that $x = x_0 + h$̶
Then H is called a (closed) <u>hyperplane</u> in X

$$X = H \oplus [x_0]   [x_0] \text{ 1-d sub sp gen}$$
$$x_0 \neq 0. \notin H$$